Tank Warfare in the Second World War

Tank Warfare in the Second World War

AN ORAL HISTORY

GEORGE FORTY

Constable · London

First published in Great Britain 1998
by Constable and Company Ltd
3 The Lanchesters, 162 Fulham Palace Road
London W6 9ER
Copyright © George Forty 1998
The right of George Forty to be identified
as the author of this work has been asserted by him
in accordance with the Copyright, Designs and Patents Act 1988
ISBN 0 09 478010 2
Set in Monotype Photina 11pt by
Servis Filmsetting Ltd, Manchester
Printed in Great Britain by
St Edmundsbury Press Ltd
Bury St Edmunds, Suffolk

A CIP catalogue record for this book
is available from the British Library

Contents

List of Illustrations

7

A US 1st Armored Division tank crew prepare a hasty meal (*US Army via Author's Collection*)
Christmas cheer in the desert (*Tank Museum*)
Crew members from 1 RTR perform their ablutions (*Tank Museum*)
A Cromwell tank crew, January 1945 (*Tank Museum*)
US Marine Corps tankers drying their clothing (*US Army via Author's Collection*)
Tank crewmen get their hair cut in the Western Desert (*Tank Museum*)
Inside the turret of a British Comet tank (*Tank Museum*)
A radio operator tuning his Wireless Set 19 (*Tank Museum*)
A 3 RTR crew tighten one of the tracks on their Comet (*Tank Museum*)
The driver of an M3 General Lee medium tank works on his engine (*Tank Museum*)
Red Army tankmen work on their KV1 (*Tank Museum*)
Bombing up a KV1 heavy tank (*Tank Museum*)
Bombing up an M3 medium General Lee tank (*Tank Museum*)
A South African tank crew get rid of their empties (*SA Museum of Military History via Author's Collection*)
Three German tank crewmen (*Panzermuseum via Author's Collection*)
The crew of an M10 tank destroyer replenish their ammunition (*US Army, via Author's Collection*)
The desert bivouacs of a German panzer crew (*Panzermuseum, via Author's Collection*)
2Lt Norman Plough of 2 RTR and his crew beside their tank (*N Plough via Author's Collection*)

between pages 160 and 161

A cruiser tank being loaded on to a tank transporter during training (*Tank Museum*)
Refuelling a Stuart M3A1 light tank from a petrol bowser (*Tank Museum*)
Part of the echelon of 7th Armoured Division, August 1944 (*Tank Museum*)
Two Churchills outside Le Havre, 1944 (*Tank Museum*)
A Sherman Crab mine clearer (*Tank Museum*)
The bow flamegun of a Churchill 'Crocodile' in action (*Ground Photo Recce Unit Kinema Branch HQ 2nd Army via Author's Collection*)
A Shermann DD amphibious tank entering the water (*Tank Museum*)
A Shermann DD with its screen lowered (*Tank Museum*)
A Rocket Launcher T34 mounted on a Sherman tank (*Tank Museum*)
The Mine Exploder T1E3 (M1) (*US Army, via Author's Collection*)
Matilda Mk I tank crew getting ready for action (*Tank Museum*)

Acknowledgements

I have many people to thank for allowing me to use their reminiscences, and as their names appear with their quotes I will not repeat
them again here. However, there are two others who merit a very
special 'thank you'. First and foremost on this side of the Atlantic is
Mrs Nancy Langmaid, who works as a volunteer at the Tank Museum
Library in nearby Bovington Camp. For a number of years now she
has been collecting reminiscences, both written and spoken, which
are concerned with all aspects and all periods of tank warfare, from
the earliest times in the First World War up to the present day. I have
dug deeply into these records as far as the Second World War is concerned, then, where possible, contacted those concerned to get further
information. Nancy has done – and is still doing – a magnificent job
and we who use the library regularly owe her a great debt of gratitude
for her scholarship, determination and perseverance, without which
the Tank Museum archives would be so much the poorer.

On the other side of 'The Pond' I had the great good fortune to get
in touch (via *Armor Magazine*) with Mr Aaron C. Elson, who, over the
past few years, has been collecting oral history from ex-members of
the 712th US Tank Battalion, who fought in North-West Europe. He
has generously allowed me to use some of these reminiscences and I
would commend his two privately published books: *Tanks For The
Memories* and *They Were All Young Kids*, which tell the full story of
these gallant young GIs, some of whose reminiscences now appear in
this book.

Introduction

Ever since the tank appeared on the battlefield it has been a potent force for shock action whose main characteristics of firepower, protection and mobility have made it a truly formidable weapon system. Although it first showed its potency in the First World War, it was not until the Second World War that it really came into its own, when it was undoubtedly responsible, within the structure of the all-arms team, for the lion's share of success in the ground battle wherever it was properly employed. However, a tank is only as good as its crew – witness the devastating results achieved by the Coalition armoured forces over the far greater numbers of Iraqi tanks in the Gulf War of 1991. It was the high standard of competence, bravery and professionalism of the American, British, French and other Coalition tank crewmen which was largely responsible for the land victory and it was no different in the Second World War. Therefore it is highly relevant to look at the tank crew and to examine in detail the part they played.

A tank crew is a team. It is led by a tank commander, who may be an officer or an NCO. If the former, then he will invariably have another important job to perform – for example, he may be a tank troop/platoon leader, in charge of up to five tanks, or a squadron/company commander, in charge of a number of troops/platoons. Of course, he may well be of higher rank – a battalion, regiment, brigade or divisional commander. However, unless he is one of those remarkable charismatic tank giants – like Generals

Patton, Rommel or Guderian, for example – he will be too far removed from the 'sharp end' to have to cope with the detailed business of fighting his tank, whilst commanding everything else. We are therefore going to confine ourselves to the lower command echelons, to the individual tanks and their crews, but to view their day-to-day wartime experiences from 'both sides of the hill', so there are German tank-crew reminiscences here as well as American, British and Russian. Those four represent the major armoured combatants of the Second World War and thus form the major part of this book, with just a few others, for example, from France, thrown in for good measure. I have also tried to mix the various theatres of war, but inevitably the majority of accounts come from the areas where tanks were mainly used, namely North Africa, the Soviet Union and Eastern and North-West Europe.

The subjects covered may appear mundane – for example: joining up, training, first action, first time wounded, taken prisoner etc., and of course the everyday tasks connected with living on an armoured fighting vehicle in battle. I have tried to use as many different reminiscences as possible, so as to introduce the reader to many armoured soldiers of all nations. I think you will be surprised by the similarity between the raconteurs about what they found to be the most important issues – as well, of course, as staying alive! Also, the humour and the 'taken for granted' bravery of men who are prepared to fight in a small, confined space, surrounded at close quarters by explosives and fuel, knowing that at any moment they could be blown to pieces, yet prepared to give of their best for their country, their loved ones and their comrades in arms. As a tank man I salute them all, irrespective of army or nationality. JFK once made headlines with the simple statement: '*Ich bin ein Berliner!*'. I am equally proud to say: '*Ich bin ein panzer soldat!*'

George Forty
Byrantspuddle
September 1997

12

1
Joining Up

At the start of the war every major combatant nation had a standing army of varying size and efficiency which was composed of a mixture of regular soldiers, who had been serving before the war began, backed up in some cases by reservists and part-time soldiers – such as the British Territorial Army and the American National Guard – together with newly joined volunteers who had rushed to the Colours in a fervour of patriotism;[1] and last, but by no means least, the mass of somewhat more unwilling conscripts who had started to stream in once it was clear to the country concerned that a major conflict was in the offing. In Great Britain, for example, the war was but a few hours old when Parliament passed the National Service (Armed Forces) Act, which made all physically fit males between the ages of eighteen and forty-one liable for military service. It would be followed in 1941 by another Act which extended the upper age limit for men to fifty-one and also made women liable for military service. By the end of 1939, only 727,000 men had registered, but in 1940 the figure was over four million and in 1941 a further 2.2 million were conscripted. Thereafter the call-up numbers dropped sharply, because by then one-third of the entire male population of Great Britain who were of working age were already in the Armed Forces, the Army taking the lion's share – over three million British soldiers were serving world-wide by early 1945. The Commonwealth nations were quick to follow Britain's lead, with one significant difference, however, because the major proportion of their new recruits were volunteers – India, for example, producing the largest volunteer army the world has ever seen.

The armoured 'slice' of these vast numbers was not initially very large, although it had started to grow even before the war began, when the Cavalry began to be mechanised. Then, in April 1939, the Royal Armoured Corps (RAC) came into existence – the Cavalry of the Line being 'combined' in a loose amalgam with the existing battalions of the Royal Tank Corps. It grew with ever-increasing speed as the war progressed and the need for armoured units of all types was recognised. Towards the end of June 1945, for example, the RAC Directorate listed its vehicle holdings as 21,933 tanks of all types and 9,994 armoured cars, while adding that 15,844 tanks and 1,957 armoured cars had also been lost in action. There was a total of seven armoured divisions in existence by 1942, together with numerous independent armoured brigades, so the number of tank crewmen was considerable.

And it was the same in France, where between the wars there had been only some twenty infantry and five cavalry divisions, mostly serving abroad, but by the time of the Munich crisis in 1938 the French had eighty-four divisions under arms. By May 1940, that figure had risen to 113 active divisions. However, within this vast army, the French had just three tank divisions with which to face the German blitzkrieg, although it has to be said that these represented just one-fifth of the French tank strength, the rest (four-fifths) of their effective, modern armoured fighting vehicles were spread thinly within the mass of infantry divisions, under the control of hidebound infantry officers who knew nothing about armoured warfare. Small wonder that the *Panzerwaffe* sliced through them so easily. The Germans, of course, were much better prepared, as Hitler had been determined to force the pace in Europe once he had taken power. However, the Germans still had to mobilise many of their forces. The recruitment, drafting, induction and training of the *Heer* (German Army) was all based upon the *Wehrkreise* (Military Districts) system, which had been set up in 1919 and worked directly under the Army High Command (*Oberkommando des Heeres* [OKH]) until 1938, when their functions were co-ordinated by the newly created Replacement Army. In 1939, there were eighteen *Wehrkreise*, divided into six Army groups. The German Army was mobilised in 'waves', a process which continued until 1944. Between 1934 and April 1940 there were nine such waves, totalling over 140 divisions. The panzer (tank) forces within this army were among the élite, there being 3,195 German tanks in service on 1 September 1939 (not including those which had been 'acquired' from the overrunning of Czechoslovakia). During the period 1940–45 the Germans built some 24,500 tanks – on a par with British wartime tank production, but mainly far superior in individual quality. In the USSR, the 'Juggernaut' that was the Soviet armed forces was already in being, with the Red Army alone numbering some four-and-a-half million men, including a staggering 21,000 tanks, although most of them were obsolescent and, like the French, spread thinly throughout a mainly infantry-orientated army. By the end of the war, the Red Army had some five hundred divisions, totalling more than six million men, a large proportion of which were armoured troops of one kind or another.

The only major nation that initially lagged behind the others was, of course, the USA, where in July 1939 the strength of the active army was a pitiful 174,000, scattered all over the continental United States and abroad. The handful of regular soldiers were backed by some 200,000 National Guardsmen, equipped with obsolete weapons left over from the First World War, who resembled the British Territorial Army in many respects (although, to be fair, the TA were much better equipped). Their total active tank strength was well under a thousand, most of which were First World War veteran vehicles, only 331 new tanks being built in 1939–40, of which 325 were light tanks, six were mediums and none were classed as 'heavy'! The immediate result of the German blitzkrieg in Europe was to stir the nation into activity, forcing the American Congress to authorise the Selective Service Act, so that by July 1941, seventeen million men had registered, although only a fraction of these had actually joined up. A few months later, on 7 December 1941, the Japanese struck at Pearl Harbor and from then on there was no more holding back. By the end of the war, the US Army was perhaps the mightiest in the world, numbering nearly six million men and exceeded in manpower only by the Soviets, whilst its weaponry, strategic mobility and logistic capabilities were second to none. The vast industrial potential of the USA would also be harnessed to the production of weapons, vehicles and equipment so that by the end of the war, for example, they had built a staggering 88,410 tanks of all types, over half of which were the ubiquitous M4 medium Sherman, generously giving many of these away to their Allies.

Regular soldiers

Induction and selection was, of course, different for different men, but for the young regulars in all armies it had all happened some years before. Dai Mitchell, now a retired major, was in 1939 a young British regular private soldier, serving as a tank crewman in the 5th Battalion, Royal Tank Corps[2] stationed at Perham Down, near Tidworth, on the edge of Salisbury Plain. He had joined the army in 1938 at the RTC Regimental Depot, Bovington Camp, near Wareham in Dorset. It was here that all such recruits received their basic training on courses lasting about thirty-six weeks. Dai told me: 'Our squad sergeant was a Sergeant Wilson, a great character, respected by everyone. In those days the squad sergeant was a man of many talents, guiding and teaching his way through the thirty-six weeks of training . . . the first five consisted of drill and more drill, mixed with lashings of PT. This was followed by thirteen weeks of tank driving and maintenance. We had Adjutant's drill parades twice a week of course, and after eighteen weeks were given ten days' leave, the squad being marched down to Wool railway station, all looking very smart in their new blue patrols, carrying black swagger canes with silver-crested knobs. After leave we went to Lulworth for our gunnery training on medium tanks – with 3-pounder guns and Vickers machine guns, and Mark VIB light tanks – with machine guns only. This period lasted for six weeks and was most enjoyable, Lulworth being noted for excellent "nosh" and the weather that summer was wonderful. It was a great thrill becoming a member of a tank crew for the first time. Then it was back to Bovington for the rest of our military education. The remaining weeks were spent putting on the final polish – pistol drill and pistol firing, twenty-four hour guards, ceremonial drill, PT tests and passing-out parades. A few fell by the wayside, squads dropping to about eighteen men, but at the end of the day the Tank Corps finished up with keen, well-trained soldiers.'

Dai was posted to the Fifth at Perham Down with other members of his recruits' squad, arriving on a wet November afternoon in 1938, and, after all the bustle and shouting of the Depot, found the ordered tranquillity of the battalion very different: 'After being shown our barrack room we were taken to the cookhouse for tea and were a little surprised to find everyone else in civilian clothes, so that we in our box-creased tunics, gleaming buttons and puttees, stood out like sore thumbs!' Dai was now a member of the medium tank section of C Company, 5 RTC, with Jock McLeod as his troop sergeant. The light tank section was under Sergeant Paddy Maloney and one can well imagine the rivalry and banter that existed between the two sections. Both McLeod and Maloney were: 'built like barrack-room doors', as Dai Mitchell explained, '. . . two splendid men, the salt of the earth. The company was about sixty to seventy men strong, billeted in two barrack blocks, with the company office about fifty yards away and the tank park about 150. Reveille was at 0600 by bugle, all the room jobs had to be completed by 0745, then on to the tank park by 0800. Crews then worked on their vehicles until lunch at 1300, the afternoon being entirely devoted to sport, in which everyone joined. In those days a great deal of trust was put on the individual soldier, permanent passes being issued after a year's service, which meant one could stay out until reveille, wear civilian clothes etc.'

Sport played a major part in most soldiers' lives in those relatively carefree days before the war. Dai Mitchell, known as 'Tweeny', was the regimental bantamweight in the 5 RTC boxing team and, during the boxing season, would spend almost the entire day training, so his main recollection of the day the war began was that it came as quite a jolt to their ordered existence: 'I remember little of the build-up to war that summer,' he recalled, 'but what does remain vividly in my memory is being woken up with a mug of tea on the Sunday morning that war was declared – we had been on the tiles all the evening before! Somebody in the barrack room switched on the radio and that dear old fogey Neville Chamberlain was quacking away. Then the penny dropped, a state of war existed between Great Britain and Germany. Life would never be the same again.' 5 RTR soon moved out of their comfortable barracks and into a tented camp, as Dai Mitchell recalls: 'The bustle and activity started within the hour and inside a week we were under canvas at Windmill Hill.' The reason for the move was so that Perham Down could house one of the newly formed training regiments. On 5 October, 5 RTR were put at six hours' notice to move, 'bombed up' their tanks with full loads of ammunition and moved into billets in the St Albans area as part of the newly formed 3rd Armoured Brigade – 'plenty of pretty girls and the black beret men were made very welcome' recalls Dai. However, they did not immediately join the BEF to go to France and were destined to spend the winter there, followed by an equally frustrating wait in the Salisbury-Fordingbridge area, this time in the thick snow and ice of a very hard winter: 'a frustrating and confusing time,' recalls Dai, as the Fifth would not be called over to fight in France until late May, much to the frustration of the tank crews.

In the tank regiments abroad other young men were also ready to fight. Major-General Rea Leakey, CB, DSO, MC, was at the time a young officer in 1st Royal Tank Corps in Egypt, having passed out of the Royal Military College at Sandhurst in 1937, then attended the six months Young Officers' 'Special to Arm' course at the Tank Corps Schools at Bovington and Lulworth. This had been followed by some enjoyable months with 4th RTC in Catterick, North Yorkshire, but, in March 1938, he found himself entering Alexandria harbour on board a troopship – soon to become one of the thirteen young officers commanding tank troops in the 1st Battalion RTC. 'We moved into tented accommodation adjoining a British barracks at Helmeih, some ten miles outside Cairo, and our outlook was the desert. This was to be our uncomfortable home for the next eighteen months. However, the pay was good, the sporting facilities excellent, and, above all, there was the Gezira Club in the heart of Cairo. This was where we met many of the British residents, who welcomed us into their homes. Inter-Regimental sports were highly competitive and I soon found myself involved in most of them – athletics, rugger, cross-country (desert) running, cricket and boxing. On two occasions brother officers entered me for individual open competitions without my knowing, and only told me when the entries were published and certainly, on the first occasion, I did not withdraw my name.

'I was entered for the Army of Egypt boxing competition, fighting at middleweight, and one of the other entrants was my batman. I fought my way to the finals, which were held in Cairo. The arena was packed with soldiers. The fight of the evening was the middleweight, "2nd Lt Leakey versus Pte Tyler" – and written up for all to see was added the explanation: "His Batman"! To the delight of the crowd, my batman won. When he woke me up the next morning with a cup of tea he took a good look at my face, gave me a mirror, and with a grin, said: "Sorry, Sir." I had two black eyes and a broken nose. What neither of us knew was that I had broken a small bone in my wrist for the second time; it never healed and thus ended my boxing career.'

Then came Neville Chamberlain's meeting with Adolf Hitler in Munich and, as Rea recalls: '. . . even in distant Cairo the clouds of war loomed heavy.' Twenty-four hours later the 1st were moving out of Cairo in a train bound for Mersa Matruh, 100 miles west of Alexandria, where they unloaded their tanks and moved out into the desert to await an expected attack from the vast Italian army based in Libya. But thanks to Neville Chamberlain's 'Peace in our Time', the war would not start for another year. In the meantime the 1st, along with the other British units in Egypt, got down to serious training, so let us skip forwards a few months to 3 September 1939 and hear again from Second Lieutenant Rea Leakey of his recollections of that fateful day: 'When the war started, we were once again back in the desert, not far from Mersa Matruh. We were now in 4th Armoured Brigade – part of the 7th Armoured Division. We had been well trained by General Percy Hobart, who was forever taking us out into the desert. One of the exercises we took part in was of interest. General Sir Robert Gordon Finlayson, Commander-in-Chief British Troops, organised one of the largest manoeuvres ever in the Western Desert. The enemy was 7th Armoured Division. A defensive line was built from the coast, stretching south into the desert for a distance of some fifteen miles. When the infantry had "dug in", barbed wire had been erected and dummy minefields laid, the exercise started. General Hobart ordered his armoured car regiment (11th Hussars) to reconnoitre the defences and they soon discovered where they ended. He then moved his Division some thirty miles into the desert and entered Mersa Matruh by the back door, so winning the battle without "firing a shot". I happened to be one of the officers who attended the conference at the early conclusion of the exercise and I shall never forget it. There must have been some four hundred officers assembled at the open-air cinema at Mersa Matruh. On the platform were the senior officers and the C-in-C addressed us. He complimented the infantry divisional commanders on the layout of their defences and then described the story of the so-called conflict. "What happened? The enemy carried out a manoeuvre which in war would have been quite impossible. General Hobart moved his whole division deep into the desert and entered our strongly defended position from the rear."

'Not long after this episode, Gordon Finlayson was posted back to Whitehall in an influential position. Hobo was "sacked". I happened to be in Cairo on the evening that he and his wife left Cairo station for Alexandria by train on their way back to England. I was one of the many who came to say "goodbye". Outside the station there was chaos, the soldiers of the Desert Rats had taken the matter into their own hands and had driven their vehicles into the streets of Cairo, abandoned them and then joined the throng on the railway platform. Hobo was "demoted" to the rank of Lance-Corporal in the Home Guard. But he was not forgotten, particularly by the Cavalry officers. It was they, I am told, who petitioned His Majesty to have him re-instated as a Divisional Commander. And so he was, but in England.'[3]

Rea Leakey's pre-war Commanding Officer was Lieutenant Colonel (later Brigadier) J. A. L. Caunter, CBE, MC, known to all as 'Blood', an RTC officer of considerable fire and ability. He had this to say about the pre-war desert navigational training that he gave all his young tank commanders: 'I believe the Italians were lacking in knowledge of desert navigation and were always frightened of losing their way, even by day. With us it was different. I must go back to 1938 to explain: I was CO 1st R Tanks in Egypt until May 1939. We did a lot of training in the desert, including night-battle practice . . . in order to familiarise all my junior officers, sergeants and many corporals with the desert, every week I sent out a party of five tanks, say, four subalterns, ten or eleven sergeants and corporals, on a week's recce of the desert, over 500 miles of "going". I used to draw lines on the unmapped spaces of the map to the south of the escarpment in the shape of a triangle and each week one of these triangles, 500 miles in perimeter, had to be covered and reported on by successive parties. From this we build up "going maps" and the confidence of junior leaders. They were in wireless touch with RHQ all the time in case of emergency, but we did not have a single instance of a lost patrol!'

Major Norris H. Perkins, DSC, late US Armor, had been out of college for some five years in the summer of 1940. He was an industrial engineer, but had a reserve officer commission and had decided to go back to school to study medicine. Hitler had just invaded France, so Norris thought it would be a good time to get his year of active duty over with, before returning to his studies. He remembers being in a great hurry: 'I requested immediate active duty, sent a letter down to the Presidio, 9th Corps Area headquarters in California, but then didn't get my orders. They didn't come and they didn't come. Meanwhile, the War Department announced the organisation of two armoured car divisions and they turned out to be the 1st and 2nd Armored Divisions. I put in for that immediately and got my orders for Fort Benning. As soon as I got to Fort Benning, I received belated orders from California. I had failed to put on enough postage – airmail requiring more postage in those days. My buddies in the 381st Infantry Reserve Regiment in Portland went off to the South Pacific. They ended up in the Philippines. Many were killed or spent years in POW camps. Some of them died in the Bataan death march. So, I had, instead of that, a wonderful experience with the 2nd Armored, met my future wife and married her, all for the lack of a postage stamp!'

Lieutenant James L. Gifford from Gloversville, New York, was a private soldier in December 1941 and was on leave in Louisville, Kentucky on 7 December, the 'Day of Infamy', when the Japanese attacked Pearl Harbor. 'A bunch of us had taken a hotel room for the night,' he recalled, 'that was the cheapest way out for soldiers, when we heard a noise down the street. I looked out of the window and people were running around. So I went down to the lobby and someone says, "We just got attacked in Pearl Harbor." I said: "Where's Pearl Harbor?" someone said, "All I know is that they are telling soldiers to get back to camp." So I went upstairs and told the guys. We all grabbed our stuff and went into the street. The civilians were pulling up in their cars and saying, "Soldier, we'll take you back to camp." Soon every car is full of soldiers and we're heading back from Louisville to Fort Knox, which was about thirty miles. The next morning they lined us up and they started reading off names: "You're going to Fort Lewis, Washington." They thought the Japs were gonna hit the West Coast. Fort Louis, Washington, they're reading all these names out. When they came to Jim Gifford, they said: "Armored Force School." I said, "What? I don't believe this. There's a goddamn war on and I'm going to school?"'

Major Forrest Dixon of Munith, Michigan, who would become the battalion maintenance officer of the 712th Tank Battalion, had initially been commissioned into the cavalry wing of the ROTC at Michigan State University. He would also find himself destined for 'school': 'When I got hauled into the Army I went directly to Fort Knox, to go to school. From Fort Knox I was sent to the 4th Armored Division at Pine Camp, New York. Then the 4th Armored produced the cadre of the 10th Armored Division at Fort Benning. Meanwhile, the 11th Cavalry Regiment was supposed to ship for Australia, but a lot of its members came down with jaundice from their yellow fever vaccinations. So they sat out there in California and all of a sudden somebody decided to send them to Fort Benning to be part of 10th Armored. So the 10th had a cadre from the 4th Armored plus the 11th Cavalry. For a while, the armoured people and the horse cavalry didn't get along. Each outfit was allowed so many twenty-four-hour passes, so many weekend passes and so many furloughs. But the armoured force couldn't get them. It seemed like they all went to the Cavalry. That's when I got in trouble. I gave three twenty-four-hour passes to a kid who supposedly had a sick mother. See, a company commander could give a twenty-four-hour pass, but he was limited in number. So I gave him three twenty-four-hour passes, because the regiment wouldn't give him a three-day pass. Then he went AWOL [Absent Without Leave]. He was supposed to be back for reveille on Monday morning and he finally made it Wednesday afternoon. He came into the orderly room and said, "Sergeant Hensley reporting for duty, sir." I said, "Well, Private Hensley, explain." He looked at me: "Private Hensley?" "I reduced you to the grade of private this morning," I said. "I don't know what they're gonna do to me." I got called over to regimental headquarters and chewed out good. Then each of the majors there put a letter on my personal file. So I was the oldest first-lieutenant in the 10th Armored Division. I didn't get promoted for a long, long time.'

The Volunteers

'I wouldn't take a million dollars for what I went through,' says George Bussell, a slight man of about five-foot-six from Indianapolis, 'but I wouldn't go through it again for a million dollars either. . . . My father never knew it, but I volunteered.' He added with a chuckle, 'My mom knew it. In front of my name there was a "V", but it looked like a check and that's what I told Dad. He went to his grave never knowing I volunteered. Because he told me: "Don't you volunteer. They'll get you soon enough." My buddy and I, we got three sheets to the wind and I said to him, "Hell, let's volunteer." So we went downtown. And they took me first, but my buddy Carl, he was married. When he got ready to sign up they said, "Are you married?" And he said, "Yeah." They said, "Well, you can't sign." We were figuring on going into the same outfit. Instead he waved goodbye to me when I went in!'

Alan Rowland, a young British volunteer, was initially desperate to join the RAF, so in September 1940 he joined the Air Training Corps (ATC) and attended evening classes three evenings a week, fully intending to join the RAF when he reached seventeen. 'In September 1941, having reached the required age, I went along to the Recruiting Office and enlisted in the RAF. A few weeks later they sent me for a medical examination which I duly passed with flying colours. At the time I worked on the railways for the LNER in the electrical signalling section, which was termed in those days to be a "Reserved Occupation". And now my problems started. Shortly after passing my medical, I received a letter stating that, owing to my type of work, the RAF would not call me up for another three months, so I waited patiently. At the end of the three months another letter arrived containing exactly the same information. By this time nine months had passed and I was still in Civvy Street. So I went along to the Recruiting Office once again, explained to the RAF that I wished to join as soon as possible – only to be told my job was a "Reserved Occupation".

'After a cup of tea in the canteen, which gave me time to appreciate the situation, I came to the conclusion I should try next door and see what the Army could offer. So into the Army office I went and was greeted by a sergeant in the Irish Guards. I explained what the situation was with the RAF and, as I had a lot of experience with horses, asked if there was any chance of enlisting in a Cavalry regiment. After pondering this question for a few minutes he replied: "I think there are a couple of regiments which still have horses." The problem with the RAF seemed to be no obstacle, also the matter of my reserved occupation seemed to be irrelevant, so I enlisted straight away. About three weeks later I attended another medical and passed A1 again, so I knew I must be fit. Two weeks later I was on my way to Bovington. The "horses" there were made of steel and, although you could ride them, they had no saddles. I enjoyed my training at Bovington and Lulworth, taking a keen interest in driving and gunnery. After training for six months came the passing-out parade and the choice of regiments to go to. I chose the 1st Royal Gloucestershire Hussars (1 RGH). Why? Because rumour had it they still had horses! After a spot of leave I joined 1 RGH, but the only horse they had was one owned by the CO. The rest were made of steel and were called "Centaurs". That is how I became a tankie or a "Donkey-Walloper", as the RTR boys used to call the Cavalry Regiment tank crews. Happy days!'

Some American volunteers also had to be persuaded into choosing tanks. For example, Sergeant Lester J. Suter, from St Louis, did not want to be in the tanks when he was first at Fort Benning. There was a parachute school there as well as 10th Armored and, as he recalled: 'I liked the way they wore their hats and the clothes they wore; they wore better boots than we did. They had a rugged attitude too, like a commando attitude. I wanted to be a tough guy, so I was going over there and join the paratroopers. And when I got over there, they said, OK, so they took me up this big goddamn tower, 750 feet. I looked down at the ground and they said: "Now, you put on this parachute and you jump." I said: "No way, I'm not jumping off this son of a bitch, take me down!" So they took me down and let me out. I went back to the tank battalion and was happy.'

The Conscripts

'My story began in March 1940,' recalls ORQMS Sam Storm, late of 155 Regiment, RAC (15th DLI). 'I had been through the normal routine of registering for National Service at the local office of the Ministry of Labour and been graded "A1" by the subsequent medical board. I had spent nine years of my young life in an office, but the very official-looking communication which I then received was, I thought, going to change all that. I had been drafted into that worthy county regiment, the Durham Light Infantry, and was ordered to report to Brancepeth Castle by 1100 hours, 15 March. To be truthful, I was not entirely pleased with my posting, even though I was Durham born and bred. Needless to say, in the fullness of time I became extremely proud to belong to the mob and woe betide the delinquent who dared make disparaging remarks about "My Regiment" in my hearing. So I entered the Army full of misgivings, but determined to make the best of things as they presented themselves. For the benefit of the unlearned, Brancepeth and its surrounds was the Infantry Training Centre at which militiamen, recruits and volunteers for the "Durhams" were trained . . . it was reputed to be one of the best training centres of its kind and, after my sojourn of about three months there, I had an excellent grounding in the rudiments of infantry soldiering and, though still raw, required only that very essential and valuable experience of service with a unit to vie with the old sweats. With all modesty I would admit that I had reached the unbelievable pinnacle of being able to wear a tape at ITC – yes, it was "Acting and Unpaid".'

Together with three hundred other new recruits, Sam was then sent by train to West Hartlepool to join No. 3 Infantry Holding Unit, not knowing that they were scheduled to be shipped over to join the BEF in France. However, this was the time of, as he puts it, 'the dark days of Dunkirk', so, after spending a few days in West Hartlepool, they were scheduled to be put on a train south and called upon to sign the usual draft warning certificate. 'That very day, however, the news of the great withdrawal through Dunkirk occupied the headlines and the train got no further than Rugby. . . . For some inexplicable reason I was one of a dozen or so chaps left behind in West Hartlepool – and

I had very personal reasons for finding that good fortune very acceptable.'

Sam's unit had now been renamed as the 50th Battalion, Durham Light Infantry, and was destined to become a training unit for a few months, but then, on 15 October 1940, it was redesignated yet again as 15th DLI. He recalls: 'On 15 October 1940, therefore, the unit proper was formed – we have now seen how it was born and weaned and now it was beginning to walk. All ranks from the CO down to the humblest private soldier were deadly keen to give a good account of themselves. The battalion had been entrusted with an operational role. Besides all-round defence of the Hartlepools in the event of an invasion, we became charged with the ceaseless vigil of stretches of beaches from Hart Station to Seaton Carew, later to be extended to Blackhall Rocks. Much hard work was put in during this period.' However, they were not destined to remain in this role for long either. In May 1941, they were relieved of their duty for the defence of the beaches and became the reserve battalion in a reserve brigade, earmarked for overseas service. This heralded a period of hard, hectic training which everyone enjoyed – fighting mock battles all over the north of England. Finally, a few months later came the end of the infantry phase of their lives, with the startling news that the 15th Battalion DLI was to be mechanised. It was to become the 155th Regiment Royal Armoured Corps – with '15 DLI' placed afterwards in brackets, one of three armoured regiments in the 35th Army Tank Brigade. The other two units in the brigade were 151st RAC and 152nd RAC, which were being converted from the 10th Battalion, King's Own Royal Regiment (Lancaster) and 11th Battalion King's Regiment (Liverpool) respectively. 'Altogether these were momentous and busy times . . .', recalls Sam, 'and ere long the side cap was discarded and replaced by the black beret. Almost every officer, NCO and man was sent in cycles on courses of instruction at the 53rd and 54th Training Regiments RAC and the AFV Schools at Bovington and Lulworth, to begin from scratch and learn, this time, the art of tanking.'

Dennis Young was another conscripted infantryman, who was then 'mechanised': 'It was never my intention to be a soldier,' he recalls, 'but war and conscription changed all that. Six weeks' compulsory basic infantry training did nothing to inspire me, but thankfully I found myself being groomed for tank duties in the Royal Armoured Corps. This completely changed my attitude, apart from now being able to ride to war – preferable to walking with the infantry – I found the training and working with expensive vehicles, machinery and equipment very interesting. This was something I would never have had the opportunity to do in civilian life. Also the type of people involved were more my type. Without wishing to sound bigheaded, I think that Tankmen are a special breed, I found this also the case with other nationalities, including the enemy. . . . I trained on Crusader tanks (2-pounder gun) and Besa machine gun, obsolete Matildas and Valentines being used as statics. Early training days were geared to desert warfare, but as the fortunes of war improved in the Middle East, the scope for being posted to a Service regiment in another theatre increased, whilst the tanks themselves improved greatly, for example, the Churchill. . . . Joining the 153rd RAC (The Essex) Regiment, who were stationed near Canterbury from the 61st Training Regiment (Barnard Castle) was an experience not to be forgotten – oil and grease replacing spit and polish. . . . I was always referred to as "The Young 'Un" by an endearing bunch of comrades, my name being Young, and I was the youngest in just about everything – name, age, service, regimental status, etc. Although I was tank crew, I was sometimes deliberately left out of schemes and arduous exercises to do internal duties, guards, etc. This used to annoy me at first, until I realised it was a deliberate ploy by the older element to protect me, looking on me as the youngster of the family. What a great lot they were. However, it was because of this that I grew a moustache to make myself look older!'

'I was the first draftee out of Winnetka, Illinois,' recalled Ed 'Smoky' Steuver; 'there were twenty-nine volunteers ahead of me so I was number thirty. Roosevelt picked me out of the cherry bowl. The first number picked was 158 and mine was 185. The headline in the paper said 158 was the number one draftee. I thought that was me, my equilibrium was off and I gave the damn paper a kick, and the boss came running out of the house in his bathrobe. "What in hell is the matter with you, lad, you going be-zerk?" He was a corporate lawyer, with a red nose and cheeks from drinking scotch. I was his driver. I picked up the paper and told him, "I'm sorry, sir . . . Oh lookit here,

158, that ain't me. My number is 185.'" "Oh, that's a good reason to celebrate. Come on in, me lad." And he pours me a shot of scotch. I'd never drunk scotch before. I had four of 'em. So I drove him to work, downtown Chicago, in an open touring car. I pull up, drop him off. He says, "Ed take the car and enjoy yourself. Have a good day. Take your lady out to dinner." So I drove up to where my wife was working and said, "Come on, take the day off."'

'Smoky' got his nickname shortly after he had joined up and was at Camp Lockett, working on cavalry horses. He recalls: 'At Camp Lockett, there was a lieutenant who seemed to have a kid every year. This one particular time when he became a father he gave each of us a cigar. That morning I lit my cigar and there was a horse brought in that had a stub in its rear foot. I knew that horse, he was a mean one to work on and nobody dared to tackle him. I had worked on him before and I said, "Ohhh, watch my smoke!" I had this cigar in my mouth and I picked up that horse's foot and I said, "All right, give me those tongs," and I was about ready to pull the stub out when that horse started laying down on me, so I turned my head, that cigar hit the horse's hind end and I went flying through the air. "There goes Smoky!" someone said, and the nickname stuck with me.'

'I was working in a foundry when I got drafted,' remembers Tony D'Arpino from Whitman, Massachusetts, who became a tank driver in the 712th Tank Battalion. 'The day I was supposed to go for my physical, I told my father – he also worked at the foundry – I said: "Don't tell them where I am." They were deferring guys because they were doing government work and I didn't want to get deferred. I can remember my father being shocked, because the morning I didn't go to work, the foreman comes to him and says, "Where's Tony?" And my father says, "I don't know, he didn't come home last night." And the foreman says to my father, "Is he shacking up?" And, of course, my father said that his Tony would never do anything like that. Anyway, I passed the physical and they gave us two weeks to report. So the next morning I didn't go to work. I wasn't going to work no more, the hell with it! I was making thirty-five cents an hour. That's what they were paying. Thirty-five cents an hour. I take it back, it was forty-five cents an hour.'

'Snuffy' Fuller, also of the 712th, was twenty-seven when he was drafted. As he was older than most and already settled in a good job, he did not like being called up: 'I worked right down the street here when I was drafted. I come from Tonawanda, North Tonawanda, that's eleven miles down the line here. I was manager of a chain store, in fact I resented the Army, I was making such good money at that time. I was working for Acme Foods; they're now out of business. I was one of the top managers and to go down to twenty-one dollars a month made a hell of a difference. From there I went to Fort Niagara for indoctrination, then Fort Knox for the basic. Then war was declared and I was shipped to Fort Benning, Georgia. Stayed there a very short time and then shipped to Hawaii and got there in January of '42. And everybody was worried about invasion, but we had it pretty easy. We had these old light tanks, M2A2 something like that, with little 37-calibre machine guns . . . old clunkers, they were, with a diesel engine. We were in Scofield barracks, Oahu, Hawaii, then they moved us to Kauai, the other island, and we had to build a camp there. And that's all we did; we'd take reconnaissance around the islands but we didn't do any fighting. We'd just ride around and set up outposts once in a while. I enjoyed Hawaii, you could say I loved it. I made it as far as tech sergeant in operations and this call came through that they were looking for people for OCS [Officer Cadet School], so I put in for it, the captain OK'd it and I got shipped back to Fort Knox again. So then, after I graduated from OCS, I was sent to Camp Chaffee, Arkansas . . . then we got shipped overseas . . . on the *Queen Mary* over to England. I came late to the 712th; I was a replacement, so I didn't get there till August.'

BASIC TRAINING

All the draftees had first to receive their basic training and in the USA this was done by the large number of Replacement Training Centers (RTCs) which were set up all over the country. Their aim was to provide a steady flow of trained men to tactical units, thus relieving units of their pre-war burden of having to give basic training to newly joined soldiers. Twelve Ground Force Centers also began to operate in 1941, including one each for armour and cavalry, and during the rest of 1941, they trained over 200,000 men. In addition there were a number of Service Schools where the individual officers, officer candidates and enlisted specialists learnt their 'special to arm' skills. For armour there was also the Desert Training Center (DTC), established in a wild and desolate area – some twelve million acres, including parts of California, Nevada and Arizona, 'a vast wasteland half the size of Pennsylvania'. Its aim was described by its first commandant, the great armoured commander, General George S. Patton, Jr, as being: 'to devise formations for marching and fighting which, while affording control and concentrated firepower, at the same time do not present lucrative air targets. It is felt that these ends have been accomplished. Formations now in use can move cross-country, followed by a combat train, and without halting can deploy into the attack formation and execute an attack, and at no time present any target worthy of bombardment.' More about the DTC later and about the major manoeuvres that were held all over the USA, but first a glimpse into the life of the 'newly joined civilian soldier'.

A day in the life of a recruit

No matter their background or upbringing, the new recruit, be he volunteer or 'pressed man', quickly found himself absorbed into 'the army system' which did not vary much between armies. Here are just two examples, one from each side of the Atlantic. Jimmie Ovendine of Oak Ridge, Tennessee was drafted into the 630th Tank Destroyer Battalion,[4] which was 'born and raised' on 15 December 1941 at Camp Jackson, South Carolina. He recalls: 'Up until mobilisation of Guard and Reserve units, Jackson had served primarily as a training facility for guard units during their summer encampments. When I arrived there were very few buildings on the post. Nearly all the buildings were used for the mess hall, supply rooms, latrines [bathrooms], some for recreational facilities, classrooms and buildings for unit headquarters. Most of the troops were housed in tents, which would be known as 'Tent City'. Many areas had to be cleared of trees and stumps to make room for the influx of new troops pouring into Camp Jackson. It would soon be bursting at its seams for lack of space. As we began to assemble under the command of our first Commanding Officer, a Tennessian, we began to learn the art of soldiering. The first orders, that of learning how to salute, then going through the many days of target practice with our individual weapons. We thought Camp Jackson had the hottest firing range in the world, with all the tall pines on the reservation – they didn't leave a single one on the ranges. I suppose they wanted you to know how to appreciate a nice shady tree if you ever got to use one.

'The very first day of a soldier's life I am sure can be his most confusing day. It started at 5 a.m. with the soft, mellow tone of the bugles blowing reveille, then the whistle of the First Sergeant. I often wondered if this fellow ever slept. He would always be up when you turned in at night and when you got up. I can honestly say that he must have been made of steel. The first order of business when you roll out of your interspring cot would be to make up your bed, making sure your blanket was tight enough for a coin to bounce when the inspection officer checked your quarters, and that the letters "US" faced correctly. Your extra shoes had to be polished and placed under the foot of the bed in correct order, your extra clothing hanging to specification and your field gear that you did not wear placed in correct order. You had to sweep and mop your area and make sure there was no dust in the tent. This seems impossible, but you did it. After cleaning your area, you rushed out to the latrine that was always located at least 200 yards from your tent. There would be one latrine per company and a company of ours would have at least 120 men. Each latrine would have about twelve commodes and twelve lavatories. Words cannot describe the scene where you have about fifteen minutes to shower, shave and do other necessary things at the same time.

'The next thing would be roll call, then the assignment of extra duty for the day, such as KP [Kitchen Police], Guard Duty, trash detail, ammo detail, target pullers for small-armor firing, latrine orderly and other duties that it would take to keep the battalion running. Soon it would be breakfast (chow time). Each company would march to the mess hall. Breakfast might consist of fresh scrambled dried eggs, toast (sometimes), jelly [jam], bacon, coffee, or it might be pancakes or French toast. After breakfast the training schedule would begin – your uniform for the day would be fatigues, web equipment, leggings, steel helmet and individual weapons. We weren't up to our full strength in men or equipment, but we made the best with what we had. We knew we had to be good, there was no question about it.'

They gave him a number

On the other side of the Atlantic it was much the same for the new recruit. Brian Brazier of Evesham joined the British Army on 19 March 1942, a day he would never forget: 'but still I didn't mind going into the Army that much, it wasn't as if I hadn't been away from home for a long time before, because I had been at boarding school since I was about eight years old. And so the time came when I was going to become a soldier. Me a soldier! I had to report to Tidworth. That was a rather awkward place to get to from Evesham station, so my father and mother took me as far as Cheltenham in the car and from there it was quite a straight run. I said goodbye as the train was pulling out and found another chap who was also going to the same place, but not to 61st Training Regiment, RAC, where I was heading for. It wasn't very long before the train pulled into Ludgershall station, the junction for Tidworth where we had to change trains. The next part of the journey was only a short distance through army camps to Tidworth. On arrival we were sorted out into truckloads (how many times have we been "sorted out" since!) and taken away to our respective regiments.

'There it was in all its glory – Army life! It was a good job we didn't know what we were going to have to do during the next six weeks! After having all our particulars taken and being given our Army numbers and our Pay Books (AB 64 Parts 1 & 2), we were taken to our barrack rooms. The way the floors were polished you would have thought it was a king's palace. In each barrack room there were ten double-tiered bunks, five down each side, with a table in the middle and two forms. At the far end opposite the door was the fireplace. By each bunk bed was an iron box fastened on the wall for putting some of your kit in, the rest had to be laid out neatly on our beds. Apart from this the room was empt; however, there wasn't a great deal of room left when twenty men were in there as well. Selecting a bunk in the room was quite an orderly procedure, much more than it would have been had we only known how awkward it was to climb onto the top bunks. Anyway, I managed to get a bottom one, so I was quite happy. The chap in charge of the room was an old soldier and was called the "Room Orderly". It was his job to see that the room was tidied up each morning before we left to go on parade.

'After visiting the stores and drawing four blankets, we had nothing else to do until the following morning, so we were free to walk about and discover the NAAFI, cinema, Orderly Room, etc. in the camp area, as we were "Confined to Barracks" (CB) for three days. The beer bar was located and, after a couple of drinks and a NAAFI supper, we wended our way back in ones and twos ready for bed. The earliest night a lot of us had had for weeks, I'll bet. The next morning we were very rudely awakened by some noisy bugler at 0630 hours. What an unearthly hour to be woken up! We all dashed out of bed, or at least we were dragged out, by the Room Orderly and were just about to go and have a wash and shave when the Orderly shouted: "It's no good you all going at once because there are only five b..... wash-basins, and there's another room to use them as well and in any case you'll have no b..... time to 'bash' (i.e.: polish) this b..... floor before you go on parade, and that's going to be b..... well done, whatever happens." Well, it was decided that one side of the room would polish their side, wash and then go to breakfast, whilst the other side would go to break-fast first and then come back, wash and polish their side afterwards; the centre was left to the Orderly after we had all gone out on parade.

'Our first full day in the Army consisted of nothing else but collect-ing kit, being fitted out with boots, battledress (BD), greatcoat and beret, etc., and by the time we had been marched backwards and for-wards from the RQMS stores to our barrack room several times we were soon fed up with marching. That was nothing, we were in civil-ian clothes with shoes on. The next day we were given all to ourselves; sounds like a holiday, doesn't it? But we worked harder that day than we had ever done before in our lives. Webbing had to be blancoed yellow, all brasses had to be highly polished and two pairs of boots had to be like mirrors. That was more like a week's work than one day's and we also had to parcel up all our civilian clothes, ready addressed home, so that they could be sent as soon as possible.

'The very next day, real Army life started in earnest. We were training to be soldiers. Reveille: 0630 hours, First Parade 0800 hours, dressed in best BD, gaiters and belts for three-quarters-of-an-hour' solid drill (square bashing) under a regular Grenadier Guards RSM. After that we had five minutes to change into denims (overalls) ready for a lecture on map reading. Of course our Troop Sergeant was always calling us long before the five minutes was up. This lasted until 1000 hours when we had half an hour for break. Having a good Troop Sergeant helped tremendously at this time of the day, because he would always let us out a few minutes before time to be first in the NAAFI queue, which by five past ten would be two hundred yards long and it was almost an impossibility to get any tea and cakes before 10.30. After break we had one hour-and-a-quarter of physical training, and after that another lecture on one of various subjects, such as mines, gas, camouflage, explosives and first aid. When this was over it was dinner time and I'm sure we all felt literally starving after all that doubling about; in fact we were ready to eat almost anything they put before us. Luckily it was all very good, clean food served on white plates and always hot. After dinner we were just about dead beat, with just enough strength to reach our beds and flop down, but that lasted only half an hour, because we were on parade again at 13.30 for some more drill. Secondly a miscellaneous period, probably rifle drill, grenade-throwing or distance-judging and thirdly more PT. After tea the day was our own, after we had blancoed our belt and gaiters, and polished our boots again ready for drill again next morning.

'This went on for three solid weeks, with hardly any alteration at all. At the start of the fourth week, things seemed to get much easier. Only half an hour's PT before breakfast and no drill. For the following three weeks we had a week on wireless, a week on gunnery and a final week on driving and maintenance; at the end of each week, a test on each subject. According to the subject we were most proficient in, we were classified as a potential wireless operator, a gunner or a driver. I had made up my mind at the time that I should like to be a wireless operator, but I'm glad I became a driver.

'And so the first six weeks of Army training were over at last and we were allowed to go home again, just for seven days, but even that was better than nothing. I was met at Cheltenham station by Mother in the car. "What? Home again? When are you going back?" "I've only just arrived, don't talk about going back already!" Well, it seemed like a couple of hours to me, but I suppose it really was seven days. . . . And then back to Tidworth for a course in Driving and Maintenance (D&M) which lasted for ten weeks, being split into five on wheeled vehicles and five on tanks. During the first half we learnt everything there was to know about a Morris, a Ford, a Bedford and an Austin lorry. We saw models and real engines which had been specially sectionised, so we could see how they worked, diagrams and drawings, until we were sick of the sight of them. We did get a week driving out on the roads which was a little compensation for all the time we were learning theory. We used to go out, usually four in each lorry, with an instructor in each vehicle, every day following the same route. It was a circular trip, so that some days we went one way round and other days the opposite way. About half-way round was a café, where we always stopped for a cup of tea and a cake, better known as "Char and Wad".

'The last Friday at the end of the first five weeks, before we went onto tanks, was the best day. We were each asked a series of questions by a sergeant-instructor and then taken on a driving test. The following day we asked our regular instructor if he knew how we had got on and he told us that we had all passed with flying colours. The next weekend didn't pass half quickly enough for us. All that time we had been in the Army and had not been told anything about a tank, but on Monday we were going to know the worst, or was it going to be the best? Again, drawings, diagrams and different parts of the engine were shown to us, until we almost looked like one. The particular engine we were concentrating on was a Meadows twenty-four-cylinder, which was used in the Covenanter tank. In one of the buildings was a Covenanter which had its turret taken off and the engine taken out and what was left had been sectionised and the pipes and tubes that carried oil and compressed air were painted different colours for ease of recognition. . . . At last our week of driving came and even after all that, we had to start off driving Bren-gun carriers and work our way up. First a day on the plains, then a day on the roads and finally, at last, the next day we were allowed to try our hands on a

Covenanter. What a treat, it was so easy, considering the weight of the vehicle – the steering could be done with just a little finger. Away we went, about four on each tank and an instructor, dashing across the plains, changing up and down the gearbox, hundreds of times to get used to it. The gear lever used to be between our legs and the two small levers for steering about hand-high on either side. I soon got used to driving it, but some of the others were crashing gears all day long. After each day's driving, we used to come back into the tank park to fill the tanks up with petrol, oil and water, grease all the nipples and generally clean up ready for the next day.

'The week soon passed and test day came along again . . . I had to take off and refit a brake band, which I managed quite successfully. The next day we had our driving test on tanks and we were told by Sergeant Burns that the examiner would be an officer. I can remember thinking at the time he would be very strict and would only pass us if we were really good. Anyway it was no use worrying. I was the first one he took out of our squad. He ordered me into the driving seat and to start up the engine, while he perched himself outside, just over my driving slit. I could see his hand wave to move me off and every time he wanted me to go one way or the other he would wave his hand in front of me. We got so far without any mishap. Then he beckoned me into a wood and told me to stop on a fairly steep incline, so that he could determine whether I was able to start off again without stalling the engine. I did that perfectly and after that we returned to the starting point. When I got out, he said I was the best driver he had passed for some time and had I driven a tank before?

'That was all the tank training I had while I was with the 61st. The next thing was, if we had passed fairly well in our D&M course, we then had to take another further advanced course on D&M and if we passed that exam we became fully fledged Driver-Mechanics with an upgrade in pay.'

Before Brian could begin his next course, the 61st Training Regiment, RAC, together with many other training units had to move up north, in order to make room for the influx of American troops, arriving for the 'Second Front' (the assault onto occupied France).

Nick Deamer, who became the Wireless Sergeant of 6 RTR, initially trained as a driver operator at Perham Down in 1940: 'After six weeks' basic recruits training, we were given a choice of trade training and I opted for wireless operator,' he recalled. 'I had built amateur radio sets as a hobby and learnt morse code in the Scouts; indeed, I would have liked to have trained as a ship's radio officer. We did a six-week course with a staff sergeant instructor, touching on the No. 9 set, but mainly trained on the WS 19 (it became the main wartime wireless set to be used in British and Commonwealth AFVs). We were taught how to speak on the radio (voice procedure), how to tune the set (netting drill), and then, most mornings, went out in fifteen-hundredweight trucks, learning how to keep the set "on net" and practising our voice procedure. I was recommended for an instructor's course but fate intervened and I was put on an overseas draft, ending up with 6 RTR in the Tobruk area in April 1941. Six RTR were taken out of Tobruk by sea and thence back to Cairo and I was sent on a second basic wireless course at Abbassia.' More from Nick Deamer later, when he becomes the Commanding Officer's operator on a command tank in Regimental Headquarters – a most responsible position.

M. E. Mawson of the 13th/18th Hussars also trained as a wireless operator, this time at 58 Training Regiment in 1942. He recalled: 'Wireless work initially was still on the 11 set, of which most details escape me, soon to be overtaken by the appearance of the WS 19 Marks I and II. Hours were devoted to its operation, accurate netting and fault finding. I have the international octal-classed valve 6K79 engraved on my heart! Unfortunately no one ever explained the "whys", only the "whats" – in fact the instructor usually did not know "why"! Added to the foregoing were hours of morse-code tapping, the whole culminating in one or two "PU" ["Public Utility" – a type of small-wheeled vehicle] outings, propelled by ATS girls whose job it was to take pairs of trainees where they desired to go (but not for the reason why they wished to go!). Practically speaking, the course was adequate to prepare us for field work. After spending a similar period on gunnery, the whole course came together for a few weeks of outdoor training – roaring around Dorset, followed by a few days under the stars in the New Forest. . . . I don't think I was alone in struggling with morse code – Class III required sending and receiving messages at twelve words per minute, Class II fifteen words per minute; the latter I just could not attain thus losing sixpence a day for three-and-a-half years.' Having joined his Regiment, Mawson returned to the AFV Wireless School during the winter of 1942–43 for a month's refresher course: '. . . Like coming home! Even the previous PT "swine" turned out to be very nice when I went to see them in the evenings.' Mawson was destined to 'swim ashore' on D-Day in an amphibious Sherman 'DD' tank, as will be recounted later.

PANZER CREWMEN TRAINING

The Germans initially trained their tank crews with great care, especially the tank drivers and tank gunners. Any potential driver, for example, who did not make rapid progress was quickly taken off driving and trained for another less important job. Tank drivers were also thoroughly trained in the servicing of their vehicles, whilst gunners were expected to be able to correct all stoppages. The maxim: 'A vehicle or gun which is properly serviced never breaks down' was repeated throughout the panzer divisions, whilst cleanliness both of vehicles and equipment was given high priority, which naturally greatly assisted in their ability to operate in bad weather and over difficult terrain. They also made much of developing the 'panzer spirit', putting great faith in physical fitness – all tank crews under training began their day with physical exercises and cross-country runs. In addition, they encouraged 'cunning, resourcefulness and cool-headedness' as part of the 'panzer spirit'. As the war progressed and their casualties mounted, the strain on their training machine increased and they were unable to maintain their high standards. *Oberst* aD Hermann Rothe told me that when he first joined Panzer Regiment 5 at Wunsdorf near Berlin: 'The passing of all military driving licences in the first few months was regarded as natural. The driving lessons for tracked vehicles were usually carried out on Panzer 1s and the teachers – NCOs – made it unmistakably clear that they did not like us to stall the engines or, even worse, throw a track. The minimum punishment for this was to spend some time running behind the tank as it drove through the training area! Most of us had a civilian driving licence, but it was quite difficult to remember the differences between driving a tank and a car. Driving the panzers required a lot of physical strength; however, we all enjoyed ourselves and, once we became young officers, it gave us great respect for our tank drivers. As well as the heat and cold, the cordite fumes from firing in battle, the greatly restricted vision when the driver's hatches were closed, conditions for drivers were strenuous both on the battle-field and on the long marches in the first years of the war – in fact it bordered on the very edge of human capability. This was the main reason why the panzer driver was always highly respected and looked after by the other members of his crew.' Another ex-panzer crewman, Horst Reibenstahl, also had special words of praise for tank drivers: 'In battle the skills of the tank driver were of outstanding importance. It was the task of the driver under the supervision of the tank com-mander to try to find a suitable firing position and to reach it quickly, in order to ease the task of the turret crew. Quite often the fate of the entire crew depended very much upon the driver's skills. Therefore it was absolutely essential that he had the capability to think tactically as well as having the necessary technical skills. The crew commander always tried to take his driver with him if he had to go to command another tank for some reason.'

2

Continuation Training
then on to the Regiment

In Britain, the outbreak of war saw the small peacetime RTC Training Centre at Bovington – now the Army Armoured Fighting Vehicles School – begin a massive expansion into a country-wide organisation which had to train both instructors and recruits for the entire Royal Armoured Corps that at its peak comprised some 190 Regular, Territorial and war-formed units, added to which were two mechanised regiments of the Household Cavalry and seven armoured regiments of Foot Guards. The first step in the expansion was for each regular unit of the Cavalry and Royal Tank Regiment in the UK to form a Militia Training Squadron, which then received periodical intakes of recruits. These Militia Training Squadrons became the nucleus of the RAC Training Regiments – by the end of the second year of the war, eleven of these Regiments had been formed (51st at Catterick, 52nd at Bovington, 53rd at Tidworth, 54th at Perham Down, 55th at Farnborough, 56th at Catterick, 57th at Warminster, 58th at Bovington, 59th, 60th & 61st at Tidworth). The vital gunnery tank-firing ranges were improved/established at Castlemartin, Redesdale (Catterick), Kirkcudbright, Warcop and Minehead, whilst Lulworth was greatly increased in size. In 1943, when it was necessary for the coming invasion to find homes for the incoming Allied units etc., the southern-based training units were moved northwards. Throughout the war, however, the Army AFV School at Bovington remained the most important part of the RAC training machine.

Germany, of course, had the training 'edge' on the Allies, as they had started their expansion a lot earlier. However, they were not without their problems. 'One of the biggest difficulties,' *Oberst* aD Albert von Boxberg told me, 'was that we were ordered to operate in our tanks (PzKpfw I) with the turret hatches closed, which made it hard for the commander to observe, having only the vision slits to look through. The commander had then to depend upon the driver to help observe through the hull-visor slits or go against the rules and leave the hatch open.' The only means of command and control in those early years between 1935–37 was by semaphore as no radios existed: 'a set of six flags were issued to every tank. They had to be held in different positions out of the turret to tell the other commanders of the other tanks in the unit or sub-unit what they had to do next. This made flag drill on foot an important part of tank-crew training. In battle the turret hatch was always left open, so injuries, especially head wounds, were chances you had to take in order to be able to see all round.

'I remember a big mixed training exercise in 1936, which was held near Münster on the Lüneburger Heide. . . . The order was to drive with all hatches closed to make the exercise as realistic as possible. The first semaphore signals were given by platoon and company commanders, acknowledged and carried out properly. But as soon as battle was joined every semblance of control was lost, with tanks going everywhere in all directions. Most ended up in a marsh, where they got stuck! The criticisms were bad and the matter was discussed afterwards at a conference. Undoubtedly, however, it was not the command that had failed but rather the means of command, which is what many officers thought all along would happen. The situation changed in 1937 as the PzKpfw II with a Maybach water-cooled engine was introduced, then radios were issued for both types of tank. The PzKpfw II had a three-man crew – driver, wireless operator and commander, who was also the gunner. Although this was still far from satisfactory, it was possible to give radio orders in battle.' He then goes on to talk about the heavier, better equipped PzKpfw IIIs and IVs, which were the cornerstone of the panzer divisions throughout the war.

'Fire and movement was the foundation of the panzer battle,' he concludes, 'which we could now fulfil. These have been built on with quick decisions and commands, giving us success in the first few years of the war.'

In a report on Soviet combat methods published post-war by the Americans and entitled: 'The Russian Soldier and Russian Conduct of Battle', a German observer wrote that he considered the training of Red Army tank crewmen to have been inadequate, especially of individual tank drivers: '... their training period was apparently too short and losses in experienced drivers were too high. The Russian avoided driving his tank through hollows or along reverse slopes, preferring to choose a route along the crests which would give fewer driving difficulties. This practice remained unchanged even in the face of invariably high tank losses.'

SPECIAL-TO-ARM TRAINING

Captain Ted Player enlisted on 5 September 1939 as a private soldier in the Royal Warwickshire Regiment, then two months later transferred to the RAC and was selected to attend for training as an officer cadet at 102 OCTU, run by the Westminster Dragoons. His formal training was, to say the least, 'sketchy', but, as he explains: 'This is not intended as a reflection on the Westminster Dragoons, who did the best they could with limited resources. Driving and Maintenance, for example, consisted of group sessions round an old Morris Cowley chassis. Motor cycling was an enjoyable excursion into cross-country riding for experienced riders like myself, but an ordeal of sheer hell for the novices. The greater proportion of time was spent on TEWTS [Tactical Exercises Without Troops], with haversack rations and, with luck, a visit to a pub. The quality of our gunnery training was symptomatic of the times. We were posted for three weeks of a freezing January 1941 to Lanark, where the accomodation was a comparatively luxurious "Belisha" barracks, overheated to suffocation. Training took place in small wooden huts, each with a single – totally inadequate – Valor oil stove. The significant feature of this phase of our training was that the ranges had been approved only for small arms at that time. Consequently, my first experience of live firing with the 2-pounder was in action eighteen months later. I was commissioned on 8 March 1941.

After some weeks at the 57th Training Regiment, I was sent on a short Young Officers' course at Sandhurst.[1] There being at that time more junior officers than tanks, this was a convenient way to keep us out of mischief and remind us that, although we were officers, as second-lieutenants we were at the bottom of the heap. My abiding memory of Sandhurst is of the RSM parading us with the reminder: "You are Sir to me, Sir, and I am Sir to you, Sir!"'

'By God, that is for me!'

Norris H. Perkins, who had had the lucky escape from being drafted to the South Pacific because he failed to put enough postage on his letter requesting 'immediate active duty', was, as he had been basic-ally infantry-trained, first assigned to the Machine Gun Company of 66th Armored Regiment when he reached Fort Benning. 'It was quite glamorous,' he recollects, 'because we had more firepower than a whole old-style infantry regiment. Then one night in the bachelor officers quarters at 4 a.m., I woke up to a terrible racket. It sounded like a hundred giant iron cogwheels rolling unclad down a vibrating iron roadway. Then my dream changed. It was a battalion of ancient Trojan chariots, their metal wheels pounding the stony plain. Finally, fully awake, I remembered that I was in Fort Benning, Georgia. It was August of 1940. I felt my way over to the window to see what the hell was going on and here was a column of tanks going by. There was a tremendous wonderful gnashing of steel sprockets, the roaring of motors, the fire shooting out of the exhausts, the tank commander in each turret wearing a crash helmet. I thought, "By God, that is for me!" So I applied for an Armored Force School tank-maintenance course at Fort Knox. After three months of that, I came back to Company H, 3rd Battalion, 66th Armored Regiment.

COLLECTIVE TRAINING

Norris Perkins' first company commander was a member of a very prominent Columbus, Georgia family, whom he discreetly refers to as

'Captain Harry Bumpkin' when he recollects: 'You will see why in a minute! When Colonal Patton, not quite a general, was conferring with the city fathers and the mayor of Columbus about integrating this big, new division into the community of Columbus and Fort Benning, somebody said, "Colonel Patton, you will be very happy to know that we have a member of a very prominent family going to be in your division, his name is Captain Harry Bumpkin." Colonel Patton said, "Goddamnit, I am not looking for breeding stock, I am looking for fighters!" Well, they made a fighter out of Captain Bumpkin. He was my first company commander. He was a roly-poly fellow, thirty-six years old. He had a high-pitched voice which went higher when he got excited. He was a fatherly figure. He was like a daddy to his little recruits and the men liked him, but he did some funny things. One time, he put a green light on the back of his turret so we could see which was his tank on manoeuvres. Of course they called it: Captain Bumpkin's rolling prophylactic station! Another funny thing he did was when he was guiding us into a bivouac one night – black-out, low lights – he said, "Watch my light; keep your eyes on my flashlight. If I go this way, you go that way if the light goes that way. You follow me now. Keep your eyes on the light." The light disappeared. The crew got out to see what had happened. Captain Bumpkin was down in the bottom of a deep pit – they had to help him get out.

'Now all about the "Wild ride of Captain Bumpkin" which gives me a chance to tell you about the M2A4 light tank. Eleven-and-a-half tons, you could get it up to sixty-five m.p.h. on the highway. It had a seven-cylinder Continental radial air-cooled engine which was really too powerful for that little tank. Each track weighed 1,600 pounds. Our company got delayed once in a road march in Tennessee. Captain Bumpkin was scared to death that he was going to lose the tail of the regiment, so he took off at top speed in his tank to catch up. I happened to be in a jeep. I soon found out that he was strewing the company all along the road and a lot of people just moved off to the side of the road and gave up; they couldn't keep up with him and couldn't find him; didn't know which way he went. I decided I had better catch him and slow him down. After about fifteen miles I finally caught up with him, at about sixty-five to seventy m.p.h. in that jeep. Here was a phosphorescent monstrosity, a beautiful sight. The unmuffled exhaust was spouting red and blue flames; a tremendous roar of the engine; fantastic roar of the tracks going forward from the rear idlers over to the roaring sprockets and static electricity shimmering along the sides of the tank. It was truly an awe-inspiring sight, and that is my lasting vision of the M2A4 tank.'

Norris also took part in the famous 1941 manoeuvres in Louisiana, when Patton did what General Hobart had done to Gordon Finlayson on the manoeuvres around Mersa Matruh. He recalls: 'Patton took the entire 2nd Armored Division across the Sabine River in southern Louisiana into East Texas. Then we went north for 100 miles and came back into northern Louisiana in the rear of the enemy north of Shreveport and won the manoeuvres – stopped the whole thing a day early!' *En route* they had almost run out of fuel, '. . . at 100 miles we began running out of gas; we outdistanced our supply and Patton privately bought some local oil company's gasoline to keep the division going. According to him, anything is fair in love, war and manoeuvres.

'We were surprised at the realism of simulated combat between units of all sizes. Movement action, co-ordination of effort, excitement, noise, hunger and exhaustion approximated to the real thing. The firing of large and small blank ammunition could scarcely be heard above the roar, clatter and rumble of armoured vehicles. Giant Army sound trucks off in the forests broadcast amplified recordings of bombs, sirens, cannon fire, rifle and machine-gun fire, the hissing of gas canisters and the roar of aeroplanes and motors. This added realism was so loud that we had to shout to be heard. The presence of burned powder, diesel exhaust, smoke and dust left nothing to add. The news writers and photographers were having a field day.'

However, on occasions, training was spontaneously made even more realistic by those taking part, as Norris recalled: 'A base of fire of three medium tanks was covering the attack of two other tanks a quarter-mile away on a simulated enemy strong point. Impulsively the men in the base began shooting live 30-calibre ammunition at the manoeuvring tanks. The target tanks heard the pings of the bullets and began dodging, getting into the spirit of things, and they had a lot of fun shooting at moving tanks at a quarter-of-a-mile range.'

JOINING THE REGIMENT

Peter Comfort, known to his friends as 'Cosy', trained with the 54th Training Regiment and then joined the 13th/18th Hussars: 'I escaped at last from Perham Down, Tidworth somewhat battered and bewildered; the 54th Training Regiment, Royal Armoured Corps had that effect; with seven other child soldiers [Cosy was aged seventeen years and ten months when he joined the 13/18H] I arrived at Chippenham Park, Suffolk – lambs to the slaughter – amongst old sweats, the Lillywhites. Three in a Nissen hut; within five minutes my precious tank beret had disappeared; my initiation had begun. But I was a 3 & 8.

'That evening I sewed on my Panda, the 9th Armoured Div Sign, looked at my first 13/18 capbadge and collar dogs. Later housey-housey in the canteen; I never won, but Jo Mears, bless him, bought me a tea and a bun – a Cavalry man. Morning, Acres-Douglas, Captain, I believe, mentioned Kent and hops, smiled kindly and welcomed me to the Regiment. As a gunner/operator I was temporarily posted to Transport Troop, to fill a gap of which there were many at the time. Driving with six hours' previous instruction was not my forte, my first encounter with a fifteen-hundredweight truck, a somewhat light vehicle with a fearsome large engine, a nightmare clutch and gearbox, which soon showed me who was the master. Indeed, it – the truck – purposely failed to negotiate the wide entrance to Chippenham Park, graciously marked by the two brick pillars surmounted on top by two-foot – or perhaps larger? – concrete balls. Rather stately, rather grand, or *was*, for with a crash, it – the ball – toppled, not slowly, embedding itself into the bonnet before my horrified eyes. A crowd gathered; no wrath, no words, just grins. The silence was broken; one word: COR! I thought fourteen days cook-house fatigues was quite reasonable. Bless Acres-Douglas, who also grinned.

'To Skipton in Wharfedale, strange cobbled streets and cotton mills; the lows, virginity lost; rather sad; rather unromantic; more like rape of a youth; no Esther Rantzen in those days, she was twice my age, hair curlers under scarf, clogs on feet and ate fish and chips. Ah well, it happens to us all. Sad. The highs of Skipton? The Moors, the Hole-

46

in-the-Wall pub, one of many; the free drinks from the wonderful townsfolk: 'Come home to supper, lad. I have three unmarried daughters.' The sudden click of the brain after weeks, or was it months, the morse code flowed, never to be forgotten. Sergeant Vickery smiled quietly, success after so much patience. Now in my present older age, I listen and it helps me to sleep; strange. . . . The lows again; the Adjutant's parade, the guard duties on a Saturday night, the boils on my neck especially in the tank turret; the low spirits of that period; defeats in the Near and Far East; my mother aged forty-eight died; my elder brother, twenty-two, killed in action; the family business destroyed by bombs; my younger brother seriously wounded in the bombing.

'And so to Suffolk, Wickham Market; the highs were great, the laughs were many. Early summer, the park, lake, schemes, bell-tents, evening walks, even the night guards were warm, mainly wonderful country perfumes, dawn mists, the cuckoo, the drone of returning bombers to Mildenhall filled the air, Godspeed to safety. A further laugh, should I say: "Fire Picquet"; Fairbanks shaving in a Nissen hut by the light of a candle balanced on the table by a knife stuck in the woodwork. "They'll never miss us, Cosy; a pint at Wickham Market." Was it the Lamb? Returning rather later than planned, a glow in the sky, lots of shouting. Fairbanks' Nissen hut was well ablaze. "Did you put that bloody candle out?" A solemn shake of the head, a marvellous organist but very absent-minded. We joined the fire-fighters silently, then stole away into the darkness with our secret.

'The lows of Suffolk? Why, of course – Provost Sergeant Cahoolie, that connoisseur of the English language; "Nah then boy, come 'ere. Stand steel. Stand up straight. What's yer bleedin' name? Number?" I never saw him write, perhaps he . . . but how did he become a sergeant? And dysentry in a bell-tent, five hundred yards from the loo, thank God for the fir trees. Another laugh, the redoubtable Sergeant Cahoolie hospitalised with sunburn while haymaking. The whole regiment, officers and ORs, smirked and quietly celebrated.

'The DD Valentine² on Fretton Lake, Brigadier Brian Palmer, erect aft, and suddenly stopped – no petrol! Whose feet didn't touch? The Sherman with engine doors tied with string, discovered by the Brigadier – same one – on his dawn sortie. Bog-eyed Hussars, unwashed, unshaven. Dickie Harrap checked for a haircut, shudders all round. When the Brigadier was about, everyone, but everyone, jumped. Some man, some leader. But long hair or short, Colonel Harrap was to die in June next year. A high was Linney Head, Pembrokeshire, a firing range, the 'Water-lilies'; the boulders, raw, forgotten in the surf. White bread and eggs in rural Wales; the Welsh loved their table, as did Buckshot Smith, the regimental butcher and poacher extraordinaire; soup and stew, feathers, bones and all, I have never tasted better. The low of Linney Head, an upturned tank, the officer crushed. "You and you and you, to the Squadron Office. Funeral firing party." Duffy was kind and sympathetic. "Now, now. That won't do on the day lads. Let's get it right. Reverse arms again; Present arms; prepare; fire; again fire; re-load, fire." We were right on the day and his parents stood silent by the graveside. The Regiment always looked after its own.

'So north to Scotland, Hodden Castle, Echefechan, Annan, Lockerbie, such names and people. The highs were the dances and Scottish reels on Saturday nights in Annan; the lows, missing the lorry and walking ten miles back in the snow and, dare I say it? Sergeant Poley-Moor – enough said. And still further north to Fort George. January 1944, 0800 hours Inverness Station. The 3 and 8s arrive, six inches of snow. The Hussars, ever hopeful, look for transport. What transport? Duffy squares himself to the wintery blast. "Come on, you lads. Form up. We'll march." Hussars never march, but we did. Hours later, Fort George, the Dartmoor of the north. How did the Seaforths manage in the winter in kilts? The highlights? A shave after schemes on the Firth, hot meals, sweet tea and bed. Loch Ness, the heather; sleeping under the stars, grouse calling; larks and, finally, the tank train to Hampshire. Three days or was it five? The engine driver who stopped to shoot a rabbit or two; the Camp coffee made with steam from the engine; the jamjars of tea and sandwiches in the middle of the night at stations who knows where, by wonderful ladies. Britain at war. Petworth. Highlights before they close the gates; a civilised tea in the old tea-room; the peace and calm of the park; the excitement of preparation, the activity, the comradeship. King George VI, General Eisenhower, "Tally-ho! Godspeed Hussars." A low note, my poisoned finger, Major Cordish-Simpson, the dipping of said finger into boiling water! And his remark: "Now, lad, you won't feel a thing when the skin grows again." What a cordy! What a man! What a great man! We all loved him so.

'Then Gosport, high notes: seeing my old school OTC Royal Marine instructor, Sergeant Padden, all of sixty, recalled to duty as a traffic marshal; he gave me a toffee. His son, Jack, my school friend, he said, had been rescued from the *Ark Royal*, sunk in the Mediterranean. War is strange. Low notes: the heat, the traffic queues, the narrow streets, wandering people, the fumes from a thousand engines, the revs and stalls, the curses of tired drivers; and then the sea.'

'The best training I had.'

The trade and crew training continued, of course, even when men had joined their units, as Ted Player recalls: 'The best training I had was probably the spell when I joined 41 RTR. They were initially stationed in the Farnham area and later moved to Worthing. It was largely a matter of being thrown in at the deep end and learning the job by doing it. I had command of 1 Troop in 'A' Squadron, three Valentines called 'Ajax', 'Achilles' and 'Anzac'; they were tough and reliable, but I am thankful I never had to go into action in one. It asked too much of a troop commander, to control his own tank and two other tanks, load the gun and operate the radio in a turret not much roomier than two dustbins and with no commander's cupola. After several months of exercising around the South Downs, there was still no sign of the Division being selected for a more active role, so I entered my name for overseas service.'

In other units, such as 44 RTR, a Territorial Army battalion, most of the basic crew training was done in the unit. They had been embodied as a tank battalion on transfer from the infantry (6 Glosters), so, as Arthur Soper recalled: 'At that time none of us knew anything about armour or its usage. Enthusiasm and black berets were our limit at the time.' An initial weeding out was necessary and, '. . . those who were not considered to be "tank material" were posted away to other arms and units. Then followed *the treadmill* [selection for crew training]. It began with a squadron parade, SSM with a clipboard. "Fall in on the right anyone who holds a driving licence." This group were tested on wheeled vehicles and put on locally run courses, at the end of which tests were set. The "fliers" were earmarked as potential tank drivers, trade tested and those who passed were awarded a five-pointed star to be worn on the left sleeve and were henceforth known as "Driver/Mech III". Their basic AFV trade training then began in earnest – on our antiquated equipment. Trade pay was one shilling a day.

'Another day, another squadron parade – same SSM, same clipboard. "Does anyone know anything about wireless – apart from listening to it?" Some responders, mostly "don't knows". Question and answer session and initial selection made for training as Driver/Operators – it was considered necessary in those days to have knowledge of a second crew trade in case of emergencies. Wireless training followed, in basic fault finding and rectification, RT operating procedure [voice] and WT [morse code] up to twelve words per minute. WT was very rarely used, except in the Western Desert when units were beyond RT range. As far as I know, driver/operators were rarely called upon to drive, except in light tanks. The second trade for operators was obviously gunnery.

'Once the requirement for these trades was satisfied, up to basic standards – the local training for gunners was very basic indeed, the main armament being the obsolete 3-pounder of the Medium Mark II tank which we never used in action. The light tank carried a Vickers machine gun, which we also never used in action. Gunners, once identified, were sent to Lulworth [the Gunnery Wing of the Army AFV School] for training on the good old 2-pounder and the Besa machine gun.

'Of the original group of driving-licence holders, those who were not identified as AFV drivers, or were surplus to initial AFV requirements, became "B" Echelon wheeled-vehicle drivers. Subsequent operational requirements often required reallocation from wheels to tracks and sometimes vice versa.

'All of this selection and training took place in step with learning how to be soldiers. We were lucky in this connection, as soon after the outbreak of war, we received a fairly large intake of regular soldiers and recalled reservists who, with their experience, taught us lots of things not specifically to be found in any training manuals, but nevertheless essential to our calling, like living and working together, etc.'

Continuation training

In some cases, this training did not finish even while they were in progress to, or when they had reached, their overseas theatre. For example, Norris Perkins was a member of the American element of the Operation 'Torch' Task Force which landed in North Africa in November/December 1942. He recalled: 'Training on the high seas, December 1942. We constructed out of trash and cardboard, dummy traversing and elevating wheels, mounted on boxes, simulating tank cannon controls. A target scene was painted on canvas. The instructors drilled gunners in speedy adjustments of fire for pretended high or low shots, teaching rapid bracketing of targets. . . . Further training in Morocco. After the successful three-day campaign against the French in November, and further landings in December, intensive training was continued in the Cork Forest of Mamora north of Rabat, the capital of French Morocco. We found that the 75mm tank cannon was extremely accurate because of its excellent controls and heavy stability of the gun platform (the tank). As an example, we hit the trunk of a tree a mile away and knocked it down on the third or fourth bracketing round. Even the .30-calibre ball-mounted bow gunner's machine gun, without any gunsight, was accurately controlled by watching the tracer through the periscope. We could roll a burst of fire into a hat at a couple of hundred yards.

'A daring innovation by Lieutenant-Colonel Harry Semmes was to have tanks close in on an objective all buttoned up, while supporting artillery fired airburst shells directly over them. General Patton, Corps Commander, gleefully rode through one of these exercises in one of our tanks, firing the bow gun. The crew reported that he melted the gun barrel!'

MOVING TO NEW THEATRES – TROOPSHIPS, ETC.

Getting to a new theatre or even to a new part of the country presented our young hopefuls with new problems and new experiences, nowhere greater than for the GIs who normally had to move long distances in the vastness of the continental USA before reaching their port of embarkation for that 'great adventure' – the journey across the Atlantic in a troopship. This was, of course, in the days before mass movement by air, so most of the moves were completed by train. 'Movement by train is quite an experience,' recalls Jimmie Ovendine; 'there weren't enough pullman [sleeping] cars available for troop movement, so we had day coaches. Each man was issued with two barrack bags, called "A" and "B" bags, upon entering the Army, for packing his individual equipment in. The natural thing to do was to put the least used items in the bottom and the things you would need on or near the top. Guess what? You would inevitably do the opposite! Each bag had a draw cord and the best way to carry both bags was to tie them together and sling them around your neck. I have never figured out why no one was hanged. It was something to watch men trying to enter the door of a troop train with two bags wrapped around their necks. Our equipment was loaded onto flat cars and baggage cars and us into day coaches. Two men per seat. We knew that it would take several days to get to our new camp at Fort Hood, in Texas (the new Tank Destroyer Training Centre), so we would have to improvise a bed. We would take our bags, stack them on the floor of the coach between the seats, turn the back of the seats so when you sat down you would face the fellow across from you. In doing this you could put your feet on the seat and he could do the same thing and this would allow you some room to stretch out. No one dared take his shoes off. The Kitchen Car would be located next to the cars which carried the company. While *en route* to Hood only two meals a day were prepared.'

Across the Atlantic

After further training at Fort Hood, it was off to the east coast ports from where the main UK-bound convoys departed. Jimmie Ovendine continues: 'When the ferry that carried us reached the unloading dock, we were greeted by an Army band playing and Red Cross ladies serving milk, coffee and doughnuts. The *Queen Elizabeth* and the *New Amsterdam* were in dock. We began loading onto the *New Amsterdam*, which was the third largest liner afloat. It had been on service in the Pacific prior to this trip. This would be her first voyage in the Atlantic.

It was a huge vessel. Its cargo doors were open on the side, with gang-planks entering them. Each one of us had a duffel bag, individual weapons and most were carrying some office equipment. We began loading onto the ship. It had beautiful stairways that led to each level. We went up those stairs, then back down. Seems they didn't know just where to put us. Soon we were led into the theatre of the ship. The seats had been removed and bunks installed, seven deep. All the battalion would be quartered in this auditorium for the voyage – some 800 plus. It would be rather crowded conditions.

'The ship began its journey late in the afternoon of 3 June 1944. On 6 June we were awakened by the noise of gunfire. This really frightened all of us. Here we were, in the middle of the Atlantic with no protection except for the weapons on the ship. Soon the ship's commandant came on the intercom instructing all troops to remain calm and in their assigned quarters. "This is an enemy attack," he announced. I don't have to tell you it scared the wits out of everyone. When we were at Kilmer we had gone through the practice of climbing down a rope ladder just in the event of our ship being attacked. Now it appeared we would be going through the real thing and not just another dry run. There were about eight thousand troops on board and we weren't sure that there would be enough lifeboats to cater for everyone.

'Above us on the top deck there were 20mm and 40mm anti-air-craft guns, mounted for the ship's protection and they began firing continuously. Everyone felt sure we were under attack by enemy air-craft. Every once in a while there would be the sound of cannon fire and it felt as though the ship had been struck by a torpedo. We all began making preparations to abandon ship. One of the fellows put on his overcoat, then his life jacket, with his duffel bag over one shoulder and his rifle over the other. Someone asked him why he was lugging all that equipment with him and he replied that he wasn't going to leave anything behind because he didn't want to pay for it! This was funny to everyone even at a time like this.

'Soon the firing ceased and a voice came over the phone for all pas-sengers to go to their assigned stations at once. We all marched orderly out of the theatre and lined up on deck to await orders to abandon ship. As you looked out across the ocean there was nothing in sight and, as the old saying goes, the closest land was straight down! All the troops were now on deck and the ship's commandant announced that today was 'D-Day'. Allied troops had landed in France and this was his way of celebrating the landing, plus giving the ship's gun crews some practice. Everyone was excited over the news and very happy that we had not been under enemy attack. It turned out to be a very joyful day. I'm sure everyone uttered a prayer to Him above for those men taking part in the invasion and perhaps for himself as well.

'There were so many troops aboard the _New Amsterdam_ that they only fed twice a day. The food was so bad you could hardly stomach it. Everywhere you looked you could see sick men hanging on the side rail, although I'm sure the ship's kitchen staff did their best under such conditions. . . . The "Ink Spots" were on board and they entertained the troops in the Grand Ball Room which had been converted into the mess hall. They had to put on their show at three different times for everyone to see it. It was great entertainment. There was not much we could do on board due to the crowded conditions, other than play cards or dominoes and read. One day each soldier received a bottle of Coke. It was hot and there was no way to cool it, so one of the fellows decided that if he tied his bottle to a tent rope and dropped it into the water alongside the ship, it would be cold in a short time. This sounded like a good idea. Some fellows gave him their tent ropes so he could tie them end to end. It would require about forty feet of rope. After tying the ropes together and the Coke on the end, we all watched as he lowered his Coke down to the water. As soon as it reached the water the rope snapped and down went his Coke. It's probably still somewhere at the bottom of the Atlantic Ocean now, if a shark didn't drink it. None of us realised how fast we were going until that Coke bottle hit the water. . . . We were allowed to take a shower at certain schedules. I'll never forget my first salt-water shower using GI soap. That was an experience in itself. Someone remarked that it was as rough as a corn cob!'

On to France

Their journey across the Atlantic ended at Glasgow on 13 June, so the voyage had lasted ten days. Their next sea voyage would be considerably shorter – by LST (Landing Ship Tank) across the Channel to France, which took place almost immediately: 'a very pleasant trip,' recalled Jimmie; 'the water was calm and no one was seasick. Late that afternoon we could see the coast of France and thousands of ships near the beach. It was a sight to behold. Many small craft had been sunk near the beach to serve as a breakwater, so the small landing craft could continue to unload men and supplies. Not very far from our LST we could see the remains of the Mulberry harbour[3] that had been destroyed about two weeks after the invasion by a hurricane. It was nothing now but a mass jumble of steel and concrete jutting out of the water. They told us to bed down because we could not unload until the next morning when the tide would be out and we would be sitting on the sandbar of the beach. We took our blankets, spread them on the steel deck and lay down for what we knew would be our last peaceful night of rest. Off in the distance you could hear the rumble of artillery fire and see the flash of guns and every once in a while you would hear a shell explode on the beach.

'No sooner had we bedded down for the night when all of a sudden the ships, and on the beach AA guns, began firing into the sky. "Bed Check Charlie", as he was called, was overhead. A few bombs fell off in the distance, but it sounded as though they exploded right next to our LST! It was a nerve-racking experience. We survived the night and early the next morning, after our breakfast of "K"-Ration ham and eggs, we began driving off the LST. Up the sand road away from the beach, as we unloaded, you could look all around and see pillboxes and other fortifications the Germans had constructed to guard the beach from the invasion forces. You looked in awe and wondered how those fellows in the first wave of the landings had ever made it. Words are not adequate to describe the destruction that was all around us.

'The assembly area selected for the battalion turned out to be an apple orchard for some of the companies. I'm sure this suited the fellows very much. It was located near Colombieres, a short distance from the beach. The drive from the beach-head to the assembly area was not a very pretty sight. The roadsides were littered with equipment that had been destroyed or abandoned in the battle for this area. German dead lay in the ditches or their bodies had been collected and stacked like cordwood. To us it was an awful sight and terrible odour.

One we would become accustomed to. Each company moved into its assigned area and began setting up bivouacs immediately. We had been told we would be in this area at least two days and nights. Each platoon would be responsible for its own security and defence. There were a few foxholes or slit trenches in the area that had been dug by troops who had occupied the area before we arrived, but not enough for everyone, so those who didn't find one already prepared began the task of digging theirs. It had been real dry and the ground was like concrete, much harder than the ground in Tennessee. After hours of digging, most everyone had his foxhole for protection when off the vehicles. One fellow became disgusted with digging his foxhole, threw down his pick and shovel and said, "If they get me, it will be on top of the ground. I'm not going to dig any more." His trench was not more than six inches deep.

'During the day we spent checking and re-checking our weapons . . . We checked radios to make sure they worked, re-packed our vehicles . . . we welded a bar about six feet long on the front bumper of all the jeeps. This bar had a sharp leading edge with an indent cut in it about three inches from the top. This was done in order to cut any cable or wire the Germans would tie across the road in order to sever a man's head if he hit this wire in an open vehicle or on a motor cycle. If we didn't have anything else to do, someone would start up a card or dice game. The *Stars and Stripes* newspaper was passed around for all the troops to read. All this helped pass time away. About 2300 hours it began to get dark and everyone made preparations to bed down for our first night in France. We had been told that if you cover yourself with a blanket, it would offer you some protection from falling debris, such as shrapnel from exploding shells. Everyone made sure he had a blanket. Soon after midnight "Bed Check Charlie" made his round. It seems as if every AA weapon fired at him, never scoring a hit. The sky became bright as day with exploding shells, tracer bullets and searchlights. For new, green troops, this would scare the shit out of you – and we were all green troops! We each grabbed a blanket and made for our hole in the ground. We made up our minds to stay in them for the rest of the night. During the night you could hear someone chipping away at the earth and the next morning we heard a voice crying out: "Help! Someone get me out of here!" The fellow who had made the remark that he wasn't going to dig his hole any deeper had dug down about eight foot deep and couldn't get out. Everyone had a good laugh over this.'

Via the Queen Mary *to Metz and blow-up rubber tanks*

Snuffy Fuller was a later arrival in the ETO (European Theatre of Operations), having first served in Hawaii, then attended OCS in the USA, so he did not join the 712th Tank Battalion until August 1944. His journey over the Atlantic had been uneventful: 'It was worse going to Hawaii at the beginning of the war, they took so much time zigzagging and fooling around, as safety precautions. The *Queen Mary* was nothing, just like a pleasure cruise, except for standing watch on the deck at night, submarine watch. That was OK, because we, the officers, had cabins instead of troop compartments. Those were all right on the *Queen Mary* but not on the trip to Hawaii, those were brutal. They were hammocks four high and common toilets – they had one big trough almost like half of the ship, you sit on one side here and do your job and turn your head and puke on the other side. That was a really rough trip. But anyway, England was fine, the usual. Sitting around and waiting. We bounced around these replacement depot areas. Then finally we got shipped over to France and we landed – darn, I forget the name of the town. This was way after D-Day, this was in August, and we bounced around the repo depots for a while, I think the last one was Fontainebleau; got to see Bing Crosby there, I had a first-row seat too, that night. I loved his music.

'Finally we got shipped out to the 712th, they sent me to "B" Company, Captain Vutech was the O. C. We were in a farmhouse outside of one town the other side of Metz, doing indirect firing. So every once in a while they sent somebody up with one officer, we had to register the guns, just to see where you're shooting. I got up to this little town of Gravelotte, it was beat up pretty bad, but this had been my first taste of war and of course we got some shelling up there. One night I tried to walk down the road towards Fort Metz and they threw a bunch of mortars at us, we got the hell out of there in a hurry! There was this small group of soldiers in Gravelotte and, of course, your

57

infantry was down below. That was all right, we enjoyed that. Somebody killed a pig one time and we had a nice pig roast. We were staying there in a farmhouse and Captain Vutech told me that our next move was towards Metz. They were gonna get a bunch of these rubber tanks and halftracks, these fake vehicles, and have a sound system. And he said: "And you're gonna lead 'em. That's your job." He was giving me the bullshit. But they did have some of those fake vehicles, I read somewhere they used them.'

To Egypt round the Cape

Having completed his training as a Driver Mechanic at the AFV School, Bovington, Brian Brazier found himself rigged out in tropical kit, 'including sun topees which were more trouble than they were worth because we never wore them and on reaching Egypt they were taken off us'. However, at this stage he had no idea where he was going, the first rumour being India, then at 0530 hours on 24 October 1942, he found himself marching down to Wool station for the last time, although on arrival there they still did not know where they were going. The train took them to Salisbury, Bath, then on to Avonmouth, where at 1330 they arrived right alongside the SS *Arawa*, a converted Argentine meat boat, with three decks below the top deck, all filled to capacity with British troops 'going to war'. He recalls: 'The deck we were on was similar to the other decks on the ship that accommodated troops. It had tables bolted down each side of the ship, and onto the portholes which were always kept firmly shut. At each table sat about eighteen men, each man keeping the same place throughout the journey for his meals. Our kit was stacked up in racks above our heads, so that whenever anything was wanted it probably meant moving several other fellows' kit beforehand to get it, and someone nearly always got a clout on the head with something that fell down. Getting to bed at night was a real pantomime. I never thought I should live through it. If you can imagine fifty or sixty chaps all trying to sling a hammock at the time in a very confined space, get undressed and get into it; the smell of dirty feet, no fresh air, kit everywhere and blankets falling on the deck, you've got a pretty good idea of how it was. I'd never been under such circumstances before and I most certainly hope I never have to be pressurised to suffer the same situation ever again. It was absolutely foul. The atmosphere was almost thick enough to cut with a knife. Perspiration from sticky bodies, smelly socks, the occasional fart, all intermingled with fag smoke; it was a wonder half of us were not choked to death before morning. After four whole days the ship was at last full to the brim with troops and just about ready to put to sea.'

The SS *Arawa* left port early on 28 October and steamed north to meet up with other ships from Liverpool and Glasgow and then the convoy moved off and, as Brian recalls, 'there was nothing but water, water and more water. After the next three days the sea began to get very rough, making the ship roll and toss quite heavily. Up till then I had been feeling reasonably well but before long I began to feel the effects of being on the high seas and for the next week felt like nothing on earth. I used to amble up on deck first thing in the morning and find a storage box close to the rail to sit down and there I would stay until night time. I rarely had anything to eat, although being continually advised to do so, but I knew that it wouldn't stay down long enough to do me any good. The feeling of sea-sickness is something never to be experienced. The continual retching all day long began to make my whole body ache and I'm sure the colour of my face looked exactly like the sea water – a very pale green! Anyway, as time passed I began to feel better, getting used to the ship's roll and finding my sea legs. From then on life wasn't too bad at all, although we were always kept busy all day long, having lectures on different subjects and the usual PT classes. Day after day went by with nothing to see except water and the occasional school of flying fish keeping up alongside the ship and at night it was possible to distinguish luminous fish in the dark. The climate gradually got hotter and hotter, until it was possible to walk about on deck in nothing but a pair of shorts, but we were always being warned about getting sunburnt; it was classed as a self-inflicted injury and could mean being put on a charge (Army Form 252).'

Unfortunately this is just what Brian Brazier did. One free afternoon he decided to have a nap on deck. He sensibly chose a nice shady spot under an overhanging part of the upper deck, but when he woke he was out in full sunshine (because the ship had had to alter course to deceive marauding submarines) and the whole front of his upper body was soon red raw! 'There was nothing I could do, I had no soothing cream or sun lotion to put on and there was no question of reporting sick to ask for any. Having to wear any clothing close to the skin for several days after that was sheer agony but it was no good complaining. Eventually the redness turned brown and every shred of skin peeled off and at last I was back to normal and able to stand any amount of sun from then on.'

After about six weeks they reached their first port of call, which was, surprisingly, Bahia in Brazil, but they were soon off again across the south Atlantic to Durban in South Africa, where, as they approached the harbour he could: 'hear a lady's voice singing all the favourite tunes, such as "Land of Hope and Glory", "There'll always be an England" and the "White Cliffs of Dover", but it wasn't until we came very much closer before we could make out where it was coming from – there standing on the edge of the quay was a rather stoutish blonde-haired woman, dressed all in white, with a large straw hat on and a megaphone in her hand, singing at the top of her voice. She sang continuously while the whole convoy was moving in and apparently, we learned afterwards, she stood there singing every time a convoy came in or went out of the harbour. She must have had some inside information on the movements of ships.'

Whilst they were at Durban, the soldiers were allowed on shore in relays, drawing lots to see who would remain on board to look after the kit and Brazier was clearly impressed with the town: 'it all seemed so lovely and clean and well spaced out, all the streets being very wide avenues with trees on each side.' The shops he described as being 'packed with goodies of every conceivable kind which back in England at that time were almost non-existent', whilst at nighttime it was 'so lovely and bright everywhere, compared with Blighty and its black-out'. The convoy left Durban after refuelling, sailed on to Aden, then up the Red Sea to Port Tewfig (Port Taufiq), 'our final disembarkation stage, very close to the southern entrance to the Suez Canal. I think we were all pretty glad the long sea voyage was at last over, after being cooped up on board that troopship for so long.'

Air trooping

Movement of troops by air was of course still in its infancy as compared with modern air trooping. However, the Germans, for example, did make some use of aircraft to fly troops across the Mediterranean and thus avoid the hazardous journey by sea. Lieutenant Ralph Ringler, who joined 104 Panzer Grenadier Regiment in North Africa, kept a personal diary of his journey from Germany in August 1942. The first leg was by train, over the Brenner Pass and down through Italy to Brindisi, via Rome. Then, on 6 August, in the rainy darkness of an early morning, he and fifteen others flew off in a Junkers Ju 52. He recalled: 'I was in a Junkers Ju 52 with fifteen men, nine of whom were officers, with all our weapons and luggage stowed away. I flew for the first time. It felt odd to begin with, the sight of the world from above was unique. The people were little dots, the ships in the harbour like toys, then the endless sea. The monotonous noise of the motors and the heat and tiredness made me fall asleep. When I woke again I saw the Greek islands somewhat covered by haze, still indescribably beautiful. As the water became shallower by the shore the islands were surrounded by the whole spectrum of colours from deep blue to bright green. The aeroplane banked over towards the landing field at Maleme in Crete. Under us there were piles of destroyed Ju 52s, signs of the hard battles that had raged there a year ago.'

After spending a few hours in Crete they flew on to North Africa. Here is how Ringler described the final landfall: 'We flew low over the British-controlled Mediterranean Sea. Bashfully Gunter asked if there were any life jackets. The pilot only grinned. They were totally useless. We were flying so low so that "Tommy" would not see us, but if in spite of this he did, then any attempt to escape would be impossible. We couldn't climb and if we were shot down we would plunge into the water within seconds. Nobody would be able to get out of the machine so why bother with life jackets? He was right. "But we've got a machine gun," I interjected. The pilot laughed again, "totally full of sand and roasted, not one shot will come from that again." This was my first taste of the attitude of "Kismet" [it is up to Fate to decide] of those who fought in Africa. The dark green sea with its white crests, the regular buzzing of the engines and the heat finally made me fall asleep. I awoke confused, the sun seemed even more powerful. My uniform clung to my body. Then I saw a flash out of the sun and started – an enemy hunter! The pilot had seen him a long time ago and was amused at our fear. "German fighter cover from Tobruk." "Haven't we had any fighter protection all the way from Crete?" "No, Lieutenant, we've been lucky. Yesterday a formation of JUs was shot down completely."

'Whilst I once more pondered the meaning of the Arab "Kismet", the pilot dug me in the ribs and pointed below. We had climbed higher and I should see the sea below us and, as if drawn by a ruler, the African coast, and the dazzling orange yellow plain – the desert. "Tobruk!" That was a couple of white spots around a bay. My eyes were blinded by the glare when the Ju 52 jolted to a halt. Suddenly the pilots became very hurried. "Quickly out, come on hurry; we don't want to be caught with our trousers down in the desert. Hurry!" We could only just throw out our kit and then the corrugated iron bird rolled off. Africa and the desert received us with sun, heat and a wind that threw sand into our faces in handfuls. In an instant one's eyes were gummed up. We didn't know whether to ask or to order the soldiers to carry our officers' chests. They formed up and marched off. Where should we go now?

'"Posted to the DAK" – that's what it said on our marching orders. We tried to orientate ourselves. On the huge airfield planes took off and landed constantly, so we had to get away from there as quickly as possible. To the north we saw dust clouds a long way away – perhaps a road. Swearing and sweating we dragged ourselves and our chests with their "equipment necessary for Africa" towards it. Mosquito nets, small and large, sheets, underwear, body belts, shirts, socks, boots and so on. On our heads we wore the most important item – the tropical helmet. *Heia Safari!*'

My first job

And having arrived, one could find oneself thrown in at the deep end, as Lieutenant 'Snuffy' Fuller of the 712th US Tank Battalion remembers: 'My first job, they gave me a platoon of "C" Company and they told me, well, you've got to go down there and take this next town – pointed it out on the maps – you go down here a certain distance, your infantry's gonna meet you and you're gonna take the town. I'd never taken a town before, I didn't know anything about it. So we load up the tanks, got down outside of this town in a field and we're waiting. No infantry. Well, we wait and wait. Finally, off to the right of us somebody started shootin' at us, and the shells were dropping right around us in this field. I said, "Well, move the tanks around so they don't get a target," and it started to get pretty late, almost dark, so I said to Sergeant Rudd, "Rudd, what are we gonna do?" "I don't know Lieutenant," he said. I said, "Well, let's go into town." So we saddle up, hit the road into town, come to the first house and they have got a bunch of farm machinery across the road – oh, graders or tractors, something like that. So I said: "Put a shell in the first house." So we put one in the first house. These farmers come tearing out and I could speak German, so I asked them if there were any German soldiers there. They said no. I said, "OK, then get this stuff off the road," which they did. So we rolled into this town, no opposition whatever, and got in the centre of the town, started outposting the tanks, found a CP [Command Post] for the night. This was all without infantry yet; they hadn't shown up. So we got into the centre of the town, just beyond you could see the mines right in the road; they had mined the road. So I said, "This is as far as we go for the night." So we got ready and maybe around 9 o'clock at night I said, "Well, I'll go out and check the tanks." So I went out and got to this one tank. There was a Corporal Wac. I said, "How ya doin', Wac?" He says, "Fine, Lieutenant, but give me a magazine for this gun." He had about a hundred prisoners standing in front of him and no ammunition. An empty gun. Corporal Wac, that's what we called him. I forget his regular name. That's one thing that stands out, here's this poor guy setting on top of the turret with a grease gun[4] with no ammunition. Well, by morning the engineers came and took the mines out, so we headed for the next town and that wasn't so bad.'

3

First Actions

DRIVER ADVANCE!

No matter what the circumstances, the first time one goes into action the 'butterflies' of fear and apprehension are there even in bellies of the most insensitive and 'gung ho' of soldiers, feelings which are in some ways heightened by being inside a moving steel box with only a limited view of what is happening outside. However, the proximity of the other crew members undoubtedly helps to lessen this fear and one is soon too busy getting on with the job to have time to be afraid, the entire tank crew working as a team to fight their tank effectively. Here are a number of 'first actions' and I have deliberately not tried to put them into any particular order, although some do follow logically on due to the circumstances, theatre of operations, etc. However, first, to set the scene, a vivid description of moving into action for the first time, as recalled by Major David Ling, MC, written about the time when he was a young troop leader in A Squadron, 44 RTR in the Western Desert in 1941: 'If the morning had been colder I don't think we could have managed to squeeze into our Matildas at all. A turret four feet in diameter and chock full of the claptrap of war – 2-pounder breech, wireless set, ammunition, etc. – is not conducive to easy entering. Swathed as we were in greatcoats and leather jerkins, the operation was one requiring time and skill with much final shrugging and twisting to bed down in comfort. It was still night and the red glow of the radio warning light was the only tiny splash in the spacious darkness around us, as the engines individually snorted into wakefulness, merging their tones with each other till the air vibrated to a monotonous buzz.

64

'We were ready to advance. Yet only ten minutes earlier we were asleep, huddled by the sides of our tanks, fully clothed and with the stiff and heavy tarpaulins over us. Now the vapourings of our dreams were replaced by the cold shock of our purpose and speculations of what was to come. It is natural that a false excitement and desire should suffuse the warm blood of those who meet action at the throat of the enemy for the first time. So it was for us on that cold night of 21 November 1941. This excitement had been growing, each day becoming greater, more anxious, as in the van of the New Zealanders we pushed along the desert shelf between the Bardia-Tobruk coast road and the Trigh Capuzzo. Gambut aerodrome, into which we roared, sitting on the tops of our turrets, oblivious to danger, and from which we could see, as we approached, the breathless frantic fleeing of the last of the enemy, sharpened that excitement. The saucy field guns that, in full view, fired at us from the height of the escarpment, planting yellow dust balls among us, was only adding piquancy to our mission.'

A desert assault

Major (Retd) Jock McGinlay was a troop leader in 7 RTR in the Western Desert in late 1940, when, on 9 December 1940, Lieutenant-General Sir Richard O'Connor began his five-day raid 'Operation Compass', which would be the beginning of a brilliantly successful assault by the Western Desert Force, ending in the complete destruction of the Tenth Italian Army. The first phase was an assault on the forward Italian positions, a series of strong points which ran southwards from Sidi Barrani, which they had established in September 1940 and then spent the next three months building up their static defences. 7 RTR, with its three squadrons of twenty-six-and-a-half-ton Matilda II (Infantry Tank Mark II) tanks, was an extremely important part of O'Connor's force, as their tough, well-armoured tanks (soon to earn the nickname 'Queen of the Desert') were markedly superior to anything the Italians could field. 'On 7 December we gathered together for an "O" Group,' recalled Jock, 'when we learnt that we were to attack the Italian fortifications on 9 December, in the order: Nebeiwa, Tummar West, Tummer East and Hill 60, prior to taking on Sidi Barrani. We were to go in and smash up the fortified camps, destroy all vehicles, guns and equipment, capture as many prisoners as possible and then get the hell out of it!

'Throughout the 8th we made ready, arriving under cover of night on the 8th/9th, after making a long detour south of the Italian positions, guided by that splendid regiment, the 11th Hussars in their 1924-vintage Rolls Royce armoured cars, and then driving due north to a position to turn in and attack Nebeiwa from the north-west. The Italian encampments had been kept very occupied by our air and artillery bombardment and there was a feint attack further north to draw their attention while we skirted round. In the early hours of 9 December we were some four to five miles north-west of Nebeiwa; dawn was breaking. We drove in fairly close formation, until we hit a well-defined desert track, made by Italian traffic supplying their camp. We turned onto the track and headed straight for the fortified position and drove into the centre of the enemy garrison, which included quite a large number of individuals in pyjamas, hopping from one dug-out to another. We dealt with the odd field gun and the M13 tanks that came in range and effectively put them out of action. We crushed many guns under our tracks. Our Matildas were being peppered by shot and shell from field guns and numerous machine guns and small-arms fire, but we found that despite all the bangs and crashes on the turret and body, the enemy shells appeared to be bouncing off without penetrating.

'During the course of the battle I had a frightening experience. Prior to the battle, we had decided to load up with as much ammo as possible in the turret. This meant that my haversack containing my shaving kit, a tin of Ideal Milk and a jar of sandwich spread, was hanging on the sighting vane outside the tank. We had obviously received a number of hits, when I suddenly felt an awful amount of wet stuff trickling down my forehead and, putting my hand up to wipe my head, found that my hand was covered with greyish matter. In my alarm I immediately thought that my head had been sliced open and it was the contents of the inside of my brain – in fact a moment of sheer terror – until I looked up at the cupola hatch and saw something trickling through. I opened up and found my haversack had been blown up on top of the hatch, had been peppered with machine-gun bullets and, alas, my milk and sandwich spread had been really well spread! . . . We continued to drive to and fro within the camp walls, still firing on those who had gone to ground, until a white flag appeared and gradually the survivors started to surrender and we had to calm down to save ammunition. At one stage a few Italian M-13 tanks appeared to counter-attack, but after two or three had been effectively knocked out the others beat a hasty retreat and disappeared in the dust to the north-west.'

Moving on to Avranches

'It was Sergeant Joe Shedevy who spotted the enemy tanks first,' – Shedevy was commanding an M18 *Hellcat* tank destroyer in 'A' Company of the 704th Tank Destroyer Battalion, which had landed at Utah Beach on 11 July 1944 – 'T/5 Bleemel Beck, driver, whipped the tank around into a firing position. Pfc Manual Alviso shoved home a 75mm APC round, the breechblock snapped shut and Corporal Clinton Threet laid the crosshairs on the centre of the swastika and the first round fired at an enemy tank by an M18 of the Battalion tore to its mark. Before the *Hellcat* had stopped rocking, another round was in the chamber and Threet was traversing the tube with swift coolness to another tank partly hidden behind a hedgerow. The Jerry, already laid, fired and missed, which cost him his life for the second round from Shedevy's gun left the Kraut tank burning. Two other tanks in the vicinity saw the action and, panicstricken, tried to escape and exposed their positions. Four more rounds were expended and two more enemy tanks were stopped in their tracks, a holocaust of flame. The battle was won and confidence in men and machines was secure. Lieutenant Addison, instantly killed in this action, was the first officer of the battalion killed in action.'

US tankers in Belgium

'The time that stands out more clearly than any in my mind is the night of 21 December 1944, the night of the fight for the chateau in

Belgium.' So recalled Tech 4 Robert Russo, a tank driver in the 740th US Tank Battalion. 'I believe everyone in "C" Company remembers that night because it was our first real contact with the enemy in force. On that particular night we were advancing down a road with the 30th Infantry Division, with Lieutenant Oglensky in the lead. We heard him call back to tell the Battalion Commander that it was getting too dark and too cloudy to go any farther, but the answer was "to keep pushing". Just about dark, Lieutenant Oglensky hit a tank mine and he immediately set up a roadblock with his tank. We were the sixth or seventh tank back, and so I thought we would spend a peaceful night. I was wrong! I was just about dozing off when all hell broke loose. I heard a large explosion, followed by another and still another, and looking out of the periscope I saw that three of the tanks in front of me were burning fiercely. Through my mind ran the thought of my trapped buddies and you can imagine how I felt. From that moment on everything seemed to be a madhouse. I could see figures running back and forth, silhouetted by the flames of the burning tanks. I could swear Krauts were swarming all over our tank. A mortar hit just about where the transmission meets the hull of the tank and I yelled to our tank commander, Willie Morris, that the firing was coming from a chateau on our left flank. I remember our loader, Corporal Waddell, feeding rounds into the gun as quickly as the gunner fired. He did a good job of keeping all the guns firing, and when he jerked the co-ax[1] from its mount when it was too hot to fire any more, I noticed his hands were bleeding, but he didn't seem to notice it. When next I looked out of the periscope I saw that the Jerries were throwing flares right over the top of our tank. I don't know to this day what actually kept us from being hit, maybe it was the wonderful co-ordination of our tank commander, gunner and loader. They fired everything in the book at the Jerries and when we were out of ammunition Willie Morris finally told me to back up and take cover behind a house. That was music to my ears and I wasted no time in getting "Ole Bessie" in gear. What I'm trying to get over is that I sat there in that driver's seat for what seemed like ages and really sweated out one of the most confusing and darkest moments of my life.'

'Bye Baby Bunting'

'The initial attack made by my tank platoon was late in the afternoon on the day after Christmas, 26 December 1944 near Bettviller, France, right next to the German border.' That is how Colonel Owsley C. Costlow, USA Retired, and now the President of the Cavalry and Armor Federation at Fort Knox, Kentucky began a vignette he sent to me about his first tank action which he entitled, 'Bye Baby Bunting Daddy's gone a hunting' – he continues: 'We had been attached to an infantry unit (3rd Battalion, 397th Regiment, 100th Infantry Division) and upon reporting to their Colonel had been given the mission to assault a dense clump of trees in which there were reported to be several dug-in German listening or observation posts. They actually wanted us to go into the wood itself but when I explained that we wouldn't be able to turn our main gun tubes in such a dense wood and that usually we would only go into such a place with dismounted infantry working as a team, we agreed to assault by fire.

'My plan was simple enough. We would attack across a large ploughed cornfield in line formation, then as we approached the woods the second section would stop and lay down a covering base of fire whilst I would lead the first section around the left flank to catch anyone trying to escape out the back. The Platoon was briefed and out we started, not knowing what we would find or face in the woods or from the hills behind the woods that were in Germany. This being our first combat mission together, I feel certain we all were very tense; it is a time like this that really commands your complete attention!

'Off we moved in a staggered line, zigzagging as we crossed the snow-covered ploughed ground that still had many dried up brown corn stalks standing in the field. As we approached the woods to within 600–700 yards, I commanded fire and the first 75mm HE shells hit the timberline, then the coaxial and bow .30 calibre machine guns began to rake the woods back and forth in and out of the trees until the 75s repeated their fire. We were really giving the trees a good cutting, but as we moved closer a strange thing began to happen. Large Belgian hares, looking very much like, but larger than, our jack rabbits, began to pop up out of the cornfield, hop at a pretty good speed, then stop, sit, look at us, then hop for another ten yards or so and stop again. As I watched I noticed that some of the .30-calibre tracers were moving from the wood line to tracking the hares. In the middle of a combat assault the urge to try out your marksmanship on a live, moving target was simply too great. Immediately I put a stop to that, ordering all fires back to the woods – we must remember the mission!

'About that time the second section stopped, took up their base-of-fire positions while my tank and the two from the first section swung around the left flank of the trees. We all continued to fire but we didn't see anyone in or out of the woods. However, I guess someone saw us, because we were soon receiving mortar fire falling among us and it was time to return to Bettviller, mission accomplished at the cost of several Belgian hares.'

Action in Sicily

Captain Norris H. Perkins had a partially visible enemy to shoot at in his first action in Sicily, where he commanded a tank company in 2nd Armored Division and later went on to win the Distinguished Service Cross and the Purple Heart. The shoot was an 'indirect fire engagement', that is to say, one in which the tanks could not see the target they were going to fire at, so had to receive radio instructions from Perkins, who was in a good position where he could see the enemy. It is a good example of the versatility of tanks with well-trained crews and Norris recalled it thus: 'My command tank was in hull defilade[2] overlooking an open valley in the approach to Canicatti, Sicily. Our position had just been shelled by the enemy. Reconnaissance by fire from my tank caused some enemy activity (men running) on a low crest 4,200 yards to our front. Not wishing to disclose the positions of two platoons also in hull defilade, I decided to use the third platoon, in full defilade to our rear, for further reconnaissance by fire and for counterbattery.

'I laid my gun and all the guns of the third platoon on a point on a clifftop about two thousand yards to our left flank. To allow for the fact that my tank was two hundred yards ahead of the platoon, my gun was traversed 100 mils to the right before zeroing the azimuth indicator, thereby placing my gun parallel to the platoon guns. I then laid my gun onto the target area and radioed the shift and quadrant reading to the platoon. The platoon then fired one salvo at the conjectured enemy position, just beyond the crest. As this caused further enemy movements visible to me from my high position, we closed the sheaf and fired several volleys. A battery of our own 105mm Armored Artillery joined in the barrage and the enemy abandoned the position and what was later found to be their three guns.

'At this point I saw a group of thirty to forty men running across the valley to the right, away from the position. They were bunched up and running along a shallow draw visible to me. I quickly fired one round at the old position and noted with my glasses that the group of men moved 15 mils to the right during the flight of the shell. I then laid the platoon onto a bush a few hundred yards ahead of the group of men and fired three volleys when they got within 15 mils of the bush. This was repeated once. There appeared to be about 50 per cent casualties. The survivors then reached refuge behind stone buildings. I noticed a road, partially hidden by the buildings, that passed over a saddle eight hundred yards beyond the buildings. I laid the platoon on this saddle and waited. Sure enough, in about fifteen minues a few men were observed straggling up the road towards the saddle. We dropped a volley right on that area, but the distance was too great to estimate casualties, if any.' Shortly afterwards, Captain Perkins was given the task of clearing Canicatti and taking the hills surrounding it, but did not know that the enemy had set up a trap for him and his tank company. His driver, Corporal Kenneth F. Grogan of Clinton, Massachusetts recalled: 'Taking the town was easy. We rambled through and exchanged shots with machine-gun nests in the upper stories of buildings. Our mission was to keep going, so we moved through the city. Four of the Captain's leading tanks, with us in front, cleared the city and reached an open plain circled by high bluffs. Then all Hell broke loose.

'The Captain, who was in the front, spotted one of a battery of 90mm guns ringing the plain and opened fire. After the first shot, we raced for cover behind a three-foot wall. Explosive shells showered hot metal all over the tank but failed to hit it direct. Then one hit smack on the end of our gun. The whole tank seemed like a ball of fire.

Everybody bailed out, fearing the tank would go up in flames. The Captain cut off the bedding rolls which were ablaze and we then ran through machine-gun fire to get to a building 100 yards to the rear. More enemy shells spattered the armour of the tank but it didn't go up in flames. I noticed that Captain Perkins almost fainted when we stopped by the building and we made him place his head between his legs to keep him from passing out. He hadn't told us before that his left arm was broken in two places. Using slats from a chicken coop and some chicken wire, we fixed up splints for his arm and waited for the medics. But the Captain said to follow him and we edged back to the tank. I was sure sweatin' that one out. The Captain must have been crazy, for he crawled back into the tank. He didn't say why at the time, but I learned later that a secret code was inside and he didn't want it to fall into the hands of the Germans in the event of a counter-attack.

'Then we picked up Sergeant Tim McMahan of Knoxville, Tennessee, who had his leg broken when the shell hit. He had fallen alongside the tank. We splinted the sergeant's leg by using a carbine, a rifle and a blanket and carried him behind the building. Captain Perkins then hailed another tank, climbed on board and rode off to direct the attack of his company. I didn't see how he could stand the pain, but from atop of the second tank, Captain Perkins guided the attack for the next hour until the medics came to relieve him. They had a time getting him to leave, but I guess he was outranked.' 'Capt Perkins refused to leave the battlefield until forcibly taken away by a medical officer' is the way his citation put it. The company had knocked out three 90mm SP guns, four 75mm anti-tank guns and several machine-gun nests. 'About sixty wounded Germans, all gun-crew members, came down from the hills, seeking medical aid,' Corporal Grogan added, 'but I don't know how many dead there were up there.'

FIRST 'KILLS' AND OTHER ENGAGEMENTS

On the battlefield at Kursk

Among the Red Army tanks that had 'wedged' themselves into the battle formations of German panzers was a T34 medium tank, bearing the number 219 on its side and commanded by Guards *Starshina* (Sergeant-Major) Kondrin. The waves of Nazi tanks rolled on one after another. In the front ranks were the heavy enemy Tiger tanks, which although they had thicker armour and a more powerful gun, were far less manoeuvrable than the smaller, highly mobile Russian T34. However, if the Soviet tanks were to knock out the enemy then they must get in close and engage at point-blank range. Kondrin ordered his driver to speed up and zigzag to make sighting more difficult for the Tiger gunner. When they were just a few dozen metres away, Kondrin stopped his tank and fired, jamming the Tiger's turret so that it could not traverse. He then manoeuvred even nearer, coming up on the right-hand side of the massive enemy panzer. 'Kondrin then fired point-blank into its side and the many-ton giant, the ammunition exploding inside it, fell apart with deafening thunder. Kondrin looked around. The fighting was at its fiercest and several tanks were already standing still or burning. To his left another Tiger was firing from the halt. Kondrin fired but missed. Sensing the danger, the enemy began to turn its turret. The *Starshina*, trying not to hurry this time, again took careful aim and the second shell pierced the Tiger's side. At this very moment a heavy blow shook his vehicle. The left track slipped down from the rollers. Now several Nazi tanks were firing at Kondrin's machine. But the Guardsmen carried on the fight. Two more shells hit the tank. All the crew members were severely wounded, ammunition was running out, flames were spreading over the ventilating grate of the engine at the rear. Firing and feeling that in another second he would lose consciousness, Kondrin set his headset straight with his bloodstained hands, cut into the radio which was still working and sent out a message: "Disabled two Tigers. All crew members wounded. Machine burning. Farewell, dear fighting friends! Avenge our death!" As if in response to his appeal two of the Nazi tanks that had just been firing at Kondrin's machine burst into flame – his comrades-in-arms were advancing!'

Is it a tank or a halftrack?

Sometimes a target can be wrongly identified with almost disastrous consequences, as this cautionary tale from Bob Hagerty, a tank commander in the US 712th Tank Battalion, shows: 'We were in Oberwampach, which was just a crossroads with some farm buildings and a few little homes. We needed an outpost and I went up on a side road and pulled off to the right. There was a little culvert where the farmer had cut a path through to move the wagons and horses. We could see up ahead. There were some buildings on fire. Sometimes things like that are deliberately set on fire by the infantry, maybe they create a kind of super searchlight and then the Germans aren't going to come through and expose themselves when they're highlighted like that. The fires were up the road, the road was kind of a gentle rise and an infantry guy came running towards us. He said, "there's a halftrack coming." So we thought, "Halftrack, boy oh boy, where is she?" Big Andy was my driver. He eased the tank back off of the road. A fellow named Ted Duskin was my gunner. He swings the gun out, and lays it up the road. And through this smoky haze that the fire is making, here comes this German, but it ain't no halftrack. It's one of the big tanks. And I just remember thinking, "God, this is gonna hurt!" Because he saw us, I'm sure, as soon as we saw him. Ted shot right away, as soon as that bulk came through the haze, and he must have hit the turret: there was a big shower of sparks. They were heavily armoured in the front and they were only really vulnerable in the rear.

'About a second after we fired, he fired, and a big lick of flame came out of the muzzle of the gun and hit our tank. It seemed to hit it down low in the carriage, it made a hell of a sound and suddenly, the German began to move backward into the smoke. How lucky can you be? We quickly took a look at our tank and one of the bogey wheels appeared to be almost severed. He hit us down low. It had glanced off, fortunately for us, and with the track still being left intact. Andy could ease her back and we eased her back down the slope and this German didn't come after us. But talk about being scared, before he made that first shot . . . They had the firepower. They could penetrate us; we couldn't penetrate them until we got a larger gun.

'After we backed down, around a little curve in the road there was a little rock wall and there was enough room for us to get in there. Ahead of us, against the same rock wall, was a tank destroyer. They had light armour, but they had a bigger gun than we had, so they could knock out a German tank, which we couldn't. So as soon as we got behind the destroyer I ran out and told the destroyer's tank commander what was probably going to be coming so he could get a good shot at it. The German doesn't know the tank destroyer is here.

'First thing you know we could hear little click-clicks. That's about all the noise their tracks made, click-click, they were real quiet. We would make lots of noise and we'd give ourselves away. He's coming down here and he has a dismounted soldier leading him. Imagine having this as your job, because this guy is dead the first time he's seen. But he's gonna take the fire and spare the tank. So this foot soldier comes down here with a rifle and as the tank creeps up behind him, the guy in the tank destroyer fired too soon. It went right across the front of him, missed him and with that, the Germans threw it into reverse and went back up the hill. And of course the tank destroyer didn't go after him because he couldn't afford to take a hit, he would lose. But I think Andy and I were genuinely scared when we saw a halftrack turn into a big German tank.'

'BREWED UP'

'The *whoosh* of the shell close to my head surprised me and I redoubled my efforts to find a target. There should have been a trace of the gun after firing. Dust should have been kicked up and – *whoosh, whoosh*. Where the hell was the damned thing?' That is how David Ling, the young troop leader of A Squadron, 44 RTR, who opened this chapter, began his graphic recollection of being knocked out. He continued: 'I was reporting to Stump Gibbon, who commanded the squadron, that an invisible gun was disturbing my tranquillity when the next effort of a singularly poor enemy gun-aimer was successful and from a range of 100 yards he succeeded in hitting me on the fourth attempt.

'The well was reminiscent of Alice's, only it was blacker, of greater girth and infinitely deeper. In falling down I was glad that I was not turning over but kept a reasonably even keel as I sped on my downward journey. I was lying on my back facing upwards and should, by all the laws of nature, have seen an ever-decreasing disc of white daylight as the well's rim receded. But there was no daylight; all was blackness and I fell with an even but fast speed.

'I wondered if there was a bottom and whether I would be brought up with a jolt but this did not happen. Probably I would be gently slowed up. After all, to be stopped instantaneously after such a fall must kill one and that was ludicrous because one cannot be killed twice and I was already dead. Of that there was no doubt in my mind and it was in fact the only lucid truth I knew. I was dead, positively dead and presumably speeding to wherever dead people go. I had no knowledge of why I was dead or how I had died. I merely accepted it as a commonplace fact and one that should give rise to no excitement, speculation or regret.

'I was dead and I didn't seem to mind. I was aware that this was the beginning of a new journey and I remember reflecting that death after all wasn't so bad as I had imagined and there did not seem to be any reason to be afraid of it. Fortunately the thought did not occur to me to compare the remarkable similarity between this fall and that of Lucifer from Heaven.

'The humming which had started as a soft whisper grew to a gentle murmur and the moon had pushed its way through the clouds, becoming faintly visible and then growing slowly to a pearly brightness. I was still falling when I became aware of a star close to the moon, that was ruby red. Its brightness drilled into me, boring away the shroud of black that encompassed me and simultaneously revitalising my easy death to uncomfortable life.

'The star was the radio's warning light, while the moon dissolved and took the shape of the illuminated tuning dial.

'I lay still, as clarity, sanity and reality came back. I was comfortable and in no pain. I knew now that I was huddled on the floor of my tank, that we were not moving, that the engine had stopped and that my last clear memory was an urgent call on the radio that some big gun was trying to hit me. Obviously it had. It was black inside and the turret and the air was full of black smoke. With difficulty I peered across the two feet of space separating me from the face of Corporal Hill. We must have received shocks of equal intensity for he also was beginning to move. I reached to him, clutched his arm and groped his face; and he returned my grip. "Are you all right, Hill?" "I'm all right,

Sir – are you all right?" "Yes, I'm all right." I didn't ask the same of Trooper Bucket, my expert and lovable gunner who used always to make my biscuit bergoo and brew my char. He could impart to those warming concoctions a flavour which, like the shining efficiency of his gun, others could not match. Now slumped across his little adjustable seat he sprawled backwards and downwards. His head, split in twain, was poised over my chest while his hot blood poured over and through me, a black glistening stream from the back of his crushed skull. His suntanned face turned half sideways was closed and white with death, shining clearly in that black murk. I remember I struggled to get up and Hill struggled also. We were entangled and I had to move Bucket. I remember I stretched up my arm to push him forward and away – and that two of my fingers went through the hole in his skull, into the warm softness within. I wiped my hand on my blood-drenched clothes.

'The good soldier is the well-trained soldier. That is why the Hun is good and why the Guards Brigade is better. Their training is more thorough and longer. The good soldier has less need to think because a textbook answer presents itself to him on most awkward occasions – automatically and without effort. My training was thorough. Years of drill, learning and manoeuvres had fitted me for just this moment. I wish I had been a worse soldier for then I could have applied reason and acted very differently from the way I did. As it was, I repeated my textbook teachings. I was a commander and being out of action it was my duty to dismount and assume command from another tank. As simple as that.

'I told Hill of my decision. And then I remembered my driver, Corporal Ennaver, for the first time. In contemplating our own troubles we had both forgotten him. We both yelled at him and he, also returning from the land of Nod, assured us he felt fine. He tried his engines and they burst into life. This was grand and made me feel less like the proverbial rat in the sinking ship. With instructions to them to turn about, and after sighting through the periscope my nearest tank, I bid these two adieu and awkwardly clambered out.

'The warm sun, the bright clear air, the hard clean ground on which I toppled and crumbled, contrasted dazzlingly with the black cylinder smelling of hot oil from which I had emerged. The world was startlingly clear and vivid, filling me with elation. Picking myself up and gathering around me my wet greatcoat I stumblingly started to run to Sergeant Bleadon's tank. He was my troop sergeant, and on another day in another battle, I was to see him stained and grimy with his left eye nearly gouged out and resting quivering on his cheekbone while he desperately tried to thumb it back.

'The distance between our two tanks could not have been more than 150 yards, but ever growing as his tank slowly pulled away and into the battlefield. My period of unconsciousness after the hit must have been brief, for Bleadon's tank had moved no more than 300 yards. Feeling a little panicked, I ran too urgently and without looking. I stumbled continually in my straining efforts to make more speed. Once I fell headlong. My fears were merited and I had but covered half the distance when the *sis-sis-sis* of machine-gun bullets about my feet told me that the obvious, if I had only paused to reason, had happened. An eternity of boundless space separated me from the safety of my objective, and I redoubled my desperate attempt in what seemed so forlorn and pathetic a hope.

'That some unseen mind guided me, that some invisible will encircled me, only can explain the impossible fact that I gained the side of the tank without a single hit registering on me. Although it cannot be denied that I must have presented a most comical sight to the enemy, a mad Englishman swaddled in the thickest woollens on what was now a broiling day, careering, sand-tripping in crazy fashion between tanks in a desert battle, and that this sight may have affected his aim. I prefer to believe Fate protected me. Leaping onto the broad back of the Matilda with no difficulty, as her pace was no more than three m.p.h., I put the turret between me and the area from which the machine-gun fire seemed to be coming. This had little effect and the fire continued spasmodically and seemingly from all directions, making life decidedly uncomfortable.'

Action on Hill 122

On the map sheet the feature was called simply by its height in metres above sea level and it was this commanding elevation which gave the feature an unrivalled view over a low-lying sector of the Normandy invasion beaches. To the French it was part of the Forêt de Mont Castre, whilst the Germans knew it as an important strong point in the Mahlmann Line, which supposedly had to be held to the last man and the last bullet. For the 712th US Tank Battalion it was the scene of their first action, where, in ten days of fighting (3–13 July 1944), the entire tank battalion was committed in infantry/tank operations on and around Hill 122. Jim Flowers was one of the tank platoon commanders in C Company of the 712th and would be recommended for his country's highest award – the Congressional Medal of Honor – but would eventually be awarded the Distinguished Service Cross, for his bravery and leadership during the operations on Hill 122. These operations included his own tank being destroyed by enemy fire and himself being badly wounded, yet he continued to lead his men, successfully destroying the enemy opposition. This is the story of the first part of that operation, as told by Jim Flowers and a member of his crew. 'I led the tanks on into the woods,' he recalled, 'and ran the Germans in front of me until I started seeing some of our own infantry and I asked them where their battalion commander was. It turned out that this was the Third Battalion of the 358th Infantry and their battalion commander was a man named Jacob Bealke from Sullivan, Missouri, a reserve officer. When I found Colonel Bealke, he was glad to see me. To say the least, he was glad to see me.

'We planned how to get him off that hill and out of those woods. Some of that brush it was kind of like a thicket, you couldn't see through, much less walk through it, and they had been catching hell. They had managed to capture eight of the Germans that I had run down and from them we found out that this is part of the 15th Regiment of the Fifth SS Airborne parachute infantry division. These were fairly clean kids, most of them looked like they might have been in their early to mid-twenties. They had had a bath and a shave recently and had had something to eat. They had clean uniforms, the whole nine yards. We probably looked like a scurvy bunch of bums to them.

'Bealke and I made a plan on how to get out of there. I'd take my tanks and knock this underbrush and thicket down so his infantry could get out. That's one of the reasons they were trapped in there.

79

"I'll knock some paths through this stuff so y'all can walk behind me to get out." So at first the infantry was walking in front of me, but that didn't last long. We hadn't gone but a short distance and they fell back in line with my tanks. And that didn't last but a few yards, they just couldn't get through that stuff and there was a heavy concentration of German soldiers. So the infantry walked behind my tanks. Our plan was to get down the side of the hill, which in some places was pretty steep and out of the woods onto this hard-surface road that ran on the south side of the hill and go on into the fields on the other side of the road and try to get him up on the line with Pond's battalion.

'Everything worked out according to plan, except for one thing. His infantry kind of got bogged down. I ran down the side of the hill, knocked down a bunch of brush and thicket and stuff for 'em and at first the infantry was right behind me. We got down to the hardtop road and now I don't know where in the hell the infantry is. I had no idea that the Germans were decimating Bealke's infantry now. As I come out of the woods and onto that hardtop road, I look both ways and don't see a damn thing, everything looks fine, so I go across the ditch and the hedgerow on the other side and out into a field. In front of me was a swampy area. I could tell by the vegetation growing there. I got on the radio and told the other tanks to look out as they came across the road. Don't run into that marshy area there and get stuck. I went around to the right of the marsh and as Sheppard came across, why Bailey ran him out in it and got stuck. Taylor, who was in Wylie's tank, and Kenneth Titman who was in the Number 5 tank, they went around on the left side and went on. Then Sheppard got on the radio and said, "Jim, I'm stuck back here." I thought "Damn!" "What do you want me to do now?" "Well, hell, you've still got your tank gun, your 75. You can support my advance by fire." He can sit there and fire in front of me at any target of opportunity that he can see. "When I have the opportunity," I said, "I'll get somebody back there to pull you out of that marsh."

'I went on and out in this field there's bushes, weeds and stuff. And there's a hedgerow up there. I don't remember if there's any trees, though there might have been. The thing that I do remember is that the artillery and mortar fire from the German side was falling in on us

80

kind of like hail or raindrops, boy, there was a lot of it. I'd run quite a distance across the second field in after I crossed the road and Taylor's tank and Titman's tank are off to my left, nothing to my right. Sheppard's back stuck in the marsh. After I'd run quite a distance out into that second field, I recall seeing a blinding flash of light and hearing this big bell ringing. What had happened, the German had fired an armour-piercing shot from an anti-tank gun and I saw the muzzle flash and the ringing was that they had bounced this thing off of my turret. I immediately had Gary stop and back up. I'm sure I'm in a fire lane that they've cut. At the same time, I'm on the radio telling the other tanks to look out for that anti-tank gun and gave them the approximate location of it. Let's be careful. So after Gary backed up, I had him pull to the right and then go forward. Hopefully I'm out of this guy's fire line. I'm sure not going to slow down to find out.

'As we do that, we hadn't pulled up too far until, I don't know whether it was an armour-piercing shot, it might have been a bazooka, I don't know what it was but it came through the right sponson where a bunch of ammunition is stored and ignited the propelling charge in this 75 millimetre ammunition and clipped off my right forefoot and I suppose that it probably went out the other side. Instantaneously, the tank is a ball of fire.'

'We were told in training "don't freeze",' recalled Jim Rothschadl, Flowers' gunner. 'I guess a few guys did. They got so petrified or frightened they just froze. But when we went into combat I kept saying to myself, "Don't freeze. Watch." So I didn't freeze. But I was damned scared, because you're sitting there without much visibility. The turret had a toggle switch in it, to traverse the gun, but it also had a little wheel that you could use to traverse it manually. I remember that little wheel very well, because when the tank got hit, that wheel was right in front of me and it knocked four of my front teeth out.

'The Germans were dug in on this hill, hundreds of them, close together in lots of foxholes. And some were on top, working the machine guns. I was firing the .30 calibre machine gun. I was a little heavy on the trigger and the barrel was melting. We were told to fire short bursts, or the barrel would get too hot. Dzienis had a pair of big asbestos mittens and he would screw the barrel off and put on another one. The barrel got so hot that it bent a little bit and the goddamn bullets were falling in front of the tank. Meanwhile, they were firing at us, with small arms and rifle grenades, which would weld themselves onto the tank and almost go all the way through. They would aim the grenades at the turret circle. If one hit there you couldn't turn the turret.

'Then the first big shell hit. It lifted the tank about two feet off the ground. It was an 88, I'm sure of it. The 88 is a high-velocity shell. And Flowers was looking for it, that 88. He was telling me to traverse from the middle to the right. I quit firing the .30 and switched to the 75. When the first shell hit, it didn't penetrate the tank. But I remember Horace Gray, the driver, started to swear, "Goddamnit, let's get out of this sonofabitch! We're sitting ducks. Let's get the hell out of here!" And Flowers told me to traverse to the right a little bit. He was standing right behind me and poking me in the back. I was trying to pick out something through the periscope, but I couldn't see anything clearly. I did see a heatwave, where the blast was from, and I fired one round in there.

'Within a few seconds' time, it might have been thirty seconds, the second shell hit. That one came through the turret. There was this goddamn humongous explosion and racket and heat. The turret was open. It immediately caught fire. And the shell went right on through. Those German 88s were known to be able to hit the front end of a tank and come right out the back. They had double the velocity of our 75s. Double.

'I remember I was burning. I was trying to get out of my little seat. I thought just for a moment about unplugging the radio. But the tank was flaming inside. I got out by myself as far as my armpits, and then I fell back in. Flowers helped me out. I kind of revived and got some air and I got out of the turret as far as my belly. Then Flowers let himself off because there wasn't enough room for the two of us. I saw him fall backwards onto the ground. When I finally got out I let myself fall head-first onto the ground. My clothes were burning. Now I had my senses. We had been told, they went all over this in training, you've got to get the fire out. So when I hit the ground I started to roll and, lo and behold, all of a sudden, plunk! I just fell down into a hole. It may have been a bomb crater. The hole was four to five feet deep and there was a lot of loose dirt. I plunked down in there and covered myself with dirt.'

Back to Jim Flowers: 'I like to dramatise this a little bit by saying that I'm now standing in the middle of Hell. I get on the intercom and tell the crew, "Let's get the hell out of here," and I reach down and grab Rothschadl by the shoulders and yank him out of that seat and start to push him up to get him out of the turret. At this point I don't know I've been hit. After I pushed Rothschadl out on top I turned around to climb out myself and as I stepped up on that ring around where the top and bottom of the turret are bolted together, when I stepped up on that, why I didn't have anything to step with. That's when I realised that something is happening. I fell back to the bottom of the damn turret basket. To this day I don't know whether I fell or it was Dzienis climbing up my back to get out. It's immaterial anyhow. I crawled, I pulled myself and crawled out onto the turret and jumped down on the ground and looked down and that's when I saw that I didn't have much of a right foot. When I climbed out of the tank, I guess it was a reflex, I grabbed my tommy gun and hung it over my shoulder. The Germans had knocked out all four of my tanks, right then and there. They all went up in balls of fire. Even Sheppard's tank.'

Knocked out at Bardia

'The barrage was certainly good, although to us inside the tank it was minimised, for a twenty-five-ton monster does not move along noise-lessly,' recalled Jim Colclough, then a tank gunner in 44 RTR. 'The belligerents were again venting their feelings of mutual contempt by slinging everything at each other. . . . Meanwhile Wally Grainger, standing immediately behind me with his head partly out of the turret behind the cupola flap, was searching for enemy machine guns and any movements ahead whilst I was gazing through my telescope. Then our squadron in complete formation opened fire and I could see streams of tracers converging on distant points. Rat-tat-tat our Besa machine guns were going, while Wally would be directing my fire through our internal wireless communication system. At times our tank reeled and lurched, so that my gun would be pointed up to the heavens or down to the ground. Charlie was the only one unable to view the external scene, which I am sure conjured up much impatience and wonderment in him. Tracer bullets were also coming our way and landing directly on the tank, which made me blink at times, viewing them through my telescope, but luckily for us there was three inches of metal which they still had to penetrate. My gums began to ache terribly, which I attributed to the powder fumes, and Charlie's face was taking on a darkish appearance from the smoke of the Besa gun.

'A lull occured for a few minutes during which time we had halted and Wally was shouting in my ear, complimenting me on my good shooting and exclaiming "Drinks on me and all the best!" for we thought that we should get a rest after this "show" at the base, having been in the desert six months already, but it was another seven months before my battalion got much-desired rest, only after taking part in another offensive, when we were driven back to Alamein.

'Off we moved again, with moonlight streaming down and incessant gunfire everywhere. About midnight we stopped again and suddenly I saw a tremendous gun flash some 200 yards or so away through my telescope and poured enough lead into it to keep anything quiet for yards around. Soon afterwards Wally bent down into the tank asking for a fire extinguisher for it appeared that Lieutenant Moseley's tank had received a hit and it was on fire and, after evacuating their tank, he had come to borrow ours. Charlie and I inside did not know and naturally thought our tank was on fire with thoughts running through my mind of Anderton, Richards and Woodward of our troop who had burned to death a month earlier. "No," Wally said, "it's OK." And then I hardly know what happened for a few minutes, for there was a terrific noise with flashes inside the turret and all became dark. I am sure a few minutes must have passed before we realised what was happening. The small pilot light over the Besa gun had evidently been smashed and then Charlie and I found ourselves saying "Are you all right?" but no word from Wally or Jock. Three months after returning to this unit, I learnt that we had received two direct hits simultaneously.

'At the time of this tragic incident Wally was just handing the fire extinguisher out to Lieutenant Moseley. Then he must have dropped back into the turret immediately behind me, but held up by the surrounding objects. By this time my eyes had become used to the darkness but overhead the starlit depths allowed a full moon to cast its beam through the open cupola, directly onto the prostrate Wally, and then we realised he must have died instantaneously. His clothing at the back of his head was on fire but this we put out with our hands. I also realised that my left arm would not function, thinking to myself that I had put my collar bone out of joint. No alternative was left to us but to evacuate the tank for we could not get any reply from Jock in the driver's seat – he, poor fellow, was also dead. A dreaded 88mm had penetrated the tank and had got him properly. Some three months later, Charlie told me that Wally's foot had to be amputated before he could be lifted out of the tank and laid in his last resting place.

Charlie scrambled out through the top and then I followed but I don't know exactly how I got out. I can remember rolling over the cupola where the iron flap should have been standing, but it wasn't there – must have been blown off. The next thing I remembered, I found myself on the ground with four other fellows near, one of whom was groaning terribly. This was Lieutenant Moseley who had been asking for our extinguisher. Farmer Norton, who was in this officer's tank, must have followed him across but missed being injured and had bandaged Moseley's leg.'

Dead or alive?

In August 1944, Young Junior Lieutenant Alexei Afanasyev had a somewhat unnerving experience whilst recuperating in a military hospital in Lublin, Poland, a month after his tank brigade had taken part in the battle to liberate the city. He and his friend Captain Nikolai Kazakov had chosen beds next to each other in the ward, then gone out onto the balcony where the morning breeze was fresh and cool. 'Where did you give it to the Nazis?' Captain Kazakov had asked Alexei. 'Somewhere beyond that big white building,' Alexei replied, pointing with a bandaged hand towards the centre of the city. 'Suppose we go there, Comrade Captain,' he went on. The Captain looked at him in surprise, 'Will they allow you?' 'I don't see why not.

The chief physician agreed not to evacuate me to a rear hospital, so he will probably allow me to look over the scene of the battle.' Half an hour later, the two officers, accompanied by a nurse, were heading towards the city centre. They soon reached a big square in the middle of which was a badly battered and burnt-out tank, covered with fresh flowers. Alexei instantly recognised the familiar number on the tank turret – it was his own tank! Attached to the side was a tablet bearing the following inscription: 'This was the first tank to break in to Lublin. Junior Lieutenant Afanasyev, tank commander; Junior Sergeant Yakovenko, driver-mechanic; Private Zhilin, gunlayer and Private Mangushev, loader, fought to the last drop of their blood against the Nazi invaders and perished in this battle.' The young lieutenant grew cold with terror – he was standing beside his own 'grave'! He read the inscription over several times. His was the first name on the list, the others were his comrades.

There was, of course, a simple explanation of the mystery, as the following account of part of the battle for Lublin, which appeared in a Soviet magazine in the early 1960s, describes:

On 22 July Alexei Afanasyev's tank brigade took part in the battle to liberate Lublin. His own tank and that of the platoon commander, Lieutenant Maryshev, were the first to force their way into the city. The two Soviet tanks destroyed about two Nazi companies, more than twenty trucks and forty horse-drawn vehicles were smashed to a shapeless mass. The Guardsmen then headed for the city centre but encountered heavy fire. The Nazis scored a hit on the tank of the platoon commander, Maryshev, who was badly wounded. Afanasyev's tank continued to fight alone. By a daring manoeuvre, Alexei managed to advance his tank to the central square. The Nazis opened fire from the flanks. A direct hit on the side set the T34 tank on fire. By prompt action the crew managed to put out the fire. But the air inside was scorching. The men were bathed in sweat and hardly able to breathe. But they were determined to fight on. The driver-mechanic cut in the gear. The AFV sped forward at the Nazi weapon emplacements. Another direct hit smashed the driving sprocket. The machine was enveloped in flames now. The Nazis rushed out of their emplacements and darted towards the tank. 'Ibrahim, put out the fire!' the gunlayer Zhilin cried out. Without losing time he took over the machine gun. Meanwhile the tank became a mass of flames. Suddenly another tremendous blast shook the tank again. A shell had hit the side. Junior Lieutenant Afanasyev was thrown out of the burning tank onto the ground by the blast, blood streaming from his nose and ears. He lost consciousness. Suffering from shell-shock and severe burns Afanasyev was picked up after the battle by Polish patriots who lived in Lublin and they handed him over to a Soviet unit. By a decree of 22 August the Presidium of the USSR Supreme Soviet posthumously conferred on Afanasyev and his driver-mechanic Yakovenko, the title of 'Hero of the Soviet Union'. The other two crew members, Zhilin and Mangushev, were both posthumously awarded the 'Order of the Patriotic War First Class'. Alexei spent a month and a half in hospital. Gradually he recovered from his shell-shock condition, his wounds and burns healed. At the request of his brigade commander he was released from hospital early and returned to his unit. Under the glorious Colour of his unit Guards Lieutenant Afanasyev covered more than 450 kilometres in the sweeping offensive of 1945. It was under this Colour that he entered Germany.

You will find tanks in the different countries liberated by the Soviet Army from Fascism. These once formidable armoured fighting vehicles have now become unusual monuments to the courage of our officers and men. And they are cherished as memorials by the grateful peoples of these countries. . . . And the tank is the best monument to the heroic Soviet tankmen, both living and dead.[3]

Mined, then almost 'panzerfausted'

'One thing that wasn't so amusing at the time,' recalled 'Snuffy' Fuller of the 712th, 'we were on top of a hill and the little town below was where we were supposed to go for the night. A little excursion and I was kind of worried because on either side was high hills; I was afraid they might have guns to shoot at us; so we were just moseying along and all of a sudden, Wham! My tank gets it. I said, "Rudd, get that sonofabitch on the hill." He radioed back and said, "That wasn't a gun, Lieutenant, you run over a mine." So we piled out of the tank and sure enough our track was gone. I walked back to Sergeant Rudd's tank, the boys are there, I looked around and said, "Where the hell is Blackbird?" He said "Oh hell, Lieutenant, he got out of the tank ahead of you." How that guy got through the turret without me, I don't know. He was the loader that time. He was an Indian boy, we called him Blackbird, he beat me out of that tank!

'Then we could see the mines in the road down below us, there were so few of them we got around them and got to the town all right. . . . The story of Donkholz, I guess that's the next one. . . . The night before we had been in the little town of Berle, this was towards the end of the Battle of the Bulge. We had terrific artillery going over up there, then they told us the next morning we're heading for this little town of Donkholz. Berle was up on a hill and Donkholz is down in the valley. You could see across there all right, but it was too steep for the tanks to get down into this valley. And Berle was up on the side of a bluff. There was just one road going in there, so the strategy here was we'd just hit this road and barrel ass as fast as we could into the town. Lieutenant Griffin's platoon preceded us. They went first and I was second. He got into town and pulled behind the first barn, set of barns or whatever, and was waiting there. I got down over there, right behind him and said, "Well, what are you gonna do, Griffin?" And he really didn't know. We can't stay here, so I headed into town and the tanks were in a string, it's a single road, you know, you're one line, in a line, and we can see this sucker off to our right with a *panzerfaust*[4] and I couldn't get my gun around fast enough and he let go, but he didn't hit my tank, he hit the second tank, hit it right in the sprocket, the track came off and the tank rolled right straight to the left, right into a goddamn manure pile. I kept going with the first two tanks, the third tank, damnit, well anyway, that's the one Zimmer was in, he could probably tell you more about it.

'Well, they were immobilised, somebody came along and told them they had to guard prisoners. So he got stuck all night guarding a bunch of prisoners. And we went up ahead and outposted the far end of town and that was a little hectic too because we had no infantry again this time and we're waiting for them, we could see a car coming down the road down there, we didn't know what it was, but finally we figured it was one of our own recon vehicles, but then finally the infantry came across there and they captured a whole German regimental outfit, the regimental headquarters. So that's about the end of that one.' When asked what he thought when he saw the man with the *panzerfaust*, he replied: 'Well, you try to get the bastard, you don't think too much of anything I guess. That happened in Pfaffenheck, the guy was pointing right at me and I couldn't get my 50-calibre gun around to get at him – see the tank commander's only got the 50-calibre up there – I couldn't get it round fast enough and he must have got rattled too, because he let fly and it went over the top of the tank so that was all right with me, or I'd have got it.' 'That was in Pfaffenheck . . . in Donkholz did you get a shot off at the guy after he fired?' 'One of the tanks did, oh yeah, they got him. One of the tanks behind me because I went ahead, they fired the machine gun.'

4

Tank Living

THE TANK CREW

'A well-trained AFV crew is like a family and should be kept together at all costs.' So wrote ex-*Luftwaffe* tank soldier Max Flemming, who now lives in England, in a letter to me a few years ago. His particular AFV crew manned a *Sturmgeschutz* (an armoured assault gun) in one of the elite *Luftwaffe* divisions which in 1942 was enlarged to form a panzer formation – *Fallschirmpanzerkorps 'Hermann Göring'* – which fought in Italy. The StuG III used a PzKpfw III chassis onto which was mounted a 7.5cm gun in a low fixed turret with limited elevation and traverse. 'If the StuG had any advantage as compared with the conventional panzer it was because it was lower, more squat and had only four men as crew. A good driver could take advantage of the lower silhouette against the skyline and use the countryside like shallow depressions, ridges or anything offered by nature or man-made to minimise the risk of becoming a target.' Continuing his words about well-trained crews he commented: 'A good commander will foster a feeling of belonging and comradeship, often waiving the normal strict military code of relationship between officers, NCOs and men. . . . The army with its experience and training facilities seconded instructors to us, also future StuG crews went to the army ranges at Luckenwalde near Berlin, for intensive AFV training. Getting in and out of the vehicle at lightning speed was practised and practised, knocking ourselves black and blue in the process. We cursed under our breath, but how we came to appreciate it in action when life depended on it! Driving practice, gunnery and tank maintenance both by day and night had the purpose of welding the crews together. . . . Towards the end of the war a shortage of AFVs and fuel found many panzermen fighting as infantry, so the very thorough infantry training we had received in our early days of soldiering came to good use. I finished my fighting days in a bicycle-mounted company on the Western Front, ironically in front of our old adversary the Sherman tank.'

'Anyone joining a tank crew for the first time,' Arthur Soper of 44 RTR told me, 'who thought – as some did – that the sole reason for their existence lay in their own particular "trade" were due for a rude awakening, and quickly! As a member of a team, which was soon made obvious, every crew member, whatever their rank, had to muck in to make life a little easier for everyone else. No crew could afford to carry passengers. In close contact with the "angry man" and being at short notice to move, the radio operator was generally on watch, but apart from him, tasks shared included replenishment of ammo and fuel, gun cleaning (main armament barrel, etc.), track bashing, cooking when necessary and possible, and taking one's turn on guard during the hours of darkness, when all other work had been completed. This latter, particularly in the summer months, meant very little sleep but one got used to it. A bit of cat napping during the day helped out, all other things allowing.

'It will be seen and appreciated that a very close bond soon developed among crew members. Everybody knew without being told that they depended upon each other for their continued existence and wellbeing. This bond has continued into life-long friendships, and when – generally due to enemy action – a friend "wasn't there any more", the loss was felt acutely by those remaining. A band of brothers, without a doubt.'

TANK LIVING

When one is living and fighting on a tank, then there are distinct and advantages and disadvantages as compared with, say, the infantry-man on his feet. The 'PBI' cannot, for example, carry more than the very basics about their person, so must of necessity depend upon others for assistance with the essentials of everyday living, which can at times assume major importance – factors like eating and drinking, sleeping, washing, performing bodily functions, etc., etc. Second World War tank crews were lucky in having a largish vehicle on which to carry a wide variety of kit and equipment, much of it home-made or 'acquired', so that their tanks often resembled tinker's carts rather than warlike fighting machines – but then any fool can be uncomfortable! In this chapter we will look at how tank crews carried out basic battlefield living, which was, of course, influenced to a major degree (as any dedicated camper knows to their cost), by the severity of ever-changing climatic conditions.

When asked the question 'What did you carry on your tank besides the usual tank stuff?' Snuffy Fuller of the 712th US Tank Battalion replied: 'We'd carry two or three cases of rations. The back end usually had our sleeping bags, bed rolls, etc. One time we captured a town and we had ten cases of champagne on there!'

It was the same in other theatres of war, especially in the deserts of North Africa, as Sergeant Ron Huggins of the 10th Royal Hussars recalled: 'When the Eighth Army eventually linked up with the British First Army in Tunisia, fresh out from the UK, they were aston-ished to see baskets of chickens tied on the backs of our tanks all squawking away and among all the other untidy survival junk we carried. This earned us the nickname "Monty's Gypsies". We didn't mind, we had already come over two thousand miles from El Alamein. And we were on our way home to the UK, although it meant fighting all the way up through the mountains of Italy first. In Italy, we were to become "tank pig-farmers" but that's another story!'

EATING AND DRINKING

Army rations

Palatable tinned rations came into use during the Second World War, when the US Army system was widely adopted by the Allied armies. Basically there were five types of field rations known by the letters 'A', 'B', 'C', 'D' and 'K'. Ration 'A' was 70 per cent fresh food, almost the same as that eaten in barracks. 'B' was similar but with tinned or packeted non-perishable items substituted for fresh. It was also known as 'Ten in One' as each box contained enough tinned food for ten men for one day. In the British Army, they were called 'Compo Ration Packs' (Composite) and were ideal for tank crews, a five-man tank crew having two days' rations per box – yes, even sweets, 'loo' paper and menus were included (and a tin opener!). 'C' and 'K' rations were designed more for the individual soldier in well-sealed cardboard boxes and could be handily stowed in pockets, ammo pouches/small packs etc., as well as in every bin and crevice of an AFV. Before the arrival of these complete ration packs, British tank soldiers existed on more simple rations – tins of 'M & V', tinned corned beef, hardtack biscuits, etc., washed down with plenty of tea, as their fathers had done in the First World War. German rations were equally spartan, but with coffee and *Zwieback* (black bread in a carton), featuring in place of char and hardtack. One form of tinned meat, produced by the Italians, deserves special mention. It came in tins marked 'AM', was known by the Germans as '*Alter Mann*' (i.e. literally 'old men', i.e. corpses) or 'Asinus Mussolini' (Musso's backside)! Each side thought the other to be better fed and there was, for example, always great rejoicing when a British supply dump was captured in the desert and the Germans could dine on 'delicious' bully beef!

In addition to the normal fare, the occasional luxury made an amazing morale-boosting difference, especially after a period of privation as Trooper W. H. Thomas of 'B' Squadron, 8 RTR recalled: 'Dec 5 (1941). Don't know if this is the right date or not but we feel good. Had meals over at the unit cookhouse and tea made with good water. A few more cigs are contributed. Later the incredible luxury of a piece of chocolate – one bar between nine of us, but effect indescribable. Then ten Woodbines apiece and as final gesture from the gods – 'Three Bells' [whisky]. I began to feel another man again.'

The cup that cheers

'A good lift for morale,' recalled British Sherman radio operator, M. E. Mawson, 'was tea, whilst shut down, made by using the Cooker

Portable Mark 2A between the hull-gunner's legs, with goggles on, all surrounded by ammunition – another horror for the safety experts!

'When we first received bread in Normandy after about three weeks – two loaves between five men, it was simply broken up and pushed down, never mind about margarine! Compo-style rations and later part-dry goods (raisins, flour, rice and so on): we had so much that it was a job to stow, but we were helped by the REME detachment welding on large ammo boxes in a row at the back of the tank. These would also, I discovered (being tidy-minded) take the .30-calibre Browning MG ammo boxes, fitting upright like books and were 100 per cent watertight. With several jerrycans[1] of water, we were complete.

'Compo boxes could also be a problem: A to D and F packs were fine, but the meat tins in the E packs contained oxtail which was not popular. The acquisition of bottles of wine proved a problem. Something had to give – and it did – clearance of some ammo in the hull beneath the commander's feet settled that. Whilst on the subject of fluids, by the time we reached Germany each tank had two giant-sized, wide-mouthed Thermos flasks – I had one at home for years afterwards as every knocked-out tank was swiftly searched to achieve one each crewman. There was a classic example I remember from the Reichswald forest fighting, where a tank in our 3rd Troop got shot-up and the rest of us were cheering on one crew member (Trooper Perrin, an East London cockney bookies' runner) as he dashed down a firebreak to safety, with Spandau bullets zipping around him, *and yet* swinging a Thermos full of hot tea made that morning!

The robust little petrol cooking stoves were not always quite as easy to use as one might have imagined, Peter Vine of 10 RTR told me: 'On 26 June 1944, 10 RTR were in support of 15 Scottish going for the Odon bridges. From then on the whole six weeks I was in Normandy just seems a blur of a nasty dream. A few salient points stick out, I remember being both exhilarated and scared, then managing to blow myself up with two petrol cookers and waking up on Southampton station, both hands and arms covered in bandages. I complained to a medical orderly that I had a twisted knot in my stomach (which I carried with me for many years and even now on occasions). His cure was a corned-beef sandwich which he fed me! I was eventually pronounced fit enough to RTU [Return To Unit] in September.'

The use of the petrol cooker inside the tank was not confined to just British tank crews, as Master Sergeant Howard A. McNeill told me: 'I know that when we finally entered combat we did things that were not authorised and maybe would have been court-martialled for it, such as smoking and cooking inside the tank with a Coleman stove. Several times while we were on the move, I was hard boiling eggs we received from French people. I used a Number 10 can and placed the stove and can between my feet. You can imagine what would have happened if we had to go into action quickly.'

'The quickest way to make a brew-up in the desert,' recalled K. S. Watt of 7th Armoured Division, 'was by filling half a petrol tin with sand and pouring a little petrol on it. If the sand was then stirred and lit it would burn for half an hour easily. The sand, of course, is a good conductor of heat, and water can be boiled like this in under ten minutes. When boiling a dixie for tea over this fire it was almost universal practice in the desert to float a bit of twig in the water. The origin of this custom is obscure, but a suggestion is that there may be something in the idea that it collects and disposes of any stray petrol fumes. On the whole I think it is just an inherited army superstition and should come under the heading of folklore! To go with your tea I can recommend Biscoo – a biscuit porridge, named from a corruption of 'Biscuit' and 'Burgoo', which was an Indian Army word for hash/porridge. Army biscuits – the large, otherwise unedible kind – are put into a sandbag and pounded to powder against a stone. Mixed with a small quantity of boiling water this makes quite a satisfying porridge, but if you were lucky enough to have some Red Carnation tinned milk and some sugar, then I know of nothing which could be more welcome on a cold morning in the desert.'

One problem preventing tank crews having a long, leisurely 'cuppa' in the desert was the Egyptian fly, which, according to Jim Colclough of 44 RTR, was a very different insect to the one found in the UK: 'His primary desire in life is to attempt to drive the British Tommy *magnun* [mad], as the Arabic language terms it. Endowed with 100 per cent persistence, he will still loop the loop around one in spite of one's attempts to drown him. . . . To overcome boredom in the desert, bets were waged to find the champion fly killer each day – the scores gradually rose until about 150 became the average kill. Then one day a trooper spent the whole day (in October 1941, waiting for the November offensive) swatting the little teasers and bagged over 600. Another time, the midday meal had been prepared alongside the twenty-five-ton Matilda tank, we had poured out the tea into the mugs, added the necessary condensed milk and sugar and started to eat the bread and cheese. Then the climax came as twenty-five dead bodies floated in a lonely mug of tea. Death by suicide or drowning was the verdict while attempting the theft of WD char!'

'We, when the tanks were moving, always had hot coffee,' recalled Staff Sergeant George G. Moss, 'simply by having the driver place two canteens on the transmission, which was at the front end of the tank, between the driver and the assistant driver. We would have the loader warm the rations (against regulations) on the little Coleman heater, the size of a roll of duck tape. In cold weather we could be very miserable as the frost from our breath would hold to the top [ceiling] of the tank and freeze. I allowed the men in our platoon to sew one blanket in their sleeping bag, cut holes for their feet and arms and "wear" the damned sleeping bag! This started in November of 1944 when the miserable French rains began turning to snow in the eastern hilly sections of the Ardennes to the north and the Vosges to the south. This "clothing system" helped quite a lot when these young men were asked to sleep sitting or standing. One at a time could lay on the turret floor and then he had to be shorter than five feet nine inches. I was over six feet and simply used the tank commander's eight-inch seat, with a backrest to sit on to sleep. The gunner stayed in his seat, also with a backrest, on the right-hand side of the turret. It was impossible to stretch out. One could always "take a chance" when we stopped to get out and move about. A far cry from the regimental calisthenics of stateside duty.'

'In the early days in the desert we were on "hard tack",' recalled Joe Lee of the 7th Queen's Own Hussars; 'a lot of men with false teeth were returned to base. Perhaps I had better re-phrase that. Men with false teeth found it hard to masticate the biscuits, some breaking their false teeth which had to be returned to base for repair. Some of the desert wells were salted by the enemy. Although not injurious to health, it curdled the milk and gave the tea a horrible taste. After our initial successes against the Italians a lot of "booty" was captured.

Training a tank gun crew on the indoor pellet range of an RAC Training Regiment in the north of England, during October 1940.

Classroom training in progress. Although this photograph was taken just postwar nothing has changed from the basic wartime style of classroom instruction, with the use of drawings, inert ammunition, etc. carried out in spartan conditions!

A tiny PzKpfw 1 Ausf A *'ohne aufbau'* (without turret) which was used by the Panzerwaffe for training tank drivers both pre-war and early on in the Second World War.

'Mud, mud, glorious mud!' This Convenanter driver seems determined to get very wet and muddy. He is somewhere on the Bovington tank training area.

When American equipment began to arrive in the Middle East under Lend–Lease in 1941, US Army instructors came with it to teach their British counterparts. Here Sergeant J P Mauger of New York City, shows two British corporals the inner workings of the .50cal Browning machine gun, in a camp near Cairo.

Goodbye to Boots and Saddles! An M2A4 light tank of the 7th Cavalry Brigade overtakes a squadron of horse-mounted cavalry during combined manoeuvres in the USA in 1940.

Newly-trained Red Army tank crews collect their brand-new KV1 heavy tanks from a Soviet tank factory.

Ready for battle! Newly-trained and newly-equipped, panzers of Panzer Regt 3, 2 Panzer Division, on parade in their barracks, 20 April 1936.

A line of Churchill tanks on training 'somewhere in England' during the autumn of 1942.

'They went that way!' Cruiser tanks on training in leafy English lanes, circa 1940. The Rhino in a black oval was the divisional insignia of 1st Armoured Division.

An American armoured unit, equipped with Sherman tanks, taking part in a vast pre-invasion exercise in April 1944, under a dramatic sky.

'With the British troops in France'. Training still went on during the 'Phoney War' period (Sep '39 to Apr '40). Here NCOs study their maps, whilst the rest of their light tank crews take a break.

A long column of Char Leger Renault R35 light tanks moving into action during an exercise prior to the German invasion of France in May 1940.

A young Red Army tank crew pauses to study their map, during training, whilst their light tank remains hidden in the woods.

This PzKpfw IV Ausf D was being used in a tank driver school. Behind it are some *Fahrschulwanne IV* – tank training vehicles.

A British tank crew in the desert working on their Matilda Mk II, which was known as the 'Queen of the Desert' as its thick armour was impervious to all Italian tank guns.

GIs preparing their Sherman tanks for action on the Tunisian front, soon after the Operation TORCH landings in early November 1942.

A tank crew belonging to US 1st Armored Division, just out of action in Tunisia, prepare a hasty meal. Note the little 'pup' tents (two-man bivouacs), tinned rations, etc.

Christmas cheer in the desert. Two members of this Stuart light tank get ready to sample a Christmas pudding (complete with a sprig of 'holly'), using captured German jerricans as seats.

Two members of the crew of a light tank belonging to 1 RTR perform their ablutions, whilst the tank commander remains on watch atop the turret.

A Cromwell tank crew belonging to B Squadron, 1 RTR, all in their winter tank suits, enjoy a quick meal and a brew before moving off on Operation 'BLACKCOCK' which was designed to clear the area between the Meuse and the Roer in January 1945.

US Marine Corps tankers dry their clothing on ad hoc washing lines stretched between their Shermans during a lull in fighting in the Pacific area.

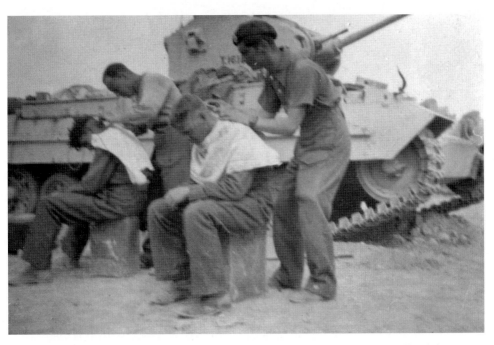

'Short back and sides please'. Tank crewmen get their haircut in the middle of the Western Desert – the barbers being other crew members.

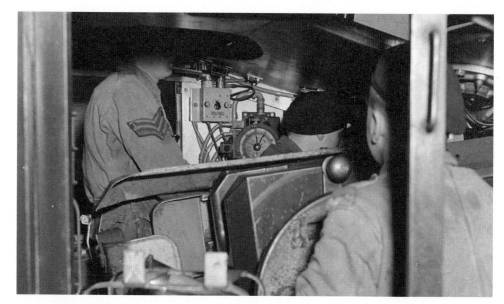

Inside the turret of a British Comet tank, looking up from the driver's position – the commander is seated on the left with the gunner in front of him, while the loader/radio operator stands on the right of the gun.

A radio operator tuning his Wireless Set 19. His tank commander's rubber-booted feet can be seen on the left, standing on his seat. The WS 19 required careful tuning but was a reliable and robust set which went on in service postwar. It provided three levels of voice communications: 'A' set for long range within the regiment; 'B' set for close range within the tank troop; 'IC' crew communications within the tank.

A 3 RTR tank crew tighten one of the tracks of their Comet. This was one of the spare tanks held at A1 as immediate replacements for battle casualties. Note that two of the crewmen wear other badges (one Royal Gloucester Hussars, one Royal Armoured Corps) so they must be new reinforcements who have not yet been rebadged.

The driver of this M3 'General Lee' medium tank is busy working on his main engine via the very handy rear doors, whilst waiting to cross the River Mu, near Chantha, north of Mandalay, in January 1945.

Red Army tankmen working on the tracks of their KV1 heavy tank on the South Western front in 1942. The KV1 was a tough 43½ton tank which first saw service in the Russo-Finnish war.

Bombing up a KV1 heavy tank. This crewman is holding a 76.2mm round for the main gun, whilst on the turret are some drum magazines for the tank's machine guns.

British tank crew 'bombing up' newly-arrived M3 medium 'General Lee' tanks with shells for their 75mm main guns. This main gun was mounted in the separate limited traverse turret on the right-hand side, while the small turret on top contained a 37mm gun and coax MG.

After a night 'blitz' on enemy positions, this South African tank crew belonging to 6 SA Armoured Division, get rid of their empties 'somewhere in Italy'.

Excellent close-up of three German tank crewmen, in the centre is *Oberst* (Colonel) Dr Bake with two of his *Hauptmann* (Captain). Note Bake's Knight's Cross worn around his neck.

The crew of an M10 tank destroyer replenish their ammunition in an ambush position in Belgium, where they knocked out two German Panther tanks, two PzKpfw IVs, a halftrack and 30–40 enemy infantry, all during the morning of 17 December 1944.

The crews of these German panzers in the desert (nearest is a PzKpfw II) dug their bivouacs into the stony ground so as to obtain some protection from enemy shellfire and bombing.

Second Lieutenant Norman Plough of 2 RTR and his crew beside their Cruiser tank at Beda Fomm, where a small British force ambushed and then defeated the entire Italian 10th Army. His tank alone knocked out 20 Italian tanks.

Clothing, new, brand new. Blokes were running around in black shirts and all sorts of other gear. It was like a circus and the brigadier, like Queen Victoria, was "not amused", so it ceased forthwith.'

A gallon can of marmalade

'We had backed off the line,' recalled Jim Rothschadl of 712th US Tank Battalion, 'and there was a rumour that another tank battalion was going to take our place. We pulled our tanks into a little field and our kitchen trucks were there. I remember driving into the field, standing up in the turret. Flowers (my commander) was outside already, talking to someone in a jeep. Sergeant Speier, he was the mess sergeant, he knew I liked pork chops. He used to call me "Po'k Chop". So all of a sudden I heard, "Hey, Po'k Chop. You hungry?" I said, "You're goddamn right." And he tossed me a gallon can of marmalade and a loaf of bread. We parked alongside the hedgerow and somebody came up and said: "You can't stand outside. You've got to get underneath the tank," because the mortar fire might come in.

'There was about two feet under the tank, so we crawled under there and took this gallon can of marmalade and the loaf of bread – we were so damn hungry. There were four of us, Ed Dzienis, our loader; Gerald Kiballa, the assistant driver; Horace Gary, the driver; and myself. We took a Bowie knife and we cut open this can of marmalade. And we broke the bread, it wasn't sliced, so we took chunks off and we scooped out the marmalade with our hands. We ate the whole gallon.'

Sometimes, however, meals were taken in more civilised surroundings as Tony D'Arpino, also of the 712th, recalls: 'Whilst we were in Maiziers, we were sent some chicken, and Klapkowski wanted to fry it. All the stuff was in the house where we were staying. As a matter of fact, they had a lot of dishes, beautiful dishes. So Klapkowski is looking for flour, he wants to roll this chicken and fry it. And he starts a fire. I said, "There's smoke in the chimney. For Chrissakes, they can see us." "Awww," he says, "they know we're here anyway. We've been here so long, they know we're here. He goes down in the cellar – there was some stuff stored there – and he gets this bag, it had some German writing on it. He says, "Is this flour?" I felt it and said, "No, that feels like plaster of Paris." He said, "No, that's flour."

'So he rolls the chicken in this stuff. And he's saved the bacon fat from the ten-in-one rations, whenever he fried anything, like potatoes and stuff, he'd use this. He fried the chicken and it came out the prettiest golden brown you'd ever want to see. But you couldn't eat it. It was tough. So he just banged it on the wall and knocked the plaster off. The plaster came off in one piece and the chicken underneath was cooked.

'Then he sets the table. He got the tablecloth and set it with five dishes. Afterwards, he said, "OK, fellas, time to do the dishes." And he opened the window, tablecloth and dishes and everything else out the window. I don't know how many plates we broke in that house.'

Meat 'on the hoof'

A fair number of veterans remember 'acquiring' fresh meat in a number of interesting ways. John Walker of 48 RTR recalled a day in Tunis in 1943 when: 'The Regiment was at rest, on the side of a dust track, which was more than likely the Tunisian equivalent of our M1. We were all doing our daily chores, when meandering through our lines came a very ancient Arab leading about a dozen decrepit-looking sheep. Idly we watched him go by and then continued with our duties, writing letters home or what have you.

'After a short while, all hell broke loose. Back round the bend came the Arab running and waving his crook, and yelling at us in fluent Arabic, which, of course, being well-educated soldiers, we didn't understand a word. But, after a lot of argy-bargy we managed to sort out that one of his sheep had disappeared. Can you imagine such a thing? And where did he lose it, why in the Recce Troop lines. Now the first recce vehicle he had passed happened to be driven by a certain crewman, who, in civvy street, had been a butcher . . . need I say more! For two days we dined on mutton stew. Much better than the regulation diet. (For the benefit of any misunderstanding, we did have a whip around for the shepherd who departed with a few francs in his pocket!)

'An army marches on its stomach. That saying was true for us in Italy,' recalled *Luftwaffe* StuG driver, Max Flemming, recalling their time behind the Volturno defence line. 'We were supporting some panzergrenadiers, it was September, still very warm and our field kitchen, further back, used to send us up warm rations by motor cycle equipped with a sidecar. The food was well and truly mixed by the time it reached us and often sour. Self-help was the answer and it just so happened that some pigs got loose close to our position. A pig hunt was agreed to supplement our rations and several of us set out. . . . I had a piece of rope which I found handy when we eventually managed to wrestle one of the pigs on to its back. The rope was fastened to one of its hind legs, but then the animal took over. It went hell for leather across the fields and attracted the English artillery observers. They didn't want us to have pork for dinner and such a barrage of shells added to our difficulties. However, the thought of a good meal gave me strength to hold on and with the help of my comrades I managed to drag the pig to a safe place and the butcher's knife. Nice tasty pork chops cooked over a fire, the pan supported by three track connecting bolts, gave us strength for the next day!'

Tea with the Bedouins

Ron Huggins of the 10th Royal Hussars did quite a lot of bartering with the desert Bedus, especially for eggs, and recalled that sometimes such dealing was not always on the 'up and up': 'Someone, somewhere in the desert thought up a crafty idea of filling empty, round cigarette tins two-thirds full of used, dried tea-leaves and then topping this up with a final layer of good, fresh unused tea. This would be offered in exchange for three or four eggs for a tank crew. I have to say that we got away with this cheating for a while, but eventually the Bedouins got wise to the trick and so before parting with the eggs in exchange for a little round tin of "tea", they would poke a forefinger into the tea and turn it over. They quickly got used to recognising the dried, used tea-leaves from the upper layer of good, unused tea. "*Musqueesh!*" they would exclaim (No good) and walk off back to their camp. However, we were still determined to have eggs whenever possible and so we came clean with them and also decided to barter for live chickens. Of course we now had to pay in a higher quantity of real, fresh tea plus tins of bully-beef and cigarettes. So it was not a rare sight to see a tank trundling along with a small Arab wicker basket tied on the back, containing a couple of live chickens, fluttering and squawking. We fed them on crushed army biscuits, mashed-up bully beef and dehydrated milk, we were the first British battery-hen farmers! Of course, if we were likely to go into action then we handed over our baskets of chickens to "B" Echelon supply lorries, with a rough label tied to each basket bearing the tank-crew owners' names.'

'We soon learned where to get eggs to eat and everything else in Germany,' reminisced GI tanker Des Tibbitts. 'In France we also had lots to eat, but you had to be careful when you stole off the French people, they didn't like it. I remember Cozzens one time, I was in a village and every house had a chimney, a big square chimney and there was a smokehouse and your chimney went right through that. All their hams and bacons and sausages hung in there on little racks. Well, I found this one up in the attic, so, boy, when I came down, and we had field jackets, so I had that thing loaded with sausage and bacon. And by God one of the sausages fell out. Old Cozzens, one of the women just got up and gave him hell for me stealing and, boy, he was eating me out and chewing me out, then he said: "You sonofabitch, now go back and get me some"! We all took our own, see, every tank ate its own food, we didn't feed the next tank. Boy, the time I killed that beef, boy, I had a lot of friends and everybody was around getting some meat, and that Kochen, he found a grinder somewhere to grind hamburger and he ground pretty near all the front quarters up, and we had frozen hamburger, we'd been cooking 'em and all you had to cook on was them little stoves about that big, boy, you'd no more than get one fried up than someone would come along and beg you for it. And we got lots of good bread off the Germans, lots of good bread, brown German bread. But we had a fine time.'

On occasions one received a parcel from home with which to supplement rations, although rationing at home meant that luxuries were few and far between. However, as Tom Bird, then a staff officer at his brigade headquarters, told me: 'I had recently received a Fortnum and Mason parcel which included a whole roast partridge in a tin. This was a suitable meal for two and unsuitable for an entire mess of four or five officers, so I brought it along for Strafer's [Brigadier later Lieutenant-General 'Strafer' Gott CB, DSO, MC] and my evening meal. Later when I was awarded the MC for my sub-unit's part in the capture of Tobruk, my brother officers were unkind enough to suggest that it was this partridge which was really responsible for my medal!'

SLEEPING

'I always said the Air Force had it rough,' mused Tony D'Arpino, 'but when they got through their mission they went back to a nice barracks, hot showers and everything else. The Navy, the same way. They're on a ship. They'd have their battles and then you've got a bunk to sleep in, they've got cooks cooking for 'em.

'Us guys, we had no heat in the tanks in the goddamn winter. I remember digging out snow, putting branches down on a blanket and a blanket on me; when I woke up in the morning I had about twelve inches of snow on me. We had a rotation plan in our tank. The engine compartment, that stayed hot almost all night. We used to take turns, one night apiece, sleeping on the engine compartment. You can just imagine, it's raining, you're soaking wet and you get cold in that goddamn piece of steel. There were no fans even. When they fired the big gun, the smoke and everything else, you've got nothing to suck that out. Today everything is different, but they didn't have none of that stuff. And those tanks were cold.' George Bussell, also of the 712th, agreed; 'You could take your finger and scrape the frost off the inside of the tanks, because they didn't have any heat. I had an assistant driver, Johnny, from Tennessee, I forget his last name. He told me, "George, if I get home and it's in the middle of July and I think how cold I was, I'm gonna build a damn fire!"'

'It was so cold,' agreed Des Tibbitts when recalling the battalion's time in the Ardennes, 'that I slept in the tank an awful lot, cold as it was. I've still got my sleeping bag out there. I had two of them mummy sleeping bags, boy, you get in one of them and zip it up and you was pretty warm. I always slept with my four-buckle overshoes on and shoes underneath and I never froze my feet. Now Herschel Payne, that particular instance, we lost him on that occasion his feet froze on him, we lost him. . . . We lost three or four men that time.'

'When there wasn't time for a bivouac [by definition a temporary encampment without shelter] we slept on the ground,' Norris Perkins told me. 'You couldn't lie down in a light tank, so you found a place between trees where you would not get run over. In the bitter cold and wet weather of the Carolinas, we managed to get quite snug in our heavy canvas bed rolls, which were water resistant. By the time you wriggled into it fully dressed, with several layers of clothing and boots. The bed roll became a round tube which would roll on a hillside. The heavy zippers worked pretty well until clogged with mud.

'War Correspondents have commented on how quickly a resting soldier can go to sleep. This is based not only on mental and physical fatigue but on the security and equanimity of being part of a well-trained team.'

'We did not dig individual foxholes or slit trenches to sleep in,' Master Sergeant Howard A. McNeill recalled, 'we dug one huge hole, eight feet long, two feet deep and the width of the tank between the tracks, then the driver would park the tank over the hole and that would be our sleep quarters.'

No room for the horse

Sometimes tank crews found other accomodation, like Brian Brazier of 46 RTR, whose squadron, after days and days of ceaseless rain in Italy, were 'allocated' part of a barn, where the farmer kept his horse and stored flax. 'Well, I've lived in some places but this was going to be the lot,' he recalled. 'It was no bigger than a rather large living room in any farmhouse; it was built of stone with only one tiny window high up in the gable wall which let in hardly any light as it was half boarded up. A manger ran along the wall farthest from the door and the whole place reeked like stables usually do. The floor was feet thick in muck and straw. An ideal home for a horse! At the time it seemed absolutely ridiculous; however, we soon realised that we would have to make the best of it. Anyway, it was that or nothing so we all got to work and began to carry out all the sheaves of flax. We had nearly finished the job when the farmer returned from his day's work with his horse, and he must have had the biggest shock of his life to see what we had done. He came up waving his arms and shouting at the top of his voice, in Italian of course, but we couldn't understand a word of what he said, although we had a good idea. In the end he got tired, realising he was not going to win and he went away, crying his eyes out.

'After we had cleared all the flax out we came across a large open fireplace in one corner, just inside the double door, which was difficult to close properly. The job was to clear the floor of all the horse muck and spread a clean layer of flax, helping to make the stone floor a little softer to sleep on. It was almost ready to move in now. A huge fire was soon roaring away in the fireplace, which helped enormously to brighten the place up, as it did look very dreary with hundreds of cobwebs hanging from walls and roof. And I'm sure the place was alive with rats and mice. To finish it off we brought in two large tank sheets which we laid on the floor and stretched them up to the manger to try to keep the rats out. It was now ready for us to bring in our bed rolls and get comfortable.

'The first night passed quite pleasantly and the following morning we all had to lend a hand to make a bridge over the brook so that we could have our tanks as close to our accomodation as possible. Two or three steel drums with tops and bottoms cut out of them were placed in the stream to let the water through, then several trees were cut down to place across these and help strengthen them and before long there was a perfectly successful bridge. We were now able to bring our tanks over by the barn and at night after dark use the batteries to give light which, with a lovely fire, made a quite comfortable home. . . .

'It got so close to Christmas now that we knew we would be staying in our present position and so proceeded to brighten up the place a little, ready for the day. Some of the sergeants were allowed to go to Naples to buy wine and nuts or anything they were able to get hold of, which wasn't a lot, we all having contributed to the cost. The large room at the farmhouse which was occupied by SHQ troop was all decorated with streamers, holly and mistletoe (not much use to us!) and the walls covered with pinups which most of the chaps had above their beds. This was where we were going to have our Christmas dinner, an occasion when all the stops were pulled out. . . . The cooks had been working practically all night to have a really good spread for the troops. . . . The sergeants and officers waited on the rest of us, as was the usual custom in the Army.

'After the feast we wandered back to our lovely warm room with our beds still stretched out on the tank sheets, as nobody was in a hurry to get up. . . . A few days more in our snug little barn, when a rumour spread around that a move was imminent. We could always tell because orders were given to work on the tanks, generally cleaning the guns, ammunition, periscopes etc. to be in position to move at very short notice. . . . It was always the same whenever there was a move; none of us wanted this to happen as we were quite happy in our little home, and yet we were always glad to be going somewhere different.'

A last word on sleeping from the North African desert, courtesy of Trooper W. H. Thomas of 8 RTR: 'Just at sunset, another column deploys on the horizon. Fresh apprehension but no gunfire so they must be ours. We hope. They settle down for the night and so do we. Lie, looking up at the moon and stars. What a contrast – the peace of the sky and the turmoil in the desert below. Used the old Lilo again tonight, that battle-scarred veteran, a big comfort from the cramped trench where six of us slept like puppies in a litter.'

AND OTHER LUXURIES

'Last night was an epoch-making affair,' continued Trooper Thomas, 'our cig issues turned up, fifty Woodbines apiece. We felt like Lord Nuffield, and then to top it all came the rum ration, quite out of the blue. A mugful among nine men. There we crouched in the rapidly gathering dusk. I was raw and cold and our fire had burned to its last safe embers and it looked as if it might be a night like last night. We were finishing a bedtime snack of bully and bread (which seemed to have a very goodly sand content, perhaps to give us grit) when the precious liquid was laid on the ground and stentorian and apprehensive yells greeted anyone whose feet wandered in its direction, as Trooper Daykin found out to his surprise. A solemn brief conference was held about how it should be doled out. We decided there was only one way – by tablespoon. So down went all the mugs on the table and our Uncle Arthur, still with the rolled balaclava on his head like a presidential cap, doled it out, going round the mugs and numbering them as he went. It was terrific stuff with a kick like a mule and a breath like a blast furnace. It tasted like an ingenious mixture of treacle, concentrated cloves and a dash of barbed wire to give it body. I kept half of mine until I was under the blankets and let the glorious fire burn down to my marrow. The SSM did the same and we lay there in the lee of the armoured car. It must have been very good stuff for our conversation ranged from the ghosts in the Forest of Dean, to nudist colonies, and to the wreck of the *Herzogin Cecilie* off Bude. And so to sleep with the stars high above. It rained again, so I am told, but I did not feel it this time.'

WASHING AND BATHING

'Our camp was within a mile of "Charing Cross" [a well-known cross-roads/tracks in the Western Desert, south of Mersa Matruh – "Piccadilly Circus" was another, some way west below Sidi Barrani],' recalled David Ling, 'the point at which the Siwa, Sidi Barrani and Matruh roads meet, and this was fortunate for us as it meant that we had unlimited supplies of water, Charing Cross being a water point and received its supplies by pipeline from Matruh to which it was shipped by tankers. Later, however, and after we had left this spot, our supplies were to be cut down drastically and for the first time in our lives we were to know what a precious thing water can be. The *birs* [wells] in the desert had been dry and unused for many years and those that did contain water had mostly a brackish greenish coloured filthy liquid with camel dung in it!'

A desert bath

Thus water was the most precious single commodity in the desert, without which no one could survive for long. It was invariably in short supply and for much of the time the troops on both sides had to exist on just one pint a day for *all* purposes, so they used petrol to wash clothes, hoarded dirty water in spare water bottles and filtered it for use in vehicle radiators. When there was sufficient for more than just a brief wash, then it was a major happening, especially when it coincided with the arrival of long-awaited food, as this account by *Leutnant* Ralph Ringler, a tank company commander in Rommel's Deutsches Afrika Korps, recalls: 'It is an inexplicable secret how it is possible that suddenly the smoking field kitchen rumbles up. How often had I sworn about *Hauptfeldwebel* Wigl and damned him as a pig and a shirker, but when things got really fiery he was always there at the right time. "We've got coffee and dried vegetables and there's a bottle of red wine for every four men." "You're an angel, start getting it out at once because we don't know what will happen in the next half-hour." Then another wonder occurred, the sun had just disappeared into the desert when all at once one of our water wagons appeared. It was hardly possible, this wagon I had sent to El Daba ten days ago and I had written it off for certain, and now here it was. I felt like embracing the driver. There were six old petrol barrels on board, full of brackish, petrol-flavoured, salty, rusty water – and there was rejoicing. Three barrels were immediately given to the field kitchen, one I kept in reserve and the other two I let be distributed among the lads. Each man received four litres of the precious liquid – four litres – the first water for a long time. We were invigorated and in high spirits. Now I could watch them – the gluttons, the spendthrifts, the bon viveurs the thrifty, the happy.

'It all depended on the way you decided to use it. First of all a hearty slug, then I washed my face – divine! I put half a litre by for shaving, then I washed my whole body, but none was spilt. A little over a litre remained now as a murky soup. Throw it away? Not on your life! Next clothing, first a handkerchief, then my shirt and finally in the thick, dark soup I soaked the tatters of my socks. What a day that was, it had started badly, got even worse, but now this luxury. I came out of it like a man reborn.'

And its continental equivalent

'When we got up to the Saar River, we took this little village,' recollected Jim Gifford, 'it wasn't even a town. I went into a house there. I went downstairs into the cellar and there was a pile of coal. . . . I decided, well, this was a good chance to take a bath. So I started to heat some water up and I filled the bathtub. The tub had a window alongside it and you could look out through the garden, you could look down the slope all the way to the Saar River. Now I'm just settled in to take my bath and soak, when all of a sudden I see a shell burst down by the riverbank. When a shell goes off, you always watch to see where the next one's coming. You walk these shells. We got so used to being hit with shells that we knew what they were gonna do. So I watch to see where the next one's gonna hit. The next one hit closer to the house. Oh, shit, they're coming this way! The next one came down right below that field. So I grabbed my nose and slid down into the water. The next thing, "Boom!" Right in the garden. Knocked the goddamn window frame and the glass and everything out. When the smoke cleared I came up out of the water. The goddamn window was gone and the glass and the frame and everything else was in the water with me. The next shell – I'm still waiting to see where the next one's going – went over the house and landed in the road. Then I got up out of the tub and that was it. That was my bath. I made sure I didn't cut myself as I dried myself off and got the hell dressed.'

BODILY FUNCTIONS

'Our arrival in Egypt had heralded the appearance of many strange maladies,' reminisced David Ling, 'among the officers in particular. Many to whom illness of any sort was quite strange went down, the commonest complaint being "gyppy tummy". None of us could explain what he put the cause down to, all of us had the same symptoms and pains. At the same time one gets a violent pain in the pit of the stomach, almost making it difficult for one to straighten the body. The worst effect is one the reader can readily find out for himself by taking a full dose of Epsom salts, syrup of figs, senna pods, calomel and No. 9 at one and the same time. The officers' latrines were situated some one hundred to two hundred yards from the tanks and daily could be seen the pitiful procession travelling to and fro between these points, much like a thin line of ants one sees making a journey between home and food store. To make matters worse, no one could offer a cure and one had to bear the malady until time, the only healer, had played his part.'

'They had a pistol port in the left rear of every Sherman turret,' recalled Norris Perkins. 'Well, nobody ever shot a pistol out of it. So the Ordnance in their great wisdom decided to eliminate the pistol ports. They heard cries of anguish and anger from the European campaign because the tank crews were using the empty shells for toilets. When they got full, they shoved them out the pistol port. After four months of production without pistol ports, they put them back again.'

One person who was undoubtedly very annoyed at the return of the pistol port was an unknown Despatch Rider, who happened to be passing M. E. Mawson's Sherman somewhere in Belgium, as he recalled to me: 'Going fast beyond Brussels to Louvain, it was my job in my crew (as nearest to the revolver port) to empty the communal urinal. This was an empty shell-case kept in the ammo rack and passed round when wanted. On this occasion I sloshed it out – very limited side vision – and it went over an M/C despatch rider! Perhaps he thought it was cold tea!'

'My tank crew obtained a twenty-pound coffee can,' Staff Sergeant George G. Moss of A Company, 714th Tank Battalion told me; 'one with a round lid in the top, a lid that would seal. We used this to defecate and emptied it when the opportunity afforded. To urinate we simply used the helmet. The assistant driver would dispose of his and the driver's through the assistant driver's hatch, and the commander would dispose of the gunner's, the loader's and his own through the turret hatch. For the three years plus that I was in a tank, that was the system.'

CLOTHING AND EQUIPMENT

Dress varied widely by theatre of operations/time of year/climatic conditions etc.; however, in general terms, the clothes worn were military – except perhaps in the Western Desert, where the Eighth Army developed a more casual approach to dress (just look at a photograph of Monty to see what I mean!), as Tom Bird recalled in a letter home: 'We have just been given some leather jerkins and here is a picture of how I look in the desert – hair two inches over the neck, scarf worn because my neck is so dirty I don't want anyone to see it, leather jerkin; map usually left behind somewhere; sort of corduroy trousers; desert boots made of suede, very chic; purely imaginary palm trees, I haven't seen one for months.' And he was a staff officer! Even their normally much more formal opponents, Rommel's Deutsches Afrika Korps, relaxed their strict code of dress on occasions, Rommel himself sporting a plaid scarf and captured British anti-gas eyeshields/goggles as a protection from the sand and wind. The eyeshields, which quickly became one of his 'trademarks' had been initially 'acquired' from amongst the litter of kit taken out of two British armoured command vehicles, as his ADC Captain Heinz Werner Schmidt recalled: 'He immediately took a fancy to them, grinned and said, "Booty – permissible I take it even for a general." He adjusted the goggles on the gold braided rim of his cap peak. These goggles were to be the distinguishing insignia of the *Desert Fox*.'

'We drew our tropical clothing,' recalled *Leutnant* Ralph Ringler of the DAK, 'I could hardly believe what wonderful things German soldiers got for war. I received as my most important bit of furniture a huge rubber-sealed tropical chest. The contents were really precious – a tropical helmet, a tent, a mosquito net with carrying case, a face veil, a sleeping bag, a pair of desert boots, a pair of tropical shoes, long trousers, short trousers, breeches, coat, blouse, string vests, a body belt of lambs wool' – here a little shake of the head – 'goggles and much, much more. Nobody thought about what would happen to these wonderful things in the future, to which was added a wonderful rucksack, blankets and the usual officers' accoutrements like binoculars, map case, pistol and ammunition pouch, etc. There are obviously no sharpshooters in Africa as we hadn't been given a steel helmet. Therefore we thought the red-lined caps must be able to give us great protection.'

'I had a pair of green-knit gloves,' recalled Ruby Goldstein of the 712th Tank Battalion, 'and a leather glove over it. When I'd post the guard outside on the tanks I had my boots and overshoes on top of the boots. It was so cold I used to take my gloves off and suck my fingers. I'd have the fingers in my mouth and suck them so that I wouldn't freeze.'

'We had a man with size 13½ shoes,' reminisced Captain Norris Perkins; 'he wore them out in Morocco. The Quartermaster didn't have spares. We sent in to a French factory in Oran to make him some new shoes. While they were doing that I had the armourer make him a pair of leather sandals out of a rifle scabbard. This worked pretty good for him, but the ejected 75mm shells kept hitting his feet and hurting him. On the other hand, he got rid of a bad case of athlete's foot!'

R & R (REST AND RELAXATION)

After months of fighting 'Up the Blue' and hard living in the Western Desert, the prospect of a few days' leave in Cairo or Alexandria was something to look forward to, but not many soldiers could take advantage of it; David Ling again: 'Leave to Cairo was started but only a small percentage of the battalion's personnel was allowed away at any one time and, therefore, to increase the number it was arranged that one truck would travel to Alex each week ostensibly to pick up 'training equipment', with one officer and a handful of ORs on board. In fact this truck carried the dirty washing of the battalion and it was the duty of the officer accompanying it to hand it over to the local *dhobi* who laundered it in time for the lorry's return to Matruh at the week's end. Generally this officer had a harassing time. In addition to wrangling with the *dhobi* over ineffective laundering, lost shirts, etc., he had to check every item in the washing list and acted as shopper for his fellow officers. There was always a long shopping list – we ran out of razor blades, soap and films, we wanted stocks of books, there were always spools of negatives awaiting development and the collection of those that had been handed in the week before and which were not ready to go at the end of the week. Nevertheless, the opportunity to go to Alex with the washing truck was one that no one missed and the competition to get one's name at the head of the list of those to go was keenly contested.

'But leave to Cairo and excursions to Alex on washing trucks took second place to the short spells one had at the Battalion's rest Camp, certainly in number and often in popularity also. It was the CO's brainwave to alleviate the same monotony of the daily desert routine (when out of action) and to prevent boredom he instituted at Gerawla a small camp on the edge of the Mediterranean. Situated amongst sand dunes, the camp consisted of nothing more than a few bivouacs, a cookhouse, a canteen situated in the open air and selling beer, canned fruit, cigarettes and chocolate from a few packing cases and a fifteen-hundredweight truck, this to replenish the canteen stocks, to draw water from the conveniently situated water point at Gerawla and to deal with any unforeseen circumstances. Squadrons each sent a dozen men to the camp for a three-day spell of lazing, bathing and eating, after which they were replaced by a further twelve. In addition to these, one officer was sent in charge of the party and whose duty it was to carry out the small amount of organisation necessary – appointment of a canteen keeper, ordering of stocks, arranging sports, etc.

'During their three days there, personnel were at liberty to do exactly as they pleased. Here there was no discipline, no routine, no orders, no guards, no supervision. One arose when one saw fit, to bathe in a small sandy bay around which our bivouacs nestled, to breakfast on increased rations with liberal supplies of canned fruit provided by the unexpected largesse of the PRI. After breakfast saw more swimming, or sunbathing; some got down to serious reading (there being a small library), while others preferred to stroll along the beach. The afternoon was given up to sleeping. In the evening some-times a game of cricket or football, while after supper and sundown the whole camp would congregate around the canteen for the inevitable evening singsong and story telling over many bottles of lager. And this for three days. Its effect was amazing, its popularity terrific and the CO had shown wise discretion in deciding the stay should be short, for a lazy holiday can quickly become boring, but after three days we could all go back to the unit regretfully.'

Jim Colclough was a member of 'A' Squadron of the 44th and he recalled in his diary visiting the rest camp: 'Gerawla rest camp by the sea – 3 nights with meals at 8, 12, 4 and 7. The canteen consisted of a windscreen which shielded beer bottles, chocolate, tinned fruit etc. On a board it said: "To find the Manager, (a) enquire at the cookhouse, (b) search the beach, (c) if unsuccessful the canteen is closed."'

STRANGE STORIES

Are you the enemy?

Dennis Young recalled a strange incident which occurred to him whilst in Normandy in 1944. 'One morning at the break of dawn, we saw a German tank parked at the end of the field in which we had just spent the night. Thinking it had been knocked out in a previous battle no one paid it any attention and we got on making breakfast. Then a little later on one of the chaps in our squadron went to take a look – presumably souvenir hunting. Imagine his surprise when he found the entire crew fast asleep inside! He knocked the fat tank commander on the head with his revolver and he promptly surrendered, apparently exhausted after days of travelling to the front.'

Don't shoot we're friends!

'My M4A3 Ford-built Sherman tank was destroyed at Herrlisheim, France,' recalled Colonel Owsley Costlow, 'where my division, the 12th Armored, was reported to have lost ninety tanks and two thousand men. I myself, lost four tanks, eight men killed and eight wounded from a four-tank, twenty-man platoon. When the replacement tanks were delivered, I drew the first M4A3E8 in the Battalion. It looked very much like the M4A3 except it had a larger turret, twin bogie wheels, a 76mm main gun and, oh yes, it had a muzzle break! No one else in the Battalion had a tank with a muzzle break but all the German tanks and German self-propelled artillery pieces had muzzle breaks. Also, no one had told our tankers that now there was an American tank running around the area with a very German-looking gun. My crew and I had many disquieting moments before other M4A3E8s arrived and were integrated into the Battalion.'

Swimming in the Med

'Have you ever heard of nakedness as a field expedient?' queried Captain Norris Perkins. 'On our invasion of Sicily, I was the only one in the whole tank company to know exactly where we were landing. I had a real problem getting it to my other four LCTs and to my platoon leaders. I could not break radio silence, and I knew that the minute "H" hour began, there might be all kinds of confusion. I didn't know when I could get my instructions to my platoon leaders, wondering what to do. We formed a circle out in the middle of the Mediterranean, marking time for a little bit. We were near the island of Malta with our five LCTs in a slow-moving circle. The ensign that was leading our LCT lowered the ramp down and here a naked man came walking up out of the ocean. Lieutenant Cameron J. Warren. He said, "What's up, Perk?" I gave him extra copies of my orders. He jumped back in the water and he handed them off to the LCTs as they came by. It was really daring, and he should have had a medal. The convoy might have gone off and left him swimming in the middle of the Mediterranean.'

To war with a movie camera

Lieutenant-Colonel Dick Schmidt, a US Marine Corps tanker told me about his time in the Pacific theatre: 'At Saipan, an assistant driver [bow gunner on a Sherman] borrowed a movie camera from 4 Division Public Relations section and mounted it in the periscope housing at his crew station. The result was some combat-action footage which the Commandant of the Marine Corps pronounced the best to come out of the Pacific War. Naturally more extensive coverage was planned for the Tinan operation. The bow gunner turned photographer dutifully took his motion pictures each day and stored the film in machine-gun ammo boxes next to his position. On the next to last day of the operation this tank hit a mine and burned, losing all the film. For the Iwo Jima operation a tank was fitted with a colour camera and synchronised with a recorder plugged into the tank's intercom system. The result was some spectacular footage –

especially of flame-thrower tanks in action – with accompanying sound track!

A crystallised tank

Sergeant Ron Huggins of the 10th Royal Hussars told me the strangest story of them all: 'The 10 RH had captured a sugar factory which contained at least one very large container of treacle. This had been punctured during the action and a lake of treacle had spread around the factory area and its yards, presenting a smooth, shiny and sticky surface to the occupying force, who arrived in Sherman tanks. Most of the tanks passed through the area with ease, although their tracks got very sticky; one of them, however, found a large shell crater. It found it by falling into it; only the turret protruded above the treacle line. The crew clambered out and onto the top of the turret, where they were stranded, being unable to get through the treacle to dry land; indeed they didn't know where dry land was because the treacle obscured the edges of the crater. Meanwhile the Sherman was settling into the crater and slowly filling with treacle.

'Other members of the unit realised that the crew were likely to come to a sticky end if not rescued. They found planks from bombed buildings and laid these through the treacle and onto the turret of the Sherman and thus the crew were able to make their escape. As far as is known their Sherman is still there, crystallised for eternity, in the yard of an Italian sugar factory.'

CREW TRADES AT WORK

As explained already, there were many tasks which required all members of the crew to work as a team, such as filling up with fuel. Even this apparently simple operation could turn into a major drama as Captain Norris Perkins explained: 'We had some interesting fires, the most interesting being in an M4 Sherman tank, sitting on the level at Fort Bragg, gassing up and doing our first-echelon maintenance and a check of everything. The crew was pouring gasoline in the filler pipes in the back deck. A gentle breeze wafted the fumes up and over and into the top of the open turret, down through the fighting compartment and out through the hatch where the driver was sitting. He touched his siren switch to test the siren; it exploded the entire mixture with a tremendous bang. It was heard a mile away, clear down to regimental headquarters. It bent down the floor of the turret basket. It tore fixtures off around the opening of the turret hatch and astoundingly the helmeted driver was not hurt. He was sitting right in the middle of the explosion, everything going away from him. All it did was slightly singe his ankles and wrists. That taught us quite a bit about gassing up and breezes.'

Drivers

Joe Lee of the 7th Queen's Own Hussars, drove a Stuart Mark I (the British nomenclature for the basic American-built M3 light tank) during the British retreat out of Burma in February 1942. They had come to the Far East from the Middle East, as part of 7th Armoured Brigade and acted as rearguard to Burcorps throughout the retreat into India, covering themselves with glory. He told me: 'The tanks were simple and good workhorses, no sophisticated equipment. The turrets were all manual control and the driving sprockets were at the front of the tank. So to move around in the tank the crew had to step over the prop shaft – as you will appreciate, there were many harsh words said at times, as this ran right through the turret at knee-height. The petrol switch was in a very awkward place inside the turret at the back. So to start up one had to try to reach it from the driver's seat. I'm sure my right arm finished up a foot longer than the left! The gears were simple and steering easy enough.

'The tanks had radial engines and ran on high-octane, so it was possible to catch fire when starting up, especially when the engine was cold after lying still all night. Being radials, one had to turn them over by a big hand crank which looked like a big starting handle, to move the oil that would have collected at the bottom of the pistons. This amused the Burmese, who really thought we were winding the tanks up, like clockwork, which I suppose could be a logical deduction!

'To get at the engine, there were two doors at the back of the tank, held together by bolts, I think there were about four, but we very soon saved time by using just one. They were very accessible and one could service them even under fire without being too exposed, as opposed to British tanks where the engine openings were all on the back decking of the tank.

'The driver's hatch was quite big and one could almost jump in, but the front of the hatch hinged from the top was crude and simple. . . . For my part, from landing in Rangoon until leaving the tank at the Chindwin River – some hundreds of miles north through impossible going with no proper roads through the jungle – I never had any trouble and I certainly covered some miles "to and fro".'

Gunners

Sergeant Nick Mashlonik of New York was the commander of one of the very first American M26 Pershings to fight in North-West Europe almost at the end of the war in February/March 1945, but was acting as gunner when he destroyed his first German PzKpfw VI, the awesome Tiger. He told me: 'Our first exposure to the enemy with the new M26 was very fruitful. We were hit hard by the Germans from Elsdorf. The enemy appeared to have much armour as we received a lot of direct fire which kept us pinned down. Our casualties kept mounting and the CO of our company asked me if I thought I could knock out the Tiger that was almost destroying us. He and I did some investigating, by crawling out to a position where we could see from ground level, a sight to behold. The Tiger was slightly dug in and this meant it would be more difficult to destroy. I decided that I could take this Tiger with my 90mm. Our M26 was in defilade position, more or less hidden by a little valley. I detailed my driver, Cade, and gunner, Gormick, to accompany me on this mission. I would be gunner and have Gormick load. I instructed both of them that once we had fired three shots – two armour-piercing and one HE point-detonating – we would immediately back up so as not to expose ourselves too long at the top of the hill.

'Just as we started our tank and had moved very slowly forward (creeping) I noticed that the Tiger was moving out of the position and exposing his belly to us. I immediately put a shot into its belly and knocked it off. The second shot was fired at his track and knocked the right-hand track off. The third shot was fired at the turret and the HE point-detonating destroyed the escaping crew.

'At the time three other German armoured vehicles[2] were leaving Elsdorf and were on the road driving to my right flank. I waited until all of them were on the road with their rear ends exposed and then I picked off each one with one shell each, getting the last one first, then the second one and then the first one – just like shooting ducks. Then I came back to each vehicle with HE point-detonating and destroyed the crews as they were dismounting from the burning vehicles. It was our first day in combat with the Pershing and it was both fruitful and exciting.'

Operators

Nick Deamer, whom we met in an earlier chapter during his wireless training in UK, was posted to 6 RTR in the Tobruk area in April 1941, only to be taken out by sea and shipped back to Cairo, from whence he was sent on a second basic wireless course at the Abbassia base school. 'On rejoining the regiment about the end of June, I was posted to the RHQ tank troop. At that time we had such outstanding characters as "Skip" Rycroft and "Dingle" Rogers in RHQ Troop, both later commissioned in the field. This was my first real experience of tanks – of seeing one or being inside one, so there was plenty to learn. I was lap gunner/spare operator on the command tank. I used to team up with the Royal Signals rear-link operator to try taking down the daily news bulletin sent out from Cairo at twenty words per minute – it was good for your morse reading!

'We spent three to four months in the desert and then the "Crusader" battle[3] began. Our tank was rushed back from an engine change, but Colonel Lister was already on another tank, so we went in with "C" Squadron, Sergeant Noble in command and with me as operator. 6 RTR was practically wiped out on the second day of this action, all the senior officers being either killed or wounded. We ended up at nightfall with just four tanks left – and ours was one of them. Next day Major Mitford came and took command of the remnants. We had two good scraps on our way back, but ended up in the Citadel in Cairo. This was our base for the next three months and I was put in charge of the telephone exchange with five other operators to man it twenty-four hours a day, until we left for a tented camp in the desert just behind Mena House. I did three weeks there as a Sergeants' Mess Waiter and then was told to move out and set up a wireless-store tent as our new Grant tanks were arriving and had to be fitted out with WS 19s. This was soon complete and we started regimental exercises in the desert adjacent to our camp. We had an excellent Regimental Signals Officer [RSO], Captain Pete Gudyer, at this time and I was put onto the Command Tank as operator for the schemes. Our new Colonel was H. M. Liardet,[4] ex-War Office, very efficient, a perfectionist. He rebuilt the Regiment both in discipline and operational efficiency. It was a period of very rapid learning, no mistakes, but it went well.

'On 27 May we got the call for action and were rushed up to the Knightsbridge area and into battle. I went up on the RHQ troop leader's tank, but on 9 June Captain Gudyer came over to me and said: "Get a stripe on your arm and get over to the Colonel's tank." I was in total shock, the CO had an "all-regular" tank crew: Sergeant Noble – driver; Sergeant Pethridge – 37mm gunner; Trooper Beevers – 75mm gunner; and now as operator – yours truly! This was the *"crème de la crème"* and I wasn't quite sure if you got shot if you made a mistake! However, we survived and after ten weeks of continuous action I felt that I was accepted. Colonel Mitford took over command for the last four weeks of this period and he was as tough as they came. We were no longer withdrawing, but holding our own and attacking. We were eventually withdrawn to the Delta area and I then put myself forward for an instructor's course at the base schools. I bought an advanced wireless-theory manual in Cairo which I still have, together with my course notebook to this day. I was ill on the course and also went to the base dentist, who was awful. I think today it would have been called reaction to all the stress.'

Unofficial modifications

'A Sherman turret had space but no comfort, least of all for the operator,' recalls M. E. Mawson; 'all he had was a drop-down round small stool to sit on and very little chance of getting to the hatchway past the gunshield. In Normandy we noted that the Sherwood Rangers Yeomanry had cut away their steel mesh around the turret so that one could go either way. In normal life all one had to do was to keep one's feet out of the traverse! Further, the operator had to get out over or under the gun breech recoil shield – or was expected to do so. The natural development was to remove this obstruction so that the place became positively roomy. Fine, always provided you didn't mind the recoil crashing back, hoping to share your extended accomodation! Modern Health & Safety bureaucrats would have had fits. Another "furnishing adjustment", which meant that I could stretch out straight and sleep – the only one of the crew who could – was by removing the ammunition from both sponsons and poking my head in one side and my tootsies in the other, below the gunner's seat. A situation which used to drive the rest of the crew mad, because I couldn't see why my incessant cracking of boiled sweets (from the Compo packs) "oft in the stilly night", should irritate them.

'The final interior operator comfort came in Nijmegen, where, from a knocked-out Guards Armoured Division tank, I secured the seat and backrest from the gunner's side and fastened it in so that I could sit and look through the periscope in supreme comfort, to the disgust of my crew commander gazing down from his open cupola, with the rain dripping down his collar. Incidentally, in later years he once remarked that his most abiding memory was looking down at me "spending a penny" into a tall empty shell-case, which it was my job to pass around and then empty out of the revolver port.

'I was also able to improve the Wireless Set 19 equipment markedly. As issued, only the turret crew could work the radio sets, the pair down in the "servants hall" had the intercom facility only, with just a faint indication of what was going on. I got tired of saying that there were no panzers for miles and how about a corned beef sandwich, so I soon had control boxes from knocked-out tanks and/or wiring tracks done so that they could all hear what we could "up top".

'I was very proud of the fact that all my troop could operate the tank wireless, so we disobeyed battalion orders quite deliberately as a result,' Major (Retd) Jock McGinlay admitted, when reminiscing about the early days in the Western Desert. 'RHQ had the idea that, once the radios were netted in on the battalion frequency, no one should interfere with the set. In theory this may have been right and the Royal Signals personnel attached to each battalion made sure that every set was in perfect tune. We had to have alternative frequencies in case of accidents and we were all supposed to know how to change. Each dawn, the CO's tank sent out a signal and we all had to make sure we were spot on to that signal. The result was that most tank crews were scared stiff to go near the set – quite the wrong idea, in my opinion; each tank crewman should be able to do every job in the tank.

'To this end I got my troop together and said they could listen, as I intended, to the BBC each night, just as long as they kept quiet about it and as long as they took turns each morning at getting back onto the battalion net. Woe betide anyone failing to be spot on net. The result was a very happy troop and a confident one as far as the wireless was concerned. In my own tank we even went as far as to have four pairs of headphones terminating in a tobacco tin inside the bivouac under which we slept alongside the tank, with a master lead to the set, connected up to *Hi Gang!* and all the other programmes the BBC were pumping out.'

Commanders

Colonel Owsley C. Costlow told me this cautionary tale of a problem which every tank platoon commander may have to face: 'Communication between tanks in a five-tank platoon was primarily via radio. The Platoon Leader and the Platoon Sergeant were authorised one transmitter and one receiver (SCR 528); the other three tanks only had receivers (SCR 538). However, on reaching Europe we augmented our communications capability by giving the Platoon Leader an extra receiver (SCR 508) so he could listen to both his platoon net and the company net. The three tanks with only one receiver each were given a transmitter; then all tanks could both send and receive.

'Also, because we worked very closely with the Armored Infantry and since our radio and their radio did not net, a Platoon Leader received an Infantry SCR 300, the walkie-talkie radio, that was placed in a special metal basket welded to the side of the turret. In addition to all the radios there was a field telephone tied on the top of the radio. This was designed for use in working directly with the Infantrymen on the ground. Each had an important purpose and were used whenever necessary.

'I always knew it would happen, and it did! One day my Company Commander radioed; one of my Platoon tanks radioed; the Infantry Platoon Leader, who I was working with, radioed; and yes, someone rang the telephone. What happened? Why of course I told my Platoon tank to wait, turned off the Infantry, waved to the telephone caller to wait and answered my Commander!'

5

Replenishment, Repair & Recovery

It was Napoleon who said that an army marches on its stomach but, although that old maxim is still very true, an armoured regiment's lifeblood is more than just rations. Without adequate supplies of POL (Petrol, Oil and Lubricants) and of all the various types of ammunition, fuses and other explosives, they will soon grind to a half. In addition, of course, tanks require continual attention if they are to remain fit for battle. They must be 'repaired and recovered', so, just in the same way as the Medical Officer (MO) and his staff, dealt with the human casualties of the unit, so the Electrical and Mechanical Engineer (EME) and his fitters, dealt with the mechanical casualties. In the Second World War, all armoured regiments in all armies contained a mass of soldiers, in addition to the tank crews, with vital tasks to perform. They were usually broken down into 'Echelons' (e.g.: 'A' & 'B' in British parlance), and operated in support of the fighting element ('F' Echelon). Indeed, many operated constantly as an integral part of 'F' at the 'sharp end', or visited the tanks daily/nightly to bring forward the supplies they so desperately needed. Here are a few reminiscences from these 'unsung heroes', without whom the tanks could never have operated efficiently.

REPLENISHMENT

'A panzer regiment is a gigantic organisation,' recalled *Leutnant* Dr Kurt Wolff of Panzer Regiment 5 which was initially part of 3rd Panzer

Division, but was then sent to North Africa as part of 5 *leichte* Division of the DAK. 'Ammunition trucks, fuel tanks move forward and often get blown up in the course of battle. Field kitchens and ration trucks search in the tracks of panzers for their units. However, the important movements in the dusk of the evening are the repair groups. Men who repair the engines, clean and adjust the carbs. Springs, track rollers and track links have to be seen to and fixed. Guns and machine guns have to be checked. You can hear the swearing of hard-working men, the clanging of hammers in the wet and cold night. As soon as the sun rises through the morning mist, the Regiment starts to roll forward. Thousands of other things come together before a battle is won. In the yellow moonlight long convoys of trucks move along the coast road, now and again attacked by English bombers. We disperse into the desert, but forward we go, forty to fifty kilometres per hour we read on our tacho. Water, fuel, ammo, bread, food and people, everything moves through the dark night which is no different from the glowing heat of the day.'

REPLENISHMENT WESTERN DESERT STYLE

As Arthur Soper told me: 'To give you some idea of how the echelon worked in the "Blue" – RASC trucks did not carry mixed loads – ammo, POL, rations and other day-to-day necessaries were loaded separately. Requirements were brought forward from the rear by the RASC to a brigade or divisional area, distributed to the echelon under the eagle eye of the QM, RQMS and SQMS, etc. In action, "B" Echelon were "brigaded". The idea of this was that if misfortune overtook a unit "packet" there was always another available. The effect of this was that now and again one was serviced by trucks from other regiments. In our case, if a "packet" was not our own, it often came from 8 RTR who were brigaded with us. The packet was usually led by a "B" Echelon officer or an SSM. A notable move up was led by SSM Plumley (a pre-war India veteran who but for the war would have been out on pension). His driver was Alfie Allen, a dear friend of many including myself. The echelon was subjected to attack by Stuka dive-bombers. SSM and driver dived into a nearby "slit" and a bomb followed them in. Their names are on the El Alamein memorial "RIP".'

While serving with his regiment in Italy, Arthur was 'ridge squatting' – well forward and turret down, with a watchman on the ridge looking out for movement on the other side of a river obstacle some hundred yards away. 'The rest of the crew were having a "kip", after doing all their maintenance. I was watchman, lying on my stomach, propped up on elbows with binoculars and an extension lead from the radio. Nothing happening, but no doubt the "angry man" is performing a similar exercise. Let's all be peaceful, shall we? There is a road in front of us, running across our front, on a slightly lower level and within whispering distance. Suddenly the silence is shattered by somebody (later identified as the RAPC sergeant) shouting: "Anybody want any pay?!" – I ask you! In full view of Jerry he had dropped the tail board of his fifteen-hundredweight truck, unloaded a fold-flat table, covered it with a blanket and put out piles of British Military Currency (held in place with stones), without the Boche responding, probably as amazed as we were!

'I didn't shout back. In little more than a whisper I said: "No thank you, not today" – or words to that effect and, "Oh, by the way, Jerry is watching you from across the way." Blue Watch could not have got under way any quicker. The lot was back in the wagon quicker than it takes to tell the story and he was off down the road leaving half his tyre rubber behind. Strangely, even at this later stage he (or we) didn't draw any fire. Amazing, Jerry didn't usually waste opportunities handed to him on a plate. But what could we have spent the pay on anyway? The Pay Sergeant's face was red for weeks and as far as I know he didn't get the MM!'

Guns over Capuzzo

Trooper W. H. Thomas of 'B' Squadron, 8 RTR, wrote an account of his wartime experiences some years ago and lodged it with the Tank Museum Library, 'Ten sheets of thin faded and crumpled foolscap typed' is how it is described in the museum archives. Here is an evocative extract: 'Nov 17th 1941, I am summoned to "A" Echelon. The journey lay through a fantastic country of carved escarpments, under a sky that hung draped like a huge black and purple curtain, fold on fold, shedding a lurid light on the desolate land below. I reached the squadron just as it was going into close leaguer. The atmosphere was like a scene from Dante's Inferno. In the lurid demonic light, men's faces were grey and unfamiliar and tanks and vehicles moved fitfully like primeval monsters in the half light of a lost world. It seemed as if the Grim Horseman was already riding above the land and the shadow of the dusky cloak lay over it. The jar and clatter of the tanks sounded a fitting accompaniment to the grey and grim scene before us. Round the cook's lorry, the men took their meal in the quickly gathering darkness.

'On the return journey the dark curtain folds had fused into one and the sky was a lowering mass of black. Flashes of forked lightning stabbed through the thick pall every few minutes, serving to light the way in lurid intermittent bursts. The swaying, jolting convoy showed vague shapes ahead and around, lit up for a second in startling silhouette by the lightning bursts. There was the sound of furious "revving" as vehicles became stuck in patches of soft sand. Several became bogged and the convoy had to turn about to tow them out. The straining rope – the wildly racing wheels – the sudden jolts – and then clear again. Final order – "Bed down for the night". Last picture – the line of transport with the men's beds made up alongside. A philanthropist brews tea and hands it around. Stars begin to pierce the pall overhead. Still flashes. Night air cold and clean. Deep sleep. In the morning the indefatigable PU [a small-wheeled saloon-type vehicle] does a swift round-up of stragglers and we move in to a welcome breakfast.

'Nov 19. Back to "A" and find all lined up and ready to start. Again a strange evening light and the long triple column moves out into the yellow murk. Our 2IC's PU has an argument with a slit trench and shows a marked disinclination to leave it. The night march makes its tentative way to the wire (marking the frontier) and Libya, tanks leading, POL coming behind. There are intermittent bursts of gunfire from Sidi Omar and lightning flashes to the north. The sky is lowering, the atmosphere tense and electric. At 2 a.m. we move through the wire into Libya. SSM Parry is the first to set foot in the enemy land. The wire stretches away on either side – grey streak in the gloom. "No smoking" is the rule and we are all bursting for one. We form up in a very efficient triangular leaguer about three kilometres inside. Sleep beside the staff car. What will tomorrow bring?

'Nov. 20. Dawn in Libya. Elusive difference in ground – blackish gravel and good going. Wide vista all round, but nothing to see. Sense of expectancy. 2 p.m. Move to join NZ Div, I see it all from the staff car. Most impressive sight – MT everywhere, of all kinds and sizes, in an unremitting flow northwards, shining in the setting sun and throwing long shadows across the sand and scrub, Major Sutton looks with undisguised admiration at our tanks, forging ahead on either side and looking well . . . "Good show, B Squadron." Around us are guns, motor cycles, trucks of all kinds, tiny runabouts, lumbering lorries, staff cars, bofors guns, 25-pounders – all flowing northwards – a striking sight. We reach Pt 190 at dusk. "B" Echelon comes up shortly afterwards, a tribute to Captain Butt. They must have travelled fast and well.'

Bombing up

Whenever the echelon arrived – day or night – it was essential to 'bomb up' the tanks as quickly as possible as Bill Haemmel, a loader in an M4 Sherman of 3rd Platoon, Company H, 1st Armored Regiment, 1st US Armored Division reminisced of his experiences during the Anzio operations in Italy in late January 1944: 'Dusk was rapidly settling in when the tanks carefully withdrew. As vision became more and more limited, the tank commanders personally guided their vehicles through the infantry positions on foot. Once the tanks were clear, the column reformed and the company returned to a point on the road perhaps one mile to the rear of the initial stopping place in the early morning. The exhausted crew members dropped down for some rest and sleep. Several unstrapped their blankets or bed rolls and stretched out next to or under the tanks, trying to sleep and fight off the cold. Others tried to find relaxed positions inside their tanks.

'Shortly after the men had made themselves comfortable the trucks of the Regimental Service Company arrived. The individual five-gallon cans of ninety-octane gasoline had been filled from large tank trucks several miles from the front line and stacked into 6 × 6 two-

and-a-half-ton trucks. Other trucks were loaded with crated rounds of 75mm shells and boxes of .30 calibre machine-gun ammunition. The truck driver and assistant driver unloaded the cargo as rapidly as they could and then roared down the road away from the front lines. All five members of the tank crew formed an irregular "bucket brigade" and handed the gas from the ground to the tank. While Mosman fed the gasoline into the tank, I received the ammunition and strapped each round into its place or piled it on the floor of the turret. The five of us were grey and haggard with fatigue and would occasionally snap and snarl at each other in the course of the work; however, in less than an hour the job was done. The camouflage net was unrolled and pulled over the tank. I noted it was 9 p.m. as I dropped back into my bed roll. In an instant I was fast asleep.'

Replen in the rain

'The rations and water truck used to come round just as darkness fell, making them less conspicuous to the enemy,' recalled Brian Brazier of 46 RTR; 'we were in a deep valley running down from the road. Over the ridge in front of us was the River Trigno which at the time was no mans' land as the Germans were on the ridge on the opposite side of the river, no more than a mile from our position. We had chosen one of the wettest times of the year to be in Italy but it couldn't be helped, the war couldn't be called off just because it was raining. About the third night in this camp the heavens just opened and it poured incessantly for over twenty-four hours. The ground way back up to the road was a ploughed field and just became a sea of mud, making it absolutely impossible for the ration truck to reach us every other day. So we had the tiresome job of carrying the rations down through all the mud which clung to our boots in great clods.

'It was also decided that the carrying of five-gallon water cans down this quagmire was almost an impossibility and so the driver decided to turn off the road to try and reach us. Of course it was sheer lunacy and in no time at all he was completely bogged down. The rumour quickly spread round the tank crews that one of them was going to have to tow the water truck down and return it back to the road. Each driver was saying "I'm buggered if I'm taking my tank out!" But in the Army "Orders is Orders" and I was the unlucky one. Now it wouldn't have been so bad had it not been pouring with rain and had we not had our big tank sheet tied up along the side of the tank with all our bedding under it. This had to be taken down and put back afterwards, creating an enormous lot of trouble besides stirring up the mud even more. It couldn't be helped, but I honestly can't say we did the job cheerfully. The swearing was incessant the whole time, each crew member wrapped up in gas capes and greatcoats set off to tow the water truck. We also had to fetch the rations down on the back of the tank as well as hitching up the truck. Eventually we got under way with Ged Kierans at the wheel of the water truck, slithering backwards and forwards behind us. We were like drowned rats when the job was at last completed and we could once again erect the sheet alongside the tank.

'We were always under the impression that it was the quartermaster's job to sort out and issue rations, but the chap we had was very much on the nervous side and if ever we saw him come to the front line, he got his leg pulled unmercifully by telling him shells were likely to fall at any time. He would bustle about telling us to get a move on and would be gone like a shot, leaving us to share and sort each troop's rations.'

Living off the enemy

In fluid campaigns such as were waged in the Western Desert, both sides took advantage of the capture of enemy supply dumps. *Hauptmann* (later Major) Wolfgang Everth, who commanded an armoured reconnaissance company in North Africa in early 1942, recalled just such an occasion in his diary thus: '26 Jan 42. The night passed quietly. We obtained other things from Tommy's supply depot and slowly we ourselves became Tommies; our vehicles, petrol, rations and clothing were all English. I was somewhat international too – Italian shoes, French trousers, German coat and hat, English linen, stockings, gloves and blankets. A soldier's life is fine! Devoured everything, put on some clean linen and had some rest. Tommy, this is our revenge for the things you have done to us! Breakfasted off two tins of milk, a tin of pineapple, biscuits and Ceylon tea. Unfortunately the reality of war soon returned. The English made a low-level air attack on our echelon, which had come up to us early. Four men killed and several wounded, it was reported on the wireless. . . . Until midday we loaded up English petrol, putting it into German cans which were better. The English cans were too weak. Four thousand litres – splendid work! The captured vehicles were painted with German crosses, so as to achieve at least some difference. At 1300 hrs came the order that we were once again under our Division and were to go there. We set off and found them that evening almost 25kms east of Msus.'

REPAIR & RECOVERY

Tank squadron fitters

Slim Wildman, who was a fitter in 'A' Squadron LAD (Light Aid Detachment) in the 13th/18th Hussars during the early days in Normandy, had this to say in prefacing his accounts of 'recoveries and repairs': 'One point I must make is that in my squadron at least, the two crews making up the forward echelon fitter section worked very much as a team and shared many duties so that sometimes one section would ride on either vehicle (these were: an ARV – armoured recovery vehicle; and an HT – halftrack), the exceptions being the two crew commanders who always stayed with their vehicles, certain of the REME craftsmen who stayed on the ARV and the signalman (radio mechanic) who stayed on the halftrack.

'The first job that I was involved in was on D-Day. I was riding in the HT and we were late in landing because of a traffic jam. On moving up the beach towards the exit we saw a squadron tank in trouble, track blown off and on the side of a sand dune. We stopped to ask if we could assist them, when the Beach Marshal came up and told us in no uncertain terms to get off the beach! Whilst we had been talking to the tank crew, a 3 Div carrier went past and we followed them up the sand dune. As the carrier started away from the beach they hit a mine, losing a track. Of course the road off the beach was now blocked, so we had somehow to push the carrier clear without hitting another mine – we succeeded, but not without some heart-stopping moments.

'Later in the day, we had a call for assistance from a tank crew somewhere near the village of St Aubin. As we went up the hill towards the village we came upon two carriers with the crews still in them. Both the vehicles had been "brewed up" and the road was blocked, so before we could proceed we had to push the carriers off the road. Whilst this was being done, Sergeant Spencer and myself did a foot recce to see what was ahead. We found that just around the corner the road was strewn with mines, making it impossible for us to get any further along the road, so we began to turn around and go back down the hill, when the electrician called out, "Jerries!" I was carrying a Bren light machine gun, so I dropped to the floor and fired one shot in their direction, whereupon they put up their hands and surrendered. We had a hard job getting someone to take them off our hands.

'The day finished with me asking the squadron leader if I should take the Vehicle State reports now or wait until the rest of the squadron had arrived at the RV. "Take it now," he replied; "this is the squadron state: six tanks only have arrived out of twenty." Of these, one needed urgent repairs to its steering, so I worked on it until 3 a.m. As "Stand To" was at 4 a.m. I didn't get much sleep that night! Fortunately many of the crews of the lost tanks arrived during the night, having been on "walking tours" of Northern France in the meantime.

'A few days later, both fitter crews were called to a tank that had lost a track in a minefield. The recovery was easy as it was only about fifty yards into the field and its tracks in were easy to identify, so all we had to do was to tow the tank backwards, making sure we kept to the track marks. With the aid of the ARV we started to line up the tank and track, preparatory to refitting the track, when we came under heavy shelling, so we decided to move out of danger. The line-up as we moved off was: the ARV towing the tank to which was attached the track, followed by us in the halftrack. As the ARV went around a sharp bend, the tank, which was on a solid tow, followed it closely. The track being on a wire pull swung across the corner, passing under a hut standing there, catching it up and dragging it along, so we now had going down the road – the ARV + tank + track + hut + halftrack!

'Now came a sad time for the fitters. We, the three sabre squadrons' forward fitters, together with the doctor and Tech HQ, had set up our position in an orchard just behind the forward tank positions. We came under heavy, but intermittent mortar fire. One bomb landed very close to our halftrack, causing some damage; it landed only a couple of feet from a slit trench in which were Sergeant Spencer and myself. One of the Tech HQ fitters was killed and another wounded. The Technical Adjutant[1] came to see if we were still mobile and told us that he had asked permission to move to a safer site, but then a shell landed in his trench, killing him and seriously wounding both the EME and the MQMS, also wounding the EME's driver. It was a great loss, Tony was a very popular officer.

'Next Pat, the electrician, and myself were called to a troop leader's tank with all its electrics out. We went up in a jeep and found that the charging motor was out of action. The driver had tried to carry out his own repairs and destroyed it. Meanwhile the troop leader had been transmitting constantly on the radio and had drained the battery completely. The tank was hull-down, but in a forward position, barely two hundred yards from the enemy. The officer asked us to put in a new battery and was very annoyed when we said "no way". To do what he wanted meant that we would have to stand on top of the tank and lower the battery down through the tank, so we would be standing in full view of the enemy, an ideal target for any sniper who might be around. In the end our solution was to run a jump lead from the jeep to the tank. I would get in the tank and Pat would be at the jeep, he would run the jeep engine, trying to pass enough power through to me so that I could start the tank engine. As soon as I had started the engine then I would try to reverse out and Pat would also reverse, making sure that the cable did not snag in any way. It worked well and as soon as I had sufficient power we disconnected the cable and I drove the tank to a safer place to put in a new battery and a new charger, also to give the driver a good ticking off!

'Now came the battle for a hill called Mont Pincon. We were successful but during the day things were a bit nasty. Major Wormwald's (then Regimental 2IC) tank was hit and started to brew up but then the fire went out. This meant that it was possible that important papers (e.g.: codes, marked maps and orders) in the tank had not been destroyed so the tank had to be recovered. Both "B" and "C" Squadrons' ARVs went up to carry out this job, but were both destroyed, their commanders killed and the rest of the crews wounded.

'During the fighting immediately after the Seine in the Epte valley we lost a couple of tanks. Moving off the next day we were in the HT and fell in behind a Troop Leader's tank. I noticed that one of its tracks was damaged, so ordered the crew to take the tank out of the line of march. On inspection we discovered that a *panzerfaust* projectile had gone through the track and entered the final drive. Sergeant Spencer, now acting MQMS, asked if I could repair it if I was left behind with the crew, less the Troop Leader. I said, "Yes, just get me a new casing." Whilst waiting for the new one to arrive, a Frenchman, who was the leader of the local Resistance, invited us to his farm. He gave some of his men to us to guard the tank and we went to the farm. The first thing he did was to go to the midden, clear some of the pile aside and dig out two bottles of brandy that he had hidden there in 1940, ready to share with the first troops to liberate him. We were in no state to finish the repair that day and when we did move off we were far behind the Regiment!

'Whilst in the Reichswald Forest I was crewing the ARV and was away from the vehicle, taking reports when a long-range anti-tank shell hit the ARV. After crossing the Rhine we were called to a break-down in the middle of a cornfield. We cleared up the problem and then sat down with the crew and had a brew-up. Along came a Black Watch officer. He asked us how long we had been sitting there. When we told him, he asked the tank commander to put a shot into a large building only about two hundred yards away. This was done, where-upon a large number of enemy troops came pouring out of the place.

'We received a report of a damaged armoured vehicle near the canal at Hengelo and discovered that it was a Household Cavalry armoured car still burning, only 100 yards from the enemy on the other canal bank. Then we started being mortared with small mortar bombs. Suddenly our driver said that we had been hit – we noticed a smell of food cooking and then realised that we had been hit by a tin of tomato soup from the burning armoured car! We then got orders to move in battlegroup formation towards Nordhorn from Hengelo. On the run one tank broke down – we on the ARV were to take it and the crew back to Hengelo. We were happy to comply, thinking that we would be able to stay the night in the town, but no, it was not to be. As soon as we had unhitched the broken-down tank, we were ordered to rejoin the squadron and this meant travelling on our own through the night along a road that the day before had been enemy territory – and we did not know how safe it was.

'In Cloppenberge, I was returning to the ARV when I came under machine-gun fire. I wasn't hit, but we discovered that a house just outside the town was still held by enemy troops. We were asked by an infantry officer if we could assist him in an action to clear the house. He was going to use a Wasp flame-thrower and needed our guns to smash all the windows in the house, he was then going to spray the place with flame fuel, including a small hut in the garden and demonstrate to the enemy what could happen to them if they did not surrender by igniting the hut. About twenty men jumped out of the windows when he did this!

'By now things were drawing to a close and we were near Bremen when one tank of another squadron bogged down in a very awkward position, close to the embankment of an *autobahn* [motorway], with enemy troops holding the top. The ground was very marshy and disturbed, making it impossible to tow backwards, so we would have to get in front of the tank where there was some firm ground. Of course this would put us leading the entire British Army – or so it felt! Fortunately, by getting up close to the banking we were in a covered position and the enemy could not fire on us without exposing themselves to the covering fire of our own troops. We were able to fix up a solid tow so the tank would follow our tracks out, without sliding back into the marsh. As we pulled away the enemy opened up with light mortars, but the ground being so marshy it meant that the bombs were sinking into the marsh and just sprayed us with mud. The few that landed on the firm ground fortunately missed us.'

Stuck in a gorge

Sometimes tank crews had to use 'ad hoc' methods of recovery in order to get the job done. Max Flemming was a StuG III driver in the elite *Fallschirmpanzerkorps 'HG'*, serving in Italy in 1943, defending the Volturno line. He recalled: 'Disaster struck three of our AFVs, including mine. We got stuck in front of the enemy, the StuGs being on their bellies in a ditch along a narrow dirt path. Volunteers – one driver with one NCO as a guide per AFV, together with a platoon of infantry as protection – go forward to recover our vehicles. We get there without any trouble. With one of our other StuGs acting as a recovery tractor, we pull the first bogged StuG out, when we come under heavy infantry fire coming from wooded hills close by. We continued with the recovery successfully; however, I was unfortunate enough to be the last of the three to be recovered and also had damaged steering gear. As the other two vehicles disappeared towards our lines I had difficulty in steering mine in a straight path, then to make matters worse, my guide disappeared. All the firing had stopped but I didn't feel happy sitting on my own in a damaged tank so close to enemy lines. I struggled along the path as best I could, hopefully towards our own positions. I had to cross a narrow bridge over a gorge about twenty metres deep. As I started to cross, my vehicle swerved to the right and in seconds I was hanging over the edge, rocking back and forth.

'I got out. Not a soul in sight, complete darkness. I started walking towards our lines and suddenly a figure came towards me. I took the safety catch off my pistol, but before I could fire a voice in German asked me what the hell I was doing. It was an infantry lieutenant. After explaining the situation, he managed to get about ten men to go back with me to sit on the rear end of the StuG as a counterweight. I then reversed very slowly and fortunately managed to straighten out. I drove behind our forward positions to the repair shop. Whilst I was getting something to eat we came under heavy artillery fire and I was wounded – metal splinters in my head – so I finished up in hospital in Germany.'

DESERT RECOVERY

Behind the unit LADs were the Brigade and Divisional Workshops, who would send out repair and recovery teams, to either help effect repairs in the field, or to recover more badly damaged – but still repairable – AFVs, and to take them back to the divisional workshops some way behind the front line. In the desert these recovery teams had to be completely self-supporting as Major Alfred Barnes of the REME, who worked as a recovery officer told me: 'The unit being highly mobile, everyone except the HQ staff is on individual rations and very soon the camp is awake. The vehicle crews' "cook of the day" is busily frying up his own idea of Australian tinned bacon, biscuits and eggs (if he has been lucky enough to scrounge some), whilst the remainder of the crew are washing and shaving – if there is enough water – and finally rolling up bedding rolls. After breakfast there is just time to wash up the dishes in the washing water saved for the occasion, and then out into the blue for "spade drill".

'The vehicle commanders chase their crews into a quick Diesel Oil and Water check and top up where necessary from the supply truck. During this check-over the "Q" [the senior WO] has reported to the Captain, OC the unit, who has decoded the CREME's[2] instructions during his breakfast and together they work out the day's work schedules. Eighth Armoured Brigade along with 22nd Armoured Brigade have had a night march to take up new positions and several of both 1st and 2nd Royal Tanks vehicles have ended up in a deep, uncharted wadi, some on their sides and most bogged down in the natural tank trap and are unable to extract themselves. They are urgently needed to face an expected enemy counter-attack, so the Scammels and Diamond Ts, along with the crews, are despatched flat out – at eighteen m.p.h. – to get the tanks mobile again.

'The lighter recovery vehicles are despatched to 131 Infantry Brigade to clear several vehicles BLR'd [Beyond Local Repair] back to Corps workshops somewhere in the rear. They also have to drop off two fifteen-hundredweight trucks, written off in a minefield at the "Help Yourself Dump" just off the main track. These vehicles will be picked clean by the unit fitters, who are all born scroungers and take pride in keeping their unit's vehicles running. You have to be very careful when you park your vehicle while you are "helping yourself" or you may find all your wheels missing when you return for it!

'The OC makes a quick check with his HQ Sergeant, Cook, Rations Corporal and finally with the water man, who can sometimes be the most important man in the unit, and then sets off with his jeep and driver to check how the tank recovery is going. The Recovery Sergeant has gone ahead in his jeep to have a quick "shufti". He finds the wadi and then goes back to guide the cumbersome but highly mobile Scammels down into the wadi floor. Using their powerful winches and snatch blocks and each other's vehicles as anchors, they start to get the tanks back on their tracks. After four hours' hard work five of the tanks are mobile and they set off for their own Regimental HQs. Two young German soldiers who have been hiding for two days to get away from their units give themselves up with their hands in the air. After a quick frisk over by the recovery crews they are fed with bully and biscuits, given a long drink of sweet tea and, after it is seen that they are harmless, they are only too willing to give a hand righting the remaining tanks. . . .

'After a few more hours the final tanks are back on their tracks and the non-runners are winched up behind the Diamond Ts onto their multi-wheeled trailers. It is rapidly getting dark and the final tanks and recovery crews decide to drive for a couple of hours into more friendly territory, where they settle down for the night before moving on to the Brigade workshops in the morning. The OC and his driver have not brought their bedding with them, so they set out for their camp in the dark, driving by the stars, instinct and some lucky compass work. On his arrival, the OC's batman prepares an evening meal for his officer and driver and, after the meal, some good Italian coffee is brewed and the driver sits down for a smoke and a chat with the HQ staff and the returned crews. . . . Someone has a "liberated" Jerry tank radio on which a very good German forces radio station is pounding out some excellent dance music, followed by the inevitable strains of "Lili Marlene". The whole camp joins in and sings the verses as it is a very popular tune with the soldiers; it is nearly always followed by the news and propaganda in English, which is greeted with jeers and laughter, but does provide some food for thought.

'The radio is switched off, cigarettes put out and the lucky ones that are not on guard duty roll themselves into their blankets and with the soft sand as a mattress and the sky for a roof, drop off for a wonderful sleep that only those who have slept in the Western Desert know. So ends another day in the Desert.'

OFFICIAL AND UNOFFICIAL MODIFICATIONS

Tank crews often modified the tanks to make them safer, more comfortable, etc. There was probably no tank more modified than the ubiquitous Sherman M4, some being official mods others unofficial. Here are a few of the more interesting ones: 'One of the more ingenious additions to the Sherman was an idea that one of our Warrant Officers developed,' as ex-USMC tanker Ed Bollard of Pennsylvania, who served on Marine Corps Shermans in the Pacific, told me: 'in order to provide extra protection he devised a method of attaching large boards (2 × 10 or 2 × 12s) onto the sides of the tank by means of large bolts welded to the tank. In this space he would pour concrete. After the battles of Saipan and Iwo Jima, these additions were in tatters. However, to my recollection, we only had one tank pierced and that was on Iwo by a high-velocity 47mm. He also welded extra track blocks onto the front slope plate and all around the turret sides. These not only gave us extra protection, but also gave us extra track blocks for immediate repairs in the field.'

A semi-official modification was the 'Rhinoceros' hedgerow cutter, used to cut through the extra-thick tall hedges in the bocage, in order to escape from the sunken roads which were ambush death-traps. The inventor, Sergeant G. Culin of 102nd Reconnaissance Squadron, received the Legion of Merit for his brainwave. It consisted of a steel tusklike structure, made from German beach-defence obstacles.

Colonel Owsley Costlow's 76mm-gunned M4A3E8s were, of course, an official modification, although as already explained in a previous chapter, the large 'Germanic' muzzle break did mean that they were often mistaken for enemy. However, the extra punch that the 76mm gave over the standard 75mm was appreciated. He told me: 'Upon approaching a small town, usually just a few houses on either side of the road, and not knowing when or where the retreating enemy troops would decide to make a temporary stand, if there was any sign of resistance we would fire one round of 76mm solid shot into the first house on each side of the road. We found if anyone was in there, they quickly came out with their hands up. The shot usually penetrated two or more houses; it might go through a picture on one wall, perhaps a desk on another, then on to the next house where it would go through a chair on the first wall and a sofa on the other side. I imagine seeing a hole appear on one of your walls, a red streak dashing through your living room, only to go out through the opposite wall could be enough to cause someone, especially a civilian, to give up and come outside. . . . Of course, if we suspected German soldiers were in the house, we followed the shot with an HE round into the same hole. That could really clean house and also rearrange a good-sized room.

'On our drive to "liberate" Ansbach, Germany, we began the day at dawn, moving quickly through several small villages, all without incident. At about the third village I began to feel uneasy, something wasn't quite right, everything was too easy, too routine; I felt sure that we were being set up for an ambush. Therefore I began to watch the hills and the church bell towers more carefully because we had found if someone was observing us and passing on the information from one town to another, they sometimes signalled from one high place to another. The little villages were within sight of each other all down the narrow valley road. So seeing a movement in the church steeple in the next town, I had my gunner place a 76mm HE round in the bell tower. A perfect shot! We had been told that the 76mm was more accurate than the 75 but really hadn't seen that much difference except on this shot. He placed it in the bell tower opening at about 800 yards, never hitting the outside walls at all. It really "rang them bells"!'

'Fording kits,' recalled USMC tanker Ed Bollard, 'they were not at all difficult to affix to the tank. They were shaped like a large letter "L" with the lower part fitting over the rear exhaust area so as to keep the water out of the engine. Then the long vertical line of the "L" extended several feet into the air permitting the tank to waddle towards the beach in water up to the bottom of the turret. On the side of the tank we had a pick, shovel, axe and sledge hammer attached. When we hit the beach we were accompanied by our reconnaissance teams who were on foot. They were all taught to go to each tank as it reached the beach and to knock off the fording kit. This was not hard as they were only taped on with waterproof tape. If a recon man was not in the area, one of the crew did the job. We left the kits where they fell. Perhaps someone came along later and salvaged them but I doubt it.'

NEAR MISS

Major (Retd) Jock McGinlay told me the following cautionary tale which occurred far behind the front line in North Africa, when 7 RTR were in the ordnance workshops in Cairo, being got ready to go 'Up the Blue', as the experienced desert warriors called going into the Western Desert. 'We were being made fully ready for desert warfare in every respect, the tanks changed to a sandy colour, water tanks fitted and all sorts of modifications carried out. Once completed each tank was run out onto a spare piece of ground, still within the workshop area, where final touches were put to the radios, the guns and last of all, we were topped up with ammo. Now I forget how many rounds of 2-pounder shells they carried. They were stacked in bins, some armour-piercing, some HE and we were filled right up. Now one tank finished up with all bins full, but with one shell still to be stowed. The loader was puzzled. Quite wrongly he decided that he would stow it in the gun.

'However, to be on the safe side, he removed the firing mechanism, laying it carefully on the radio at the back of the turret. Next to come in the turret was the radio operator, who objected to seeing this mechanism on his radio and promptly returned it to the gun. Now to replace the mechanism the gun had to be cocked, it would not fire otherwise. Next into the tank was the gunner who, whilst he sat in his seat examining his telescopic sights, noticed the gun was cocked. Yes, you've guessed it. He pressed the trigger to release the mechanism. The resulting bang terrified everyone. Heads poked out of turrets, people asking, "what the hell?" We were indeed lucky, the shell landed in the roadway, many hundreds of yards away, outside the main workshop gates. Being a solid shot, no one apparently was hit.'

6

Specialised Equipment

Many unusual, but extremely useful, weapons and devices were used during the Second World War, mounted on tanks. These included odd 'un-tanklike' weapons like flame-throwers, demolition guns, rockets and even strange very powerful blinding lights; mine-clearing devices such as pressure rollers, flails and explosives; amphibious screens and ships propellers which turned tanks into temporary boats; schnorkel devices so as to enable them to cross rivers via the river bottoms; bridges of various shapes and sizes; 'carpet' layers to enable vehicles to cross soft ground; dozers with various blade sizes; engineer vehicles armed with demolition guns; etc. The list was endless. Although there were examples of some of these special devices in most armies, the largest single concentration was in the British 79th Armoured Division, the 'Funnies', as they were called. Under the inspiring leadership of Major-General Sir Percy Hobart, they played a major part in the success of D-Day on the British and Canadian beaches. 'Seventy-nine Armoured Division was unique,' recalled Dennis Young of 11 RTR, 'in that it never fought as a Division, but was a collection of various unusual weapons . . . the idea was that in action they would be farmed out to whatever part of the front required them.' The Brigades within 79th Armoured Division varied, however. At one time or another there were the following:

27th Armoured Bde – DD amphibious tanks.
30th   "   "   – Flail minesweeping tanks.

1st	Assault	Bde	–	AVREs (Armoured Vehicle Royal Engineers).
31st	Armoured	"	–	Crocodile Flame tanks.
33rd	"	"	–	Buffaloes (tracked amphibious assault vehicles).
35th	Tank	"	–	CDL tanks (replaced by 1st Tank Brigade).
4th	Armoured	"	–	DD tanks for Rhine Crossing.

Also: 49 RTR and the Canadian APC Regt – APCs for troop carrying.

43 RTR – experimental unit which did invaluable work on trials on which the divisional equipment was based.

D. V. Ager of Swansea was a member of 43 RTR and recalled: 'Its chief function was to carry out experiments on all the damn-fool devices that backroom geniuses dreamed up to put on tanks! We did *nearly* go on a whole series of invasions, in fact I doubt if any unit in the British Army can have *nearly* gone on as many invasions as we did. We *nearly* went on an invasion of North Africa, we *nearly* went on the invasion of Sicily and the Italian mainland; we *very nearly* went on the D-Day invasion of Normandy and we *nearly* went on the invasion of Malaya at the end of the war. Every time we were meant to be among the first troops ashore – to clear beach defences, to blow up the mines and to make negotiable tracks across the soft beaches – we were not very optimistic about our chances. Every time some boffin came up with a fresh device for us to test and we handed over our tanks, with their curious outgrowths, to some other unit to drive into action.' One of their first major 'funnies' was the amphibious DD (Duplex Drive) tank, but many others followed. 'It was in Suffolk that we tested one device after another. The floating and wading tanks had only been the first in a long series. We had flame-thrower tanks (which terrified us as much as any potential enemy); we had tanks with chains on revolving booms that flailed the ground in front to explode mines; we had tanks that ploughed and tanks that rolled the ground for the same purpose. We had tanks that carried great fascines or bundles of wood palings to drop into inconvenient trenches and other holes (that was a slightly more sophisticated version of a device that had been used in the First World War). We had tanks carrying bridges; either long straight ones sticking out in front like a huge proboscis or folding ones like scissors that often jammed. There were tanks that filled holes with their own bodies, whilst other tanks ran on trackways over their tops. Some of the devices were almost too silly to mention.

'There was a memorable series of night experiments with infra-red light. Our tanks were fitted with special headlights and some brave soul was supposed to mark our route through a minefield or whatever with special lamps. None of this could be seen by the supposed enemy. Each tank commander and each driver had a viewer through which the landscape appeared from the darkest night, though in a ghostly and unreal form. Disconcertingly everything was reversed, though this should not have been very difficult to correct optically. Also as one moved the viewer, the guiding lights left slow trails behind them like meteors, but it worked.

'We also had radio beams, allegedly to find our way back to laager at night (they were still thinking of desert war). One heard dots if one veered to one side and dashes if one drifted off the other way. Bliss was a continuous note that showed one was heading in the right direction. Of course as always there were snags. We laid on a special demonstration in daylight for Lord Alanbrooke, the Chief of the Imperial General Staff. Our drivers had their seats in the "up" position with their heads projecting from their hatches and their eyes conspicuously blindfolded. The rest of us were battened down inside and out of sight. Since we had such an important spectator we had to get it right, so the other members of the crew watched through their periscopes and made sure the drivers went in the right direction, whatever the radios might be saying. We all dramatically converged on the great man and the demonstration was a huge success. Years later, no longer a humble trooper, I met Lord Alanbrooke. His daughter was a geologist and worked in the same office as my wife. I thought of telling him how we had deceived him all those years before, but I didn't betray the Regiment! Anyway, he was no fool and must have known the deceits and contrivances of military inspections.

'There were so many devices I cannot remember them all. One that does stick in my memory was the simplest thing imaginable. It was the tank equivalent of the Bangalore torpedo – a long pipe, not much thicker than a gas pipe, filled with explosives. The theory was that the tank pushed it into a minefield and exploded it so that all the mines would go off by sympathetic detonation. The idea was fine so long as you had a nice unencumbered battlefield and a nice flat minefield. The pipe was always lying waiting for us and we had to hook onto it by a fishing-like action through a hole in the bottom of the tank. The primary purpose of that hole (with its protective metal hatch) was for crew members to relieve themselves without emerging into the unfriendly world outside. We would duly hook onto the end of the pipe and push. Can you imagine trying to push a narrow flexible pipe cross-country in a straight line? Almost invariably the pipe would describe an elegant arc and come back to menace the operators.

'One day we were in a hurry. We all had weekend leave and were wearing our denim overalls. The technique was to hide the overalls in a convenient ditch on the way to the station as soon as one could escape from one's duties. At last that morning we got the pipe more or less straight in more or less the right position. One of us attached the electric leads and the tank backed away. We set off the charge. No doubt the pipe and its explosives had been lying around in the damp fields of Suffolk for some time. There was no blinding explosion. Looking through our periscopes with the hatches closed we watched a thin trail of smoke coming from our end of the pipe. We watched it impatiently but it just smouldered on. Our intended leave train came and went. Eventually the smouldering stopped and we went back to camp.'

43 RTR took part in many more trials but as Mr Ager has explained, they never made an operational landing. However, their final 'secret weapon' (the CDL – see below) so impressed Mountbatten, that he decided they should be used in the Far East. 'So the 43rd RTR was not involved in the last stages of war in Europe, but was busy getting ready for the final onslaught on Japan. Once more we prepared our tanks for the landing from the sea. Every crack and hole was sealed with tape and filthy black Bostick. Every moving part of every item of machinery and equipment was taken to pieces and treated for use in the humid tropics. As Europe celebrated the end of the war, we were on embarkation leave ready to embark for India and the final show-down. . . . We reached Bombay to find the invasion fleet forming up in the harbour for the forthcoming landings in Malaya. As we waited for

our tanks to arrive on another ship, we were told yet again that we, with our special devices (we still called them "funnies"), were to be the spearhead of the attack. In fact many of my friends and myself were put into a special squadron which was to be the spearhead of the spearhead. Our tanks at last arrived with their specially adapted turrets shrouded in covers for secrecy. Then the atom bombs fell and the war ended. Yet again the 43rd did not reach the invasion beaches and I survived. Who am I to complain about my almost peaceful war? I never wanted to kill people or to be killed myself for that matter.'

Harry Webb of St Leonards, near Ringwood, was also in the 43rd and after "D"-Day was given the job of ferrying AFVs from various places on the south coast over to the beaches of Normandy, on LCTs and later on LSTs. Their return loads were tanks for repair, wounded and POWs. He told me: 'A couple of incidents that come to mind about this engagement. First, while driving a Matilda – why a Matilda? we didn't ask questions, we just drove them – along the GOLD Beach, I struck a rogue mine which blew the front nearside tool box out of the hull, but did little other damage; a tough little tank, the Matilda. Another incident that happened to me regarding mines – but this time at sea: we had discharged our cargo of tanks in Boulogne harbour, pulled off the beach and dropped anchor, waiting for the rest of the LCTs to form up in convoy for the return to Blighty. Luckily we were empty, when there was a very loud explosion. We learned later that it was a magnetic mine that had exploded under the well deck and blown the best part of the deck away. But as the construction of these craft was basically rows of flotation tanks welded together, we didn't sink. We were not far from the beach so we were able to beach the craft with the help of two other LCTs, one on each side. The only casualty was the cook who had been brewing up in his galley and a dixie of boiling water had poured all over him. He was rushed off to the field hospital in Boulogne. Meanwhile the Skipper called the crew, including the two "Pongos" – as we were nicknamed by the Navy – to what was left of the wheelhouse where we "spliced the mainbrace". To the uninitiated, that is a double tot of rum all around, which went down very well!'

Later Harry had a hair-raising journey to Ostend on board an oil-tanker which had been converted into a tank-landing ship. 'The keel was removed to make it flat-bottomed for beaching and in doing so they had to reduce the rudder by half and incorporate two bow doors. I was detailed to this vessel for its maiden trip. We loaded the tanks into what had been the original oil tanks and all went well. On approaching the harbour the plan was to unload them straight onto the beach. On each side of the harbour were two very long breakwaters. As the vessel slowed for the runup to the beach, it lost steerage due to half the rudder having been removed. Instead of nosing up to the beach, we did a sharp turn to port and went crashing straight through the left-hand breakwater. Situated on the end of the breakwater was a small, manned lighthouse, so it left the lighthouse keeper marooned. Have you ever seen a very irate Belgian lighthouse keeper? Just as well I couldn't understand French!'

AMPHIBIOUS TANKS

'Our training for using DD [Duplex Drive] tanks began with Valentines – they were the first to be adapted,' recalled G. E. Masters of Skipton, North Yorkshire, who served in 1 Troop, B Squadron, 13th/18th Royal Hussars as a tank gunner. 'The training, swimming and launching trials were first carried out on Fritton Lake and we were at the time billeted in Great Yarmouth. Part of the training meant that we had to learn to use and operate the Davis Escape Apparatus as used by submarine crews – this was the part we disliked most – the first venture wearing the kit being that we had to enter a swimming pool at the shallow end and walk to the deep end, holding onto a rope stretched from end to end. Finally we had to take our places as members of a crew in a cut-down Sherman at the bottom of a thirty-foot pit. When in position, the water was poured in at the rate of about three thousand gallons per minute. After being submerged for some five minutes the hatches were opened and the crew surfaced one at a time. This practice was carried out several times during training.

'The two squadrons chosen to use the DD tanks ["A" & "B"] left for Gosport to do sea-launchings. We would load on the LCTs at Stokes Bay, cross the Solent and launch, landing on the Isle of Wight. Major-General Sir Percy Hobart, 79th Armoured Division commander, saw some of the training. A move to Fort George followed with training in the Moray Firth. During numerous launchings some tanks were lost, but the crews were all rescued, except for only one fatality. Montgomery came to visit us whilst we were there and told us the role we had to play. The launching of the DD tank could be very hazardous, for once on the lowered ramp of the LCT there was no going back. Then slowly down the ramp and into the sea, engage the twin props and get away from the ramp which would rise and fall with the swell. The crews of the LCTs were always very dubious about the whole thing and we were often told that we must be mad bastards to attempt to swim in a canvas boat with a thirty-ton keel, which, when one thinks about it, did seem a risky undertaking!

'We loaded our tanks aboard the LCTs on 3 June 1944, but rough weather blew up and D-Day was postponed for twenty-four hours; however, we set sail on 4 June about midday and once out at sea we began to form up into convoys. We spent a rough night at sea and many tank crews were seasick. Not many wanted breakfast and as daylight came we wondered if we would be able to swim. The plan was for a launch from seven thousand yards, but because of rough seas it was shortened to five thousand yards. On reaching this point the LCTs stopped and the order was given by Brigadier Prior Palmer to launch. When all tanks were in the water, we formed into columns of five tanks and headed for the beaches. When we neared the beach each column got into line abreast in readiness for the landing. The battleships standing out to sea were shelling over our heads, while the ships firing rocket salvoes were shelling the beach and some rockets were falling short. The landings at low tide had exposed what should have been underwater defences, so we could pick a way through from post to post, each with a Teller mine on the top. Once beached the flotation screens were dropped and the tanks were fully operational. During the swim in some tanks were lost with their crews, but the Regiment's "A" & "B" Squadrons landed thirty-three out of forty tanks.

'All tanks engaged beach obstacles and strong points with their 75mm guns. Immediately behind us landed the Armoured Vehicles Royal Engineers (AVRE) and the other "Funnies" of 79th Armoured Division, with the flail tanks to the fore. My main feelings during the landing were of excitement not fear. It seemed just like all the other landings we had done in training; apart from the noise of the shell fire and when a nearby AVRE went up in flames we never knew what happened to it. We were not static for very long, as soon as the flails had cleared lanes from the beach, we moved into the road and advanced in support of our infantry – the East Yorkshire Regiment. We took our first objectives and by evening all objectives had been taken and we were able to witness the marvellous sight of scores of gliders landing with the airborne lads. "B" Squadron lost ten tanks in the day, but some of these were able to be recovered.

'On D-Day+4 (10 June), RHQ (in Honey tanks) and "B" Squadron's Shermans crossed the Orne bridges and with infantry support from the Paras, put in an attack to link up with a para company which had been cut off. We crossed the start line and all was going well when several anti-tank guns in a wood on the flank opened up and two Honeys and four Shermans were knocked out. My tank was hit twice and brewed up. Corporal Hind, the tank commander, and I were not wounded and scrambled out, but the operator was badly burned on one arm and the driver and co-driver were wounded and badly burned. We pulled them out and lay together in the long grass until we were picked up by other tanks of the squadron. That was my first encounter with anti-tank guns, but it was not to be my last. My crew commander (then Sergeant Hind, MM) was later to be killed, so I was the only one of the crew to escape unharmed.'

Another member of the 13th/18th was M. E. Mawson, a radio operator in another Sherman DD, who considers he owes his life to Admiral Ramsey, because it was he who said that every DD tank should have an inflatable dinghy, and as Mawson could not swim, his chances of survival in the water without one were negligible. He recalled: 'The run-in over the last few miles was wonderful – nothing happened at all, yet looking back as the light became stronger the entire ocean was covered by lines of vessels elbow to elbow and seemingly stretching back to the UK and all rolling remorselessly along, anything that faltered just had to be run down, one of our tanks was later overtaken due to slow speed in rough water and a survivor was only saved because when he was at his last gasp, a rating on a passing vessel had managed to fling out a rope accurately. I realise now that in my awe at all this might I was gazing at the last fling of the Empire before the intellectual know-it-alls dismembered it. Henceforth my local "neighbourhood" began to be somewhat uncomfortable, despite the solid curtain of whizzing British ammunition over us. We touched land, dropped our front screen and I believe let off a round or two, but the breakers from the fast incoming tide immediately swamped us so that instead of going down the water came up. We reached the turret top just about in unison and threw out the inflatable dinghy, remembering to retain hold of the ripcord. To our joy after an eternity it swelled up and we got in, in a rather undignified haste in the midst of all the shells and mortars plopping down. In front were all the underwater devices with explosives on top towards which we drifted remorselessly, all save one using our own helmets as balers; our thoughts about him are best omitted – he has suffered headwise greatly I believe since from a mortar received in north-west Germany and is now dead anyway. On and around the obstacles were crowds of poor devils drowning as they tried to neutralise the booby traps, the sea being so rough that clinging to the obstacles they just went under the water or the armada of ships. Curiously, the rising tide saved me, it carried the dinghy right over the fuses onto the bench and also (it dawned on me later) saved us by quenching the mortars – we had no blast or splinters.

'Once upon the beach despite our weak limbs we covered the ground very quickly (!) to scrub dunes' top at which point memory fades. I know we found ourselves on the extreme left of the Orne Canal and that just to the east was a shot-up tank landing craft aground with a figure flat on the scrubby sand. This proved to be a rating with one or possibly two feet missing but still conscious. Having earlier taken heed of our canny young troop leader's thought to divide the First Aid Box among us, we had plenty of morphine syringes. These were used I hope with good effect and we searched along the beach for succour. Ultimately we did obtain a stretcher with which we tottered back to the injured party. Here let me say that I have ever since regarded the toughest task in war is to be a stretcher-bearer. How we managed to carry the rating between four of us I shall never know, yet they did all that sort of thing in mere pairs.

'By now you will gather that the immediate hornet's nest had quietened quite a lot – in fact I now know the assault was well inland, leaving the beach crowded with later technical arrivals and follow-ups. On our part we found a patch cleared of mines in the scrub, dug a trench, roofed it with the anti-sea shields thrown off by arriving Bren carriers and settled down to await events. During the late sunny afternoon I walked right out over the receded tide to some of our tanks which had not made it and secured items of tinned food. I passed the body of a fellow unit member (Trooper Schofield) and thought rather soberly how I had felt hard done by during the early hours.

'During the first night we lived in our own smudge pot smoke and a nearby ammunition dump was bombed which made a firework display, nevertheless with aid of a ration box collected from a base point (solemnly signed for!) lived very well for nearly a week, having sent a message forward as to where we were and sat it out gently until an A1 echelon appeared with a familiar face in it and took us off to the reinforcement unit. The final amusing memory which I never ever regret recalling concerns us getting our new tank (151232) ready. At the time we were loading and testing, etc., the technical adjutant fussed about to the effect that "B" Squadron was in an attack that evening. Later my hull gunner commented that he had never experienced such leaden boots as he carted the shells from the dump. Not surprisingly our rejoining occurred the next (sunny) morning in a lovely apple orchard where our OC was seen, resplendent in his only remaining clothes, to wit a civilian white jumper and grey trousers, but unfeignedly delighted to see us. Come to that we were relieved also to see him again!'

FLAME

First used by the Germans in 1914, the impact of early flame-throwers was limited by their inadequate range; however, they were perfected in the Second World War and widely used by both sides, many of the more efficient ones being mounted on tanks. Of these, the British Churchill Mark VII flame-thrower, known as the 'Crocodile', and the various flame guns fitted to the American Sherman, were the most successful. 'We had a few flame-thrower Sherman tanks in our company. I did not fire the flame-thrower in combat, but witnessed it in action and later trained in a flame-thrower tank.' This is how Nile E. Darling of Salmon,

Idaho, an ex-USMC tanker, began a letter to me some years ago. He went on: 'The flame-thrower threw a ⅝th-inch rod of heavy jelly-like napalm fuel. Good fuel would carry up to 150 feet. It would stick to a vertical target and burn. The flame and heat was so intense that it did not have to burn people to kill them. If fired into a building or cave, it would use up the oxygen from the air and people would suffocate.'

'On Iwo Jima,' recalled Lieutenant-Colonel Dick Schmidt, another ex-Marine tanker, 'a particularly bothersome strong point had defied all measures taken to reduce it and, after several days, had to be bypassed. It consisted of a central blockhouse with radiating tunnels to many other positions. Finally our engineers managed to blast a crack in it and tanks using concrete-piercing fuses at point-blank range finally managed to put a small hole into the blockhouse wall. We then moved three or four flame-throwing M4s up to the block-house and each tank poured some 250 gallons of napalm into the opening. The last tank touched off the whole lot. Smoke and flame came out of holes in the ground and unseen firing positions for almost 100 yards around the blockhouse!'

It is nice to be able to include a reminiscence of a more humane use for the dreaded Churchill 'Crocodile', as Dennis H. Young of 7 RTR told me: 'Being excused tank duties at the time, I did not take part in the Belsen Camp clean-up, only the "Crocodile" flame-throwers of the regiment engaged in this. My late friend Brigadier Reggie Wood, CO 7 RTR, told me that the first attempt to combat the disease was to spray thousands of gallons of DDT from the flame guns over the camp. When it was realised that there could be no more lives to be saved the decision was made to use the "Crocodiles" in their normal role and to burn to the ground all the huts, this being considered a more effective way of combating the disease threat. During this operation the Military Police kept strict control by only allowing personnel on essential duties into the area.'

FLAILS

The flail device for clearing a lane through a minefield was undoubtedly the most successful and was widely used from D-Day onwards.

The other effective mine-clearing device was a mine roller, used by the Americans and nicknamed 'Aunt Jemima'! However, such mechanical means of mine-clearing all began much earlier, in the Western Desert in late 1940, when Wavell and O'Connor were planning their highly successful Operation Compass against the Tenth Italian Army. The first phase of this operation was to attack the forts which the Italians had built to protect their hesitant advance over the Egyptian border. These forts were surrounded by wire, anti-tank ditches and mines. It would be the latter with which Major Jock McGinlay, then a young troop commander in 7 RTR, was going to find himself dealing. He told me: 'The next morning we were to attack the camps. What excitement. Most of us were unable to sleep, even if we could. I had been under fire on the North-West Frontier of India, but this was something different. However, sleep was not for me or my tank crew. Out of the blue, at about 10 p.m., came a convoy of lorries, headed by a Lieutenant Colonel from the Engineers. In these lorries were the weirdest contraptions, which they proceeded to fit onto the front of my Matilda. Mine was to be one of the leading tanks on the second camp attack. What this transpired to be was a forerunner of the flail tank. Two long four-inch girders were fitted on either side of my tank about four feet or so above the ground. They met at a point several yards ahead of the tank. Three cross girders gave it strength and served as the carrying arms for what was then suspended from them. These were tar barrels, or similar, filled with concrete with an axle through the middle, probably on roller bearings. These were suspended on chains and the idea was for these barrels to be fitted at the last moment before the run-in on the enemy, using the barrels to sweep the minefield. In theory, back in Cairo, and on a flat piece of desert, this might have worked, providing the enemy obligingly held his fire long enough for the barrels to be fitted at the last moment.

'In practice they were a disaster. The camel shrubs, which are small mounds of hard sand built up over the years around a shoot of grass or bush, abound on most of the twenty-mile-deep belt along the African coast. Within a couple of hundred yards, going at a snail's pace even, I had not one single barrel left. They just bounced and bounced until the chains broke. This may sound like a fair experiment, but to be landed on me at such a time was cruel. We were on the move into real action. I and my crew lost inches of skin frantically spannering off these girders which were going to hinder the full action of the tank and the revolving turret.'

ROCKETS

The most sophisticated of the high-explosive rocket attachments to be fitted to tanks was the American T34 launcher on the Sherman, which was nicknamed 'Calliope' as Colonel Owsley Costlow explained to me: 'Shortly before our drive to the Rhine River, a sixty-tube rocket launcher, T34 "Calliope", was added to one of the tanks in the company's second platoon. It seems that each of the three medium tank companies in the battalion received one. This was in addition to the bulldozer blade that had been placed on another second-platoon tank. They had all the odd pieces of equipment in their platoon. On 24 March 1945, our reinforced battalion task force prepared to attack Germersheim and to seize the bridge there over the Rhine. By this time I was in command of "A" Company, which was to be the fire support for the attack. The other two battalion Calliopes had been brought up during the night so at first light I commanded three sixty-tube rocket launchers and could deliver 180 rounds of 4.5-inch rockets at a minute's notice. It was almost like being a Division Artillery Commander! However, the rockets were noted for their inaccuracy, with a ratio of at least 10 per cent of rounds over and 10 per cent short, so they could only be used in general fire support against an area target. As the first tanks moved out for the attack I had one Calliope cover the left flank, another cover the right and the third to be prepared to fire ahead of the leading tanks into the town, if requested. I believe I was the first Calliope fire-support commander in the Division and perhaps in all of Seventh Army!'

SEARCHLIGHT TANKS

'Way back in the First World War it had been proposed that searchlights should be mounted on tanks for use in night action, but it was not until the 1930s that some interest was revived.' That is how Sergeant Brian Hutchinson of 155 Regiment, RAC and 11 RTR began his reminiscences on the searchlight tanks, codenamed 'CDL'[1] – the Canal Defence Light. He continued: 'My first encounter with CDL occurred in early 1943 after completing my training with the 60th Training Regiment, RAC, stationed at Catterick. On passing out we had the usual kit inspection – in those days you could not move a body of men from one station to another without checking that they had all their kit! At the conclusion of the kit inspection the CO told us that we were going to Lowther Camp, Penrith, to 155 RAC and he added that when we got there we would find that "they were on something special". The words made little sense to us at the time, perhaps close support of infantry or something of that nature. Next day we arrived at Penrith and were ushered into HQ Squadron Office and before any-thing else was said or done we had to sign the Official Secrets Act! The Squadron Leader then went on to say that although they had eighty tanks on charge, only a dozen had guns! He then went on to explain in some detail the workings of CDL and from then on we trained in the use of this on the moors above Ullswater. It was a topsy-turvy life which involved a lot of night training. Security was very strict, of course. When not in use the special turret had a canvas cover so that the slit in the turret was hidden from view. Nevertheless, the turret did look decidedly odd, especially as it had no gun. Later on someone had the bright idea of welding a piece of drainpipe onto the turret, hoping it would look like a gun. In actual fact it looked like exactly what it was – a piece of drainpipe welded onto an odd-shaped turret! I will never forget the face of the beach master when eventually we landed in Normandy and drove off the landing craft.

'In early 1944, 11 RTR returned from the Middle East and took up residence in Lowther Camp whilst the three previous regiments were moved elsewhere. 49 RTR eventually became an Armoured Personnel Carrier Regiment and fought throughout the North-West Europe campaign; 152 and 155 Regiments, RAC, were destined to become a training regiment and a holding regiment respectively. And so it came about that I found myself posted to 11 RTR and back to Penrith where CDL training continued. Obviously the 11th had been returned to this country with a view to using CDL when the invasion of Normandy took place and, in due course, some weeks after D-Day we duly embarked for Normandy, harbouring up first of all in a wheat field in Beauvais, followed a few days later by a field outside Tilly-sur-Seulles. We fully expected to be using our new weapon within a day or two, and at that stage we knew our weapon inside out and we thought we had a war-winner, but long after the breakout from the Normandy beach-head we were still in our field in Normandy. No official reason has ever, to my knowledge, been given as to why CDL was never used. We all felt that it would be a war-winner, and so I feel with hindsight it would have been in a First World War situation of fixed lines. In the more fluid fighting which we encountered it would, I suppose, have been comparatively easy for the enemy to come side on to us and pick us off, silhouetted against the light of the next tank, one by one. . . . It was eventually used on the Rhine crossing although not quite in the way originally intended. It was used more to illuminate the opposite bank rather than to dazzle the enemy, which had been the original intention. "A" Squadron of 49 RTR was hastily assembled and mounted on CDL tanks for this operation and my old troop corporal from 155 RAC, Charlie Dixon, had the distinction of being in action for the shortest possible time before his tank brewed up. It must have been a lucky shot but no sooner had he switched on his light than he was hit, so a few seconds was his total length of time in action!'

AND THEN ON TO THE BUFFALOES

'Meanwhile we in the 11th,' went on Dennis Young, 'were still har-boured up in Normandy while the rest of the army were into Belgium and approaching the Dutch-German border. Out of the blue one day, we were ordered to hand our CDL tanks over to another regiment and we went by lorry from Normandy to Belgium. We assembled in a cinema at Ghent where we were addressed by General Sir Percy Hobart who said that, although we had been training on CDL for the last three years or so, we could now forget that and we were to be mounted on Buffaloes – amphibious landing craft. He added for good measure that we had a fortnight to train ourselves before going into action! It turned out to be a little longer than a fortnight, but not much. Buffaloes were an American invention and had previously been used in the Pacific theatre. They were unusual in that the drive was the same for land as for water. The tracks had sort of paddles on them which gripped the earth, often muddy, on the approach to the river or canal and then on arriving at the water's edge all that was necessary was to get into third gear and proceed in exactly the same fashion across the river. On arriving at the far bank one climbed out in first gear and at the appropriate point disembarked your infantry or supplies, and returned for the next lot. They could carry a platoon of infantry, or a Bren carrier, or a small scout car and any amount of ammunition and other supplies. It was our job, after ferrying the initial assault, to keep on ferrying further troops and supplies until the bridgehead was secured or, as in the case of the small rivers, the engineers had completed their pontoon bridge across which further supplies could be carried. . . . In spite of the frustrations we all felt at the time that our CDL tanks were taken from us, we quickly adapted to Buffaloes and in a very short time became expert at loading and unloading and devising various ingenious schemes for carrying loads. We also rather wallowed in the comparative comfort that these new vehicles gave us. It doesn't take the average British soldier long to find ways and means of making himself comfortable and we quickly discovered that a chopped-off tree trunk placed between the ramp and the driver's compartment, draped with a tarpaulin which was provided, converted the Buffalo into a very comfortable home with plenty of room to move around in, while the vehicle equipment also included four kapok floats which provided very comfortable beds!'

REMINISCENCES OF AN AVRE DRIVER

Corporal Leslie Radford was originally trained at 57th Training Regiment, Catterick and passed out as driver/mechanic on Churchill tanks. After training he was posted to 80 Assault Squadron, Royal Engineers at Saxmundham as a tank driver. They were equipped with AVREs – Armoured Vehicle Royal Engineers, which were Churchills which did not have the usual main armament, but instead were fitted with a 290mm Petard spigot mortar. 'The Spigot mortar threw a forty-pound bomb of high explosive – also known as a "Flying Dustbin" – a distance of up to 150 yards and was specially designed to deal with concrete blockhouses, pillboxes and similar emplacements. The tanks were also armed with two Besa 7.92mm machine guns. After Christmas 1943, the unit moved up to Fort George, Scotland, for further intensive training, including loading and disembarking from landing craft. Early in 1944 we began to study maps of the area in which they would land; the place names were in code and gave no actual indication of true locations. What was shown on the map as Cairo, for example, turned out to be Caen.

'We landed at St Aubin, after a rough crossing, the differing speeds of the various craft combined with rough seas had disrupted the time-table. The order of landing should have been DD tanks, then AVREs, then infantry, but instead the infantry landed first and were soon swarming around the defences. One of our objectives was a block-house which stuck out onto the beach, so the spigot mortar could not be used because it might have caused injury to nearby Canadian troops. A flail tank from the same LCT landed and joined by two others began clearing a track three tanks in width. The AVRE crews then laid down white tapes to show the width of the track. Then some Sherman DDs arrived and began moving up the track but were knocked out and caused a blockage, delaying movement inland. In the afternoon, whilst I was removing amphibious exhaust extensions from tanks I was just missed by a sniper's bullet – this was about twenty-five to fifty yards off the beach. Some 105mm Priest SP guns arrived and immediately shelled the town hall area from which the sniper's bullets had come. About this time I discovered that our AVRE had been hit by a 50mm shell, which had gone through the trackguard but not penetrated the hull. We then supported local infantry with our machine guns as they captured a radar station.

'The crew of another AVRE had dismounted to lay a series of explosive charges when their AVRE was hit by a shell and some other charges inside the tank exploded. The pannier doors of the tank were found a mile away, while the entire turret was blown 300 yards and the side armour went even further, indicating the volatile nature of the explosive they were using and the great force that it had released.

Sadly nothing was ever found of the two men who had been inside the tank when it was hit. . . . In another unfortunate incident, one of our troop officers was crushed whilst our AVRE was manoeuvring and he slipped between it and the bulldozer blade fitted on the front of another AVRE, just as the rear end of ours swung round. The driver was being guided from the ground as he only had limited vision to the rear. On another occasion our crew came across some German box mines. These were linked together in fours and had the characteristic that once they were armed they could not be disarmed and had to be exploded. They were also powerful enough to blow a Bren carrier clear up in the air! They were some two feet long, four inches wide and three inches deep and were of a new type which hadn't been seen before, so we were asked to get hold of some to send back to the boffins in England. An intelligence officer was examining some of them – without the necessary technical expertise – and they exploded with disastrous effect for those nearby. I'm afraid that he just thought himself to be more intelligent than he actually was.'

7

Operations

TANK FIGHTING

In this chapter I am giving examples from as many sources as possible of tanks and tank crews carrying out their primary function of closing with the enemy and killing him, by making use of their most important characteristics of firepower, protection and mobility, which all add up to shock action. In not all cases were they successful for one reason or another. In the first account by a young French officer tank commander, the reason for failure was a total lack of radio communications – normally the lifeblood of armoured operations and the means by which commanders at all levels are able to project their personality onto the battlefield, influencing the outcome in some cases merely by the force of their individual charisma. Despite the wireless, this required armoured commanders like Rommel, Guderian and Patton to be right up at the 'sharp end', often with their leading troops – not unlike the kings and senior noblemen of a former age – and often having to physically fight for their lives, so unlike the senior commanders on the Western Front in the Great War who were for the most part ensconced in their safe chateaux well behind the trenches. However, as this is generally a 'low-level history', I have concentrated on single tank or tank troop/platoon-level battles, whose commanders were constantly at risk.

WHAT MIGHT HAVE BEEN

Abbeville, 4 June 1940

By the end of May 1940, the Germans had established a bridgehead south of the River Somme at Abbeville. General de Gaulle's 4 Division

Cuirassée (4 DCR) had tried, without success, to destroy this bridge-head on 28 May. It was then decided that a new offensive operation should be launched on 4 June, with the same aim; this time it would be made by Major General Fortune's 51st Highland Division and Colonel Perret's French 2nd Division Cuirassée, with General Fortune in overall command.

At the time Colonel (Retired) Henri Puga, was a *Sous-lieutenant* (Second-Lieutenant), commanding a troop of three Renault R40 tanks in the 2nd Division Cuirassée, as he recalled: 'The R40 was a new version of the R35, armed with an improved 37mm long gun. My troop was part of the 48th Tank Battalion, headed by Commandant André Massine, Duc de Rivoli, Prince d'Essling, direct heir of the Emperor Napoleon's field marshal and a former First World War tank man. The battalion was part of 2 DCR. On 3 June officers made a foot-reconnaissance towards Behen, south of Abbeville. Then, by night, we moved off with our tanks – no lights – coming carefully in from the east to reach our new location without being detected. We were delayed even longer as the roads had been bombed by the *Luftwaffe*. Going through Aumale was especially difficult, so we arrived at our assembly area very late, just in time to depart and so had to leave without refuelling.

'We crossed the Start Line at 0330 hours on 4 June, still in the dark, behind an impressive creeping barrage. It was the only time during the Second World War that I experienced this very effective barrage, which had almost been the rule for a frontal assault during the First World War. Our battalion was on the left of the divisional layout. Reserve Lieutenant Sebastien's company, to which I belonged, was on the far left of the battalion, while my troop and that of Officer Cadet Debeaud, were both on the far left of the company, so we were in fact on the very left flank of the attack. We advanced slowly behind the barrage, firing our guns at the enemy who were located in the edges of the woods opposite, halting from time to time to let the dismounted infantry catch up. Then, about 0800 hours, shrouded in the morning mist, the River Somme came into sight. We had greatly overshot the objective and reached the river to its rear unscathed. Here we were far to the enemy's rear, just six tanks, with no enemy anywhere to be seen, or friendly forces either, for that matter. Unfortunately, we were unable to let our headquarters know what we had achieved – we had no radio sets fitted in our tanks! The only means we had to communicate was a set of signal flags, which had to be waved from the top of the turret! In order to talk, Debeaud and I had to bring our tanks close together, open our cupolas and shout across.

'By 1000 hours nobody else had joined us, so we decided to go back and try to discover where the rest of our attacking forces were and what was holding them up. As we retraced our steps we were engaged heavily by the enemy who had obviously let us go past unchallenged at dawn. My own tank was hit no fewer than fourteen times by German anti-tank rounds, but they fortunately caused only secondary damage to the tank's superstructure and broke the episcopes. They did no serious damage and my tank kept on fighting until 25 June. My Troop Sergeant's tank received eleven hits, which did not injure any of the crew, but his tank was far more seriously damaged than mine, and so had to be back-loaded.

'By 1200 hours we were back at out Start Line once again, where we discovered what had happened to cause the failure of the attack. The main assault had been aimed on the enemy positions around Le Mont Caubert, which had been defended by strong enemy forces, using 88mm AA guns firing in the ground role for the very first time, thus "christening" their future reputation in the anti-tank role. In addition, the area around Mont Caubert had been heavily sewn with anti-tank mines which had stopped many tanks, including the entire right wing of our 48 Tank Battalion. In addition, many infantry units were also unable to make any progress due to heavy enemy artillery fire. We stayed around the Start Line area for the rest of the day, being shelled from time to time, but ready to go into another attack if called upon to do so. However, this never materialised and the following day we were moved further east, the enemy having attacked once again all along the River Somme line.

'What a disappointment! One can only dream what might have happened if just one of the six tanks in our two troops had been equipped with a radio. We could have let our headquarters know that there was a clear way through to the river from whence the enemy positions could all have been taken in the rear, which might have altered everything – but one cannot remake history. At least a tech-

A recovery crew loading a Cruiser tank onto a tank transporter trailer during training in the UK, watched by various senior officers.

Refuelling a Stuart (M3A1) light tank from a petrol bowser. Refuelling was more often done using the leaky British flimsy petrol cans or the much superior 20 litre German Jerrican (one can be seen behind the bent oildrum, but it is painted black with a white cross indicating water).

Part of the echelon of 7th Armoured Division near Chartres, France, 18 August 1944. Note the line of jeeps and other lorries, the medical post and the M 31B1 'Terrier' Tank Recovery Vehicle, which was based on the M3 medium tank.

Outside Le Havre in 1944, two Churchills, the one on the left is a Churchill AVRE with an SBG (small box girder) bridge in the travelling position. Note also the sheer-legs and rear support frame.

A Sherman Crab mine clearer coming out of the water on the Normandy beaches, the chains on the rotor are clearly visible, these explode the mines as they beat on the ground.

Graphic photograph of the bow flamegun of a Churchill 'Crocodile' destroying huts at the Belsen concentration camp.

A Sherman DD amphibious tank entering the water with its screen fully extended. The twin 26inch propellors which are connected to the running gear via a bevel gear and pinion engaging with the idler wheels can be seen to the rear. A speed of 5–6mph was possible in the water, steering being achieved by swivelling the propellors.

A Sherman DD with its screen lowered. Part of the metal frame and the 36 tubular rubber pillars which held up the screen can be seen collapsed.

This Rocket Launcher T34 which was mounted on a Sherman tank comprised 60 tubes in banks, each containing a 4.5inch rocket. It was known as 'Calliope'–see Colonel Owsley Costlow's description of firing these awesome weapon systems.

Another strange mine clearing device was the Mine Exploder T1E3(M1), known as 'Aunt Jemima', which was also mounted on the Sherman tank. It exploded mines by pressure.

Matilda Mk 1 tank crews belonging to 4 RTR, getting ready for action in a French farmyard. Despite their small size and minimal firepower, they did well against the panzers because their armour was very thick and their crews very well trained.

Despite being short of tanks in the early days, Britain still supplied them to other Allied and Commonwealth countries. These Matilda Mk IIs are being loaded in UK for shipment to Russia.

Lieutenant Joe Sweeny and Corporal Garret of 42nd RTR keep watch from the turret of their Matilda Mk II, somewhere 'Up the Blue' in the Western Desert.

This British A9 Cruiser tank with its two 'dustbin' shaped machine gun sub-turrets is beginning to look like a Christmas tree with all its outside stowage. It must have been early in the campaign as the 'Solar topees' have not yet been discarded.

Ready to advance! A column of Light Mark VICs, belonging to 1 RTR moving up to the frontier in the early days of the desert war. They were part of the newly formed 7th Armoured Division, whose 'Desert Rat' insignia (seen on the front of each tank), quickly became world famous.

Panzers IIIs of Rommel's Deutsches Afrika Korps are seen here parading in Tripoli soon after their arrival in February 1941. The unexpected initial advance would quickly sweep the British out of Cyrenaica.

Churchill tanks moving up in pursuit of the German forces in the Allied drive to clear North Africa. January 1943.

The battle for Italy. A column of Eighth Army tanks pursues the enemy on to Bologna and Ferrara. In the lead is a Sherman M4A3E2, nicknamed 'Jumbo', because its extra armour put the weight up by 10,000lbs.

Last briefing before shipping across the Channel. GI tankers study their battle maps before boarding the landing craft to take them over to Normandy.

Good shot of an M5A1 light tank moving through a French town. The strange set of 'teeth' on its front is the Culin hedgerow cutter, designed by a GI, using metal from invasion beach obstacles. Its purpose was to cut through the thick 'bocage' hedgerows in Normandy and it was very successful.

Paris is liberated! A Sherman belonging to the 2nd Free French Armoured Division commanded by General Jacques LeClerc, is cheered by excited Parisians as it drives through a Paris street, 15 August 1944.

Shermans in the snowy Ardennes. GIs stand in front of their Shermans (the one on the right is a 'Jumbo' M4A3E2). They are wearing a variety of headgear including (man on left) the tank crew 'crash' helmet, whilst all wear the olive one-piece overall and rubber foul-weather boots with metal snaps.

The tank that won the war. The Americans built a staggering 49,234 M4 medium tanks, known universally as the Sherman. Highly adaptable, rugged and dependable, the Sherman had a bad reputation for catching fire when hit – hence its nickname 'The Ronson Lighter'! This is an M4A3 fitted with track extensions (called 'Duckbills') to reduce ground pressure and make it easier to cross bad going.

A column of PzKpfw III moving through a battered village in Russia. The extra trackplates on the front glacis give more protection to one of the most exposed parts of the tank.

Silhouetted against a burning village on the Russian steppes is this most famous of all German tanks, the Tiger. It entered service in late 1942, almost three years before the Allies could produce a tank with comparable gunpower.

A Comet tank belonging to 3 RTR, moving up to the perimeter of the Rhine crossing bridgehead, March 1945.

A despatch rider brings a message to this Soviet Army tank commander. The tank is a T28C medium which had extra armour and the longer 76.2mm L/26 gun as well as four machine guns in separate sub-turrets and a fifth coaxially mounted MG.

This Sherman is well-laden with men of the 29th Marines, as it moves up to take Ghuta on Okinawa, April 1945.

Armour-piercing ammunition made a terrible mess of any AFV it penetrated – such as this German Stug 3. The anti-bazooka plates gave protection against HEAT missiles but not armour piercing.

Graves of these German tank crews are marked by steel helmets, alongside their wrecked tanks. They were caught by rocket-firing aircraft near Coutances during the US Army breakout in June 1944.

Winston Churchill and Field-Marshal Montgomery, accompanied by Major-General 'Lou' Lyne (Divisional Commander) and other VIPs, inspect tanks of 7th Armoured Division – Churchill's 'Dear Desert Rats' as he called them, during the Berlin Victory Parade, 7 September 1945.

7 September 1945 was the Victory Parade Day in Berlin, when 4,000 infantrymen and over 200 tanks representing the Great Powers, paraded in the Tiergarten. Here three streamlined Russian JS 3 heavy tanks drive past the saluting base.

nical victory: "*Vive le blindage!*" If our R40 tanks had not been so well-armoured I would not be here to tell the tale!'

SIDI OMAR

'The action that sticks most in my mind,' recalled Sergeant Paddy Bermingham of 'C' Squadron, 2 RTR, 'was the taking of Sidi Omar during the early part of the Wavell push, just before the Christmas of 1940. Although we had been to France, our actual battle experience was negligible, apart from one action against a battery of guns west of Sidi Barrani. Commanding the squadron was Captain Pat Hobart, nephew of the famous Sir Percy (our previous OC had been killed at Sidi Barrani). The squadron 2IC and my tank commander was Captain D. Wilkie; our crew was quite a "mixed bag" of nationalities – he, our operator "Tumbleweed" Green and the nearside "dustbin"[1] gunner, Bill Lowe, were all English; Corporal Sid Watkins, our main gunner, was a South African; in the offside "dustbin" was Tom Carelton (my pal since school days) and myself, driver, both Irishmen.

'Soon after Sidi Barrani we were ordered south to take Sidi Omar, a fort on the Lybya-Cyrenaica border. Prior to this, one of our main topics of conversation amongst the crew had been how we should take a fort. My idea, inspired by having read the yarns of P. C. Wren, was to circle round and round the fort firing everything we had into it. Our tank was an A9 cruiser which although poorly armoured, had quite an assortment of weapons. Our main armament was a 3.7-inch Smoke Mortar, we also had three Vickers machine guns and, mounted for Ack-Ack use, a Bren light machine gun.

I believe we arrived at the Start Line a little too early and had to wait for our supporting artillery. Due to the flat nature of the country we were spotted by the Italians who started to shell us. This kept us on the move and some lovely figures of eight were cut in the sand. Our artillery arrived and were soon putting down concentrations on the fort, which lasted for several minutes. We made the fort at best possible speed, jinking on the way so much that our tank was broadside on to the Italian gun position outside the fort before we realised it. We were so near I heard Captain Wilkie shout for his revolver! I was in a quandary in the seat as to whether I should charge the gun or trust that our speed would carry us by safely, all the time waiting for the crash which fortunately never came. My bad scare was soon forgotten when my commander ordered me to circle the fort. I did my utmost to tell both "dustbin" gunners what was happening but it must have fallen on deaf ears as both were busy using their machine guns and later we did agree that P. C. Wren had something after all. After going round the fort once, came the urgent command "sharp left!" from my commander. This move placed the tank looking at a large breach in the fort. I sailed across and with all the MGs hard at it, came to rest beside the squadron commander's tank which had become a casualty, having charged one of the buildings inside the fort and, in doing so, dropped one of its front idlers. Looking through the visor I could see Captain Hobart with steel helmet on, shooting away over the top of the cupola with a .38 pistol. I think the sight of a second tank inside the fort must have been too much for the Italians and very soon they were appearing from nooks and crannies everywhere to give themselves up.

'Later I witnessed a very amusing incident between the squadron leader's driver, John Cheasney, and an Italian. John, naturally dark, was sunburnt darker than most Italians after our couple of months on the "Blue" [i.e. in the desert]. Wearing Captain Hobart's smartly cut overcoat and sporting a nicely trimmed beard and by this time smoking Italian cigarettes, in the half light he was approached by a prisoner who whispered very confidentially in his ear for several minutes in Italian. John played the part well until the prisoner, peering closer, saw he was English and with an exclamation of "*Inglese!*" bolted for cover amongst his friends. John, not knowing a word of Italian, must have "nodded" where he should have "shook". Soon afterwards we withdrew some way from the fort and, after a very welcome rum ration, settled down for the night.'

'DUEL OF THE KNIGHTS'[2]

'"Hey Russian! Hey Sashka! Are you still alive? I thought you might burn up with your tank . . . it'll burn. I'll let it burn, if you prefer it to be your grave . . ." the strange voice came over the radio. The T34's commander *Starshina* [Sergeant Major] Aleksandr Milyukov was stunned. What kind of dog played jokes like this? But once again, the cryptic voice came across the radio. "That farm tractor will be your grave. But then again, I will meet you with my Panther[3] one on one – one on one just like the knights of old . . ." "Oh, so that's you, you son of a reptile!" snarled *Starshina* Milyukov, as he realised who was talking with him. The radio signal was coming from a Fascist. And not just a simple one, but an ace, the "sly devil" as he was called by Milyukov's crew. "I'm ready!" Aleksandr reset the frequency knobs in front of him, "watch who takes who, and the Fascist will get his!" "Now let's begin the duel. Only write out your last will and testament; we have found that your country is huge and we've studied the Russians well." "Worry about your own last will and testament!" Milyukov cried into the radio, "and the mothers of the Germans, as they say, can begin counting the dawns left to their sons. . . ."

'So the Panther tank commander was in radio contact with the commander of one of the T34s of a tank brigade on the Voronezh front, who called the T34 a "farm tractor" and who challenged him to a duel, one on one, like knights. Our tanker accepted the challenge.

'The command was given: "Mount up!" Milyukov's T34 shot off at once, with no others around it, and moved to a starting position. The enormity of the risk they were taking became obvious as the Panther fired two rounds at the T34. Milyukov's crew were caught napping, as the enemy tank must have come forward from the second echelon and immediately surprised them with well-aimed fire. By a quirk of fate they were still alive. . . . In their second engagement Milyukov's crew laid a skilful trap for the German tankers. But they weren't there! Both the gunner, Sergeant Semyen Bragin and Milyukov himself, had no time to wonder at this fact, for once again shells whistled close by their tank. The Germans had outsmarted them by spotting the trap and it was obvious that the "Knight" in the Panther was an ace. It now seemed that this wasn't a second-echelon tank, nor was it a free hunter. The loader, Private Grigoriy Chumak, more than once called the German a "sly devil" under his breath. And now the tankers entered real combat with each other.

'Milyukov was nervous. He knew that there was only one way he would come out of this alive and still be a tank commander – namely by winning the duel with a brilliant play. There would be a military court – his T34 had rolled out of its designated fighting position without orders from his battalion commander. Playing it through could lead to a real death – for no one had faced this German ace and lived to tell about it, this fellow could hit a kopek with every shot and had demonstrated it several times in a row. Things grew hushed and Milyukov's knowledge of the terrain gave him and his crew a chance for success, it was treeless, but peppered with ravines and gullies. And the T34 was a fast, manoeuvrable tank, which would force the Panther to come after it. Milyukov had himself "flown" the tank up to eighty kilometres per hour (fifty m.p.h.). Later, driver-mechanic *Starshina* Milyukov had increased the factory characteristics of the tank by at least a third. The winner of this duel would be the crew with the most mastery of its respective vehicle. With that, the victory would go to him who spotted the enemy first, he who was the first to fire an accurate shot, he who was to turn away in time to avoid a hit, and much much more.

'The main problem was to get within three hundred to four hundred metres of the Panther, where his gun could penetrate its glacis, then things would be more even. But the Germans weren't about to wait for him to close and at 700m they began accurate fire at the dodging T34. The Hitlerists had opened fire immediately the crews had spotted each other and they didn't give up a single metre of that 700m range between the two tanks, which was their reserve. A round landed right next to the Soviet tank. Can't we get some more speed up? No, on the rocky ground the T34 could only reach about thirty kilometres per hour – no more, and the increase was only just a fraction. You cannot fly over 700m like this, for the German will surely get his fatal shot in if you try. And right then Milyukov hit the brakes, cutting his speed. He decided, "Well, let the German get his sights on us." Aleksandr knew he was now dead in the other's sights. "No, you reptile, not yet! HIT IT! GIVE ME SPEED AND MANOEUVRE NOW!" cried Milyukov. The T34 shot forward just a split second before flame spouted from the long barrel of the Panther. He had timed it well, for the German's shot was very close to the mark. "There it is, Fritz, that long lance of yours isn't everything!" Milyukov had realised that if he could avoid getting hit by shells on the open parts of the terrain, he might be able to close the distance with the German ace. But here was Nikolay Luk'yanskiy, who was sitting in the commander's seat: "Twelve seconds, commander, I make it twelve seconds." "Luk'yanskiy is a smart boy," thought Milyukov.

'Now he knew that it took the German twelve seconds between his first and second shots. Picking up speed he rolled ahead for about 200m over the rough ground. But Luk'yanskiy's voice called out: ". . . seven, eight, nine, ten, eleven . . ." Milyukov suddenly pulled back on the brake levers with all his might. The tank pitched forward and stopped. The next German round screamed by the bow of the tank. "See where that came from!" The Russian tank stopped sharply, swinging this way and that, but the German shells only landed near the tank. The crew had made masterly use of every dip and rise in the ground to achieve some measure of protection. The Soviet combat vehicle managed to creep ever closer to the Panther. The German ace blasted off round after round, but the T34 was like a "spirit" and it continued to "grow" in their sights with every bound. The nerves of the German were not made of iron and they began to pull back. "Hold still, you reptile! Give me speed!" cried Milyukov.

'The enemy tank was now steadily pulling back in reverse. While there was still a German ace sitting in that tank, our tankers went after him yet again. Not once did the German show them his sides or rear to shoot at. Then there was just one instant when the withdrawing Panther hit a small bump and its long gun soared into the air, and it showed its belly. This was the moment that Sergeant Bragin had been patiently waiting for and he whistled an armour-piercing shell at that exposed place. Flames spurted from the German tank, and the Panther of the noted ace began to burn. Milyukov's crew went crazy with joy, laughing, shouting and grinning widely. All this ceased instantly when the voice of the battalion commander crackled over the radio, "Milyukov! Duelling is the least of your problems, and you will be going up before a court!"

'After the battle was over, the valorous foursome, as was verified by those who witnessed the duel between the Soviet and German tanks, during the entire fight had fired off but one single shot, just like participants in an old-fashioned duel. The observers were alert to the parallel: it was just like knights duelling in the twentieth century. After the battle, Milyukov considered the self-control of his battalion commander and his experience. During the duel he had not said a single word, for he knew the matter was out of his hands. He only expressed his displeasure and anger after the duel had played itself out and the survivor was identified. Perhaps he may have agreed with it in spirit, for battle later erupted between opposing sub-units after the "knights" had finished their duel, and Milyukov's crew would claim other victories, but what victories! His T34 met up with three Tigers, lit them up, and then plunged into the crews of several artillery weapons.'

A DAY AT HASTENRATH

'Upon recovering from wounds received in Normandy, I was transferred from hospital back to my original unit, I Company, 1st Battalion which, to the best of my recollection was located in the town of Breinig.' That is how Lieutenant Henry J. Earl of 33 Armored Regiment, US Armor, began his account of a single day of action of 3rd Armored Division in the Scherpenseel/Hastenrath area in November 1944, where his platoon of five Sherman tanks would lead the attack on Hastenrath. His graphic battle account followed a detailed explanation of the plan of action, which in brief terms was for an infantry/tank attack, with the tanks leading, following a very heavy artillery barrage. The tanks would first be led through the enemy minefields by a mine flailer and would then fan out, with the infantry still close behind. As soon as the tanks reached the first buildings, part of the infantry would go round them and take over the lead, with the tanks in support. The rest of the infantry would initially stay mounted in their halftracks until the lead infantry had reached the town, then dismount and join them. At the same time, more tanks and infantry would assault Scherpenseel in a similar manner. Lieutenant Earl continued, explaining the battle as though he were an onlooker, thus talking about himself in the third person as 'the lead tank commander': 'As I Company moved forward, enemy artillery fire became increasingly heavy. Shortly after crossing the line of departure, one of our tanks struck the minefield and was disabled. Captain Gunnarson immediately ordered the mine flailer into the minefield. The lead tank dropped in behind and followed. Each succeeding tank dropped in line and followed. The mine flailer was struck by an armour-piercing shell and destroyed. Thoughts raced through the lead tank commander's head. If he ordered his tank around the mine flailer, he would take a hit from the same gun that had destroyed the mine flailer. If any or all of his crew survived the hit, they would, as they crawled from their tank, be subject to the small-arms fire that covered the minefield. If they survived this and had not cleared the minefield, they would not last long in the minefield with all its anti-personnel mines. With these thoughts in mind, he ordered his tank to pull around the disabled mine flailer. Soon they were clear of the minefield without taking a hit. One of the other tanks must have silenced the gun.

'Orders were then given to start the gyro-stabilisers. They enabled the tank to fire its tank gun and coaxial machine guns accurately whilst the tank was on the move. As the tanks came through the minefield they took up their attacking formation, allowing the maximum frontal fire as well as maximum flanking fire. They flushed out and destroyed a reinforced infantry company that was covering the minefield with small-arms fire. In skirting the left flank of Scherpenseel it was necessary to go between the town and a fortified building with its own network of defensive positions, as had been shown in aerial photographs. As the lead tank passed this building, at a distance of about fifty feet, two Germans appeared in a window, one with a rifle, the other with a *panzerfaust*. They both fired. The tank commander who had his head out of the turret hatch, ducked a fraction of a second in time. The *panzerfaust* struck the tank, rocking it. The penetration was in a non-vital spot and did no damage. The commander hit the traversing switch, swung the gun around to the window and fired two high-explosive shells. Through the dust and the smoke it was apparent that the shells had inflicted a great deal of damage to the interior of the building. It was doubtful if there were any survivors. The entire action took less than ten seconds. As the lead tank cleared the town of Scherpenseel, it found itself looking down gently sloping terrain to the town of Hastenrath in the distance. The tank commander slowly swept the town with his binoculars. He spotted a vehicle under an archway alongside a building. The distance was too great to determine whether it was a tank, a self-propelled gun, or a prime mover for an anti-tank gun. The round in his breech was HE. He fired. It fell slightly short. The second round was armour-piercing. This struck the vehicle, setting it on fire.

'The original plan of attack was to move down the slope directly to Hastenrath. As the tank moved forward, a loud clear voice commanded, "Turn right!" He obeyed. It was not until much later that he realised that it had been God who had spoken to him. He slipped in behind the town of Scherpenseel, using the buildings in the background to help cover the movement of his tanks. He spotted a slight movement behind the remains of a shelled-out building as did the commander of the tank following on his left flank. Both fired. Debris and parts of an anti-tank gun flew in the air. The advance continued to the end of Scherpenseel. Here it made a ninety-degree turn and headed directly for Hastenrath. After following this new course for a short distance, the lead tank found itself on the edge of a cliff. The cliff ran diagonally across the entire terrain. This had not shown on the aerial photographs. . . .

'When I Company reached Hastenrath, only the lead tank and three others remained of the original nineteen-tank attack force . . . They were First-Lieutenant Henry Earl, Staff Sergeant Fred Nulle, Sergeants Mike Draganic and August Formslag. . . . Nulle's and Formslag's tanks were sent to the left end of the town, to cover a road that approached Hastenrath from the rear. There was also a small ridge that died out about fifty yards from the end of town. They were to prevent any tanks, SP guns or anti-tank guns slipping behind the ridge and surprising I Company from the left flank. The lead tank along with Sergeant Draganic's tank took up positions covering the main street, also covering a road that ran along the right side of town, preventing any armour from surprising I Company from the left flank. A report was sent to battalion stating they were on the objective awaiting the infantry, also requesting battalion to bring another mine flailer with them. The battalion advance was down a gently sloping valley approximately two miles wide, flanked on each side by wooded ridges extending two to three hundred feet in height. The 1st Infantry Division was advancing down the ridge on the right side, the

104th Infantry Division advancing down the ridge on the left side. The two infantry divisions had encountered bitter fighting. Their advance was slow. The Germans were making them fight for every foot of ground. Thus, I Company found itself well in advance, and could expect to receive enemy fire through an arc of 270 degrees. The lead tank commander whilst studying the wooded ridge on his right flank through his binoculars, spotted a prime mover and an anti-tank gun moving at high speed, break from the cover of the woods into a clearing then disappear back into the woods again. Its appearance had been so brief there had been no chance to take it under fire. It was clear that the Germans were beginning to close in from the flanks. A short time later the commander spotted a self-propelled gun, this time on his left flank. It was inching its way into a position to fire from the crest of the ridge that ran to the left end of Hastenrath. He barked a command, the guns of the four tanks swung over onto the SP gun which immediately backed off the crest of the hill and out of sight before a round could be fired.

'As the minutes ticked away, tension mounted and mounted. Since the brief action by the enemy on both flanks all had been quiet. The town looked deserted, the whole countryside looked deserted, and yet nothing could be further from the truth. To make matters even more desperate, the tanks had stopped in an open field. There was no cover and no cover to be had. The lead tank commander peered from his open hatch, desperately searching for some movement. His gun was trained down the main street. From a pile of debris not more than 100 yards away, came a tremendous blast and at the same time an ear-splitting crack as an armour-piercing shell missed the top of the turret and his head by inches. The gunner had seen the blast at the same time. The gun was slightly lowered and fired. The tank had a round in its breech. The anti-tank gun had to reload. The AP shell struck the debris exactly where the blast had been. The tank crew reloaded as fast as possible and fired a second shell, this time HE, to make certain that the gun and its crew were destroyed. The action was over. The tank commander reflected. How could the gun have missed at point-blank range? He was certain that the gun was not there originally or it would have fired when his gun was pointing to the left at the SP gun. The crew, who were lying down, must have worked the gun into position. They could do this as the gun had a very low silhouette. Once in position they were confronted with the problem of removing some of the debris, but they could not have done this by hand as the tank crew would have seen them. It was evident that there was not much debris to remove and the anti-tank gunner must have planned to remove it with his tremendous muzzle blast. This was an excellent idea and would have worked had not the tank commander and his gunner been looking directly at the gun when it fired.

'While he was contemplating this, he studied the town of Hastenrath and the surrounding countryside. With his eyes barely above the hatch, he scrutinised every detail, constantly reminding himself to be alert and to look for any movement. As he did this impatience set in. Where the hell was the infantry? Why weren't they down here? Didn't they realise his tanks couldn't last much longer in this exposed position? Then reason returned. He knew that the 36th Armored Infantry Regiment was as fine an infantry regiment as there was anywhere. He knew if anyone could get into them, they could. He remembered from experience that if you gave the Germans just twenty-four hours to dig in, you paid hell getting them out again. And here they'd had almost six weeks to dig in and prepare their defences. His thoughts were broken by a call from battalion requesting an ammunition report. He called his three remaining tanks for their reports. Then he checked with his loader as to their condition. The report was: "Just these six rounds on the floor and one in the breech." "My God!" He could vaguely remember firing forty or fifty rounds, but here they had fired ninety rounds! The reports began to come in. Two tanks had seven rounds each, the other six rounds. He called battalion, giving the report. There was a low whistling at the other end, and then: "We're trying to get in to you and we'll try some way to get some ammunition down to you."

'Time was literally killing them. They had been stationary for almost an hour. During that time, the Germans had attempted to move an SP gun into position on the left flank. They had moved an anti-tank gun right under their very noses. And what about the prime mover and the anti-tank gun spotted on the right flank? They should be in a firing position by now. He toyed with the idea of moving on into the town and fighting it out in the streets there. But even as he thought about it he knew it was ridiculous, he was positive there was a minefield between his tanks and the town and he wasn't about to lose one of his tanks to the minefield – that would be 25 per cent of his force and 25 per cent of his firepower. For what? Just to prove there was a minefield there? Even if they did get into the town, they wouldn't stand much of a chance. Every doorway, every cellar opening, every window would be a likely base for a *panzerfaust* attack. Without infantry his tanks didn't stand a chance.

'His thoughts were broken by the God-awfullest sound and by his tank being lifted off the ground and shaken. He was violently thrown against the gun guard. Bouncing from that he slammed into the back of his gunner. As he scrambled to regain his footing he knew that they had been hit, but not penetrated. That meant that the gun which had fired was firing at extreme range. As he peered out of his hatch again, he knew that the chance of him spotting the gun was very slight. He had to be looking right at it when it fired. Again he was violently thrown against the gun guard. Bouncing from this he was wedged between his gunner's right shoulder and the side of the tank. Fighting once more to regain his footing and to get his head out of his hatch, his thoughts went to his crew. My God, his men had courage! There they sat, knowing any second they could be killed or badly mangled. They knew what they were in for; they had seen the remains of other crews hauled from their tanks. It was much harder on them than it was on him. He was absorbed in the complete concentration of locating the gun. While all they could do was to sit and stare at the interior of the tank or peer through periscopes which afforded them only limited vision. They took another hit. Secured this time by a better handhold, he was not thrown against the gun guard. The hit was low on the side. The interior of the tank was lit by a ball of fire caused by the terrific friction of the penetration. A white hot eighteen-pound projectile entered the empty ammunition rack under the floor. The earlier models of the M4 Sherman medium tank did not store ammunition under the turret floor. The steel walls of the compartment prevented the molten metal from striking the interior of the hull and ricocheting throughout the tank. This saved the crew. The fact that the anti-tank gun was firing at extreme range also saved the crew. The velocity of the projectile was so reduced that the ammunition compartment was able to confine its effect. Had the gun been firing at a closer range the velocity of the projectile would have been so great that the ammunition compartment would have had no effect.

'Still searching the countryside, he felt the shoulder of the gunner pushing him up from underneath. He had been so intent on trying to locate the gun that he had forgotten they had to get out of the tank – and get out fast! He boosted himself up and out onto the rear deck, allowing his crew to scramble out. His map case was gone. No matter how dangerous it was, or how crazy, he had to get it. Dropping back inside, he felt for his map case. He spotted it on the other side of the turret under one of the rounds. Diving under the gun he grabbed it – back across the turret, up and out. As his hands were on the front slope of the turret, his knees on the edge of the hatch, his legs and buttocks over the opening of the hatch, he heard a tremendous sound. Ignoring this, he half-slipped and half-tumbled to the ground, joining his crew.' After the war, Lieutenant Earl received a letter from his platoon sergeant, Fred Nooly, who was watching all of this drama unfold. Fred said that Earl had just been clearing the hatch opening when an armour-piercing projectile struck the two open hatch covers just behind his buttocks. The hatch covers simply vanished. Had he spent an extra second or two inside the tank, his escape would have ended in the hatch opening. Earl and his crew were later captured and entered Hastenrath as prisoners of war – but more of their experiences in a later chapter.

INFANTRY-TANK CO-OPERATION IN THE JUNGLES OF NEW CALEDONIA

'January 1944 saw the receipt of our new Sherman tanks. They looked like and were a more formidable weapon with their three-inch armour-plated turret and 75mm gun. Once again the rush began to make the vehicles combat ready, to teach the crews new firing techniques and the operation of more complex equipment. Receipt of these heavier tanks proved to be another big morale booster.' That is how Colonel Gino F. Amorelli describes this part of the battle history of the 754th Tank Battalion who fought against the Japanese in the Pacific theatre and lived up to their motto: 'No mission too difficult'.

He continues: 'XIV Corps relieved the marine command on the island on 15 December and from that day on all efforts were made by front-line units to tie in all beach-head defences into a solid perimeter. Concurrently with this, the Provisional Service Command which began operating on 6 January 1944 continued the extensive job of constructing and maintaining road nets and supply installations. . . . Perimeter defences were tightened by infantry units on the line. Existing minefields were enlarged, new ones laid and perimeter barbed-wire barriers were reinforced. Infantry patrols kept running into stiffening enemy counter-patrol action and captured documents foretold a general assault against the Allied positions on or about 9 March. . . . During this period the battalion maintained a constant state of readiness.

'9–31 March 1944, saw elements of the battalion continuously committed to action. The Japanese 6th Infantry Division opened their attack against our perimeter with an artillery bombardment against the infantry front-line units, the airfield and our battalion bivouac area. It is believed that our encampment had been pinpointed by the enemy intelligence as the incoming artillery fires were not random misses of the airfield. Fortunately, this baptism of fire had no serious effect on the battalion as a fighting unit. Most shells were bursting high in the tree tops (75–100 feet) and although some personnel casualties were sustained, there were no serious injuries.

'The main attack was launched in overwhelming force in the sector of the 37th Division and against the 129th Infantry Regiment on 11 March. Diversionary attacks were launched simultaneously against other elements of the division and in the America Division sector. The sector of the line occupied by the 129th was fairly flat with some deep ravines and creeks running into its positions. This area also lay a short distance west of the Numa Numa Trail which afforded the enemy an easy route of approach into this area. The Japanese had been able to cut through the wire in this area and effect two minor penetrations. However, they were unable to exploit these penetrations due to infantry and artillery fire. Having been contained, the 129th counterattacked with the 1st Platoon of our Company "C" in support. The ground was generally flat, but due to the deep ravines in which the Japs took shelter, it was difficult to bring the tank guns to bear on them. During this period, two pillboxes were retaken and the tanks withdrawn, only to begin attacking again at 13.15. This only lasted for another hour as they had almost exhausted their fuel and ammunition supplies. The attack was suspended whilst the 2nd Platoon came up to replace the 1st and the attack was resumed at 17.30. The combined team managed to demolish all the Japanese-held pillboxes and restore the original line.

'Our months of training on Guadalcanal paid off. Tanks in two waves led these assaults, with three medium tanks leading the way, covered by two light tanks. Interspersed with this second wave of tanks were infantry troops who supplied close support to the tanks which in turn gave cover by cannister shell fire to those units leading the attack. Tanks were again engaged against the enemy on 15 March, this in the F Company sector of the line. The Japs still held a salient in our lines and couldn't be dislodged. Twice a co-ordinated attack was made, the first at 15.00 and the second at 16.45. With this second counter-attack the enemy were either killed or driven off. One tank was damaged, over 100 enemy bodies counted and four captured. Enemy troops again attacked in the F Company sector on the 17th, made a small penetration but were driven back immediately by a combined infantry-tank attack.'

YEROKHIN AND THE ELEFANTS[4]

'Look at the face of Lieutenant Aleksey Yerokhin in the snapshot taken by our special photo correspondent, Yakov Khalip, back in 1943. While much has been lost due to the age of the photo here, dear reader, believe that you are looking upon one of the Russian workhorses of the 1940s – and one whose force of will and mastery of his skills brought low German pedantries and arrogance. And now gaze again on this portrait of a tanker. He won acclaim for his skills, even from another of our special correspondents of the time, Konstantin Simonov, who wrote about him thus: "Yerokhin is a slightly stocky twenty-four-year-old with a ruddy face, blessed with bright grey eyes that sparkle with mischief. This Russian fellow is a gay sort, one you can learn to like in short order, and as is usually the case, also blessed with a keen wit. He is always called upon for the tasks requiring the greatest care and he carries them out with the greatest deal of cunning and attention to detail. These two qualities have permitted him to rise above the others in recent days in smashing the Germans. Right now he has managed to combine them with great satisfaction in using his cunning and our methods to overcome what appear to be new and unknown machines."

One of these 'new and unknown machines' which Simonov was talking about was the 'Elefant' tank destroyer (also called the 'Ferdinand' after its designer Ferdinand Porsche). The sixty-five-ton SP anti-tank gun (*Sturmgeschutz mit* 8.8cm PaK43/2) used the hull of the Tiger(P) but with extra 100mm-thick armour plates bolted on to give a staggering 200mm of frontal armour. Combined with its long 8.8cm gun it was a formidable weapon, although only ninety were ever produced (in April–May 1943). Dokuchayev rightly comments that: 'To engage an Elefant in a duel, it must be stressed, was very, very difficult . . . this machine was a real threat to any tank within one kilometre of it.' Nevertheless, during the battles of the Kursk salient, Lieutenant Aleksey Yerokhin managed to destroy six Elefants over the course of two days and this is how he did it.

'On the evening of 11 July 1943, the tank company under the command of Lieutenant Cherneg moved out to take up its initial combat positions. The T34 of Lieutenant Yerokhin moved ahead of the rest of the battalion, since it was part of the forward patrol of the advance guard. Suddenly his patrol found itself under enemy fire. He and his crew knew at once that their tank was under direct fire, not indirect fire. Yerokhin immediately directed the tank to roll behind a copse, then climbing out of the turret and moving forward, he began scanning the area. Roughly one-and-a-half kilometres away he spotted a German vehicle on top of a small hill. "That's no tank; not with that box-shaped hull," Aleksey Yerokhin thought to himself. "Whatever it's armed with is powerful, from the sound those shells made when they flew by." It was also soon clear that this weapon was on the move in the direction of the German offensive.

'They closed the distance to the German combat vehicle – perhaps it was somewhere around 1400m. At that range they opened fire. One round, then a second . . . the T34 commander put three rounds "on the way" into the glacis of the Elefant. But as it turned out they were three ineffective shots. After manoeuvring closer, he fired two more rounds, after which the German began to burn. But now let us hear the words of Lieutenant Yerokhin as to how he carried this out.

"'After that we knew that even as powerful a German machine as this could burn," he recalled, "and the battalion began to deploy, taking up positions to the left and right of the place where we were supposed to provide support to the infantry in case of a German attack. We were soon able to see things pretty well through the smoke clouds (caused by the burning Elefant) on our right flank, where we spotted several more of the huge German machines. The first of these was now silhouetted on the top of the same hill. We immediately gave it a company salvo. It was hit and halted. The rest of their unit deployed and once on line to the front began firing back at us from the halt. After getting permission from my commander, I began to move my tank to the left, taking advantage of the dips and hills until I could take the Germans in their right flank. I was successful in getting into position and moving up onto a small hill and using great care and skill, put five aimed rounds one after the other into the nearest of the German machines. It began to smoke after the fifth round. The other Elefants, sensing what had happened, began to withdraw, as they could not turn their turrets and my appearance on their flank placed them at a disadvantage. If they turned to engage me, then the rest of our tanks could shoot at their vulnerable sides and if they stayed in their present positions, then their opposite flank was open to my fire. Therefore, they elected to pull back. It was soon obvious that the German attack had been broken up."

'Things remained this way all night, as the Soviet tanks remained in their positions. While that took place and once things were quiet, Lieutenant Yerokhin and one of his crew members went out to familiarise themselves with the machine they had destroyed. This is what they found: four of their shots had gouged the armoured side over the running gear and left big pits. Considering that they were shooting at the thick armour at a range of 1,400m, this wasn't surprising. But yet the machine had caught fire. Why? The reason was obvious once Yerokhin and the crewmen looked in through a round hatch in the rear armour plate. Right where Yerokhin had hit the vehicle with his shells was an auxiliary fuel tank. The violent shell strikes had caused the fuel to ignite and the burning fuel was what had burned out the tank, even though its armour had not been penetrated. He also saw that there was no way that any tank shell would penetrate the vehicle's glacis. But the sides could be penetrated at close range and at longer distances, the next best thing was to shoot for the area of the auxiliary fuel tank. And once this was determined the fate of the Elefant was sealed. These conclusions were proven on 12 July, when combat started up once again. On that day Lieutenant Aleksey Yerokhin increased his score of destroyed German SP guns. But first he would have to encounter one of the German tank aces, fighting in an Elefant with an experienced commander and crew. The first shot from this vehicle blew up a light Soviet tank, the second took out a T34. Yerokhin never gave him a chance to take his third shot. In a short period of time he fired a large number of shells, the bulk of which hit their target. After his second direct hit the Elefant fell silent and when it took its fourth direct hit, the top hatch flew open and its crew bailed out. The T34 commander decided to play the game to the end, since up until now the Elefant had not begun to smoke or catch fire so he kept firing until it did. Six of the heavy German Elefant weapons eventually fell to Lieutenant Aleksey Yerokhin. A truly unique accomplishment!'

TWO TANK DESTROYER ACTIONS

Sergeant John Henle, MM (nicknamed 'Gannet' as he would eat anything!), joined his local Territorial Army battalion at Buckfastleigh, Devon – the 5th Devons (POW) Battalion. He recalls: 'It was a heavy-machine-gun battalion and stayed that way until about 1941. It then became the 86th Anti-Tank Regiment (Devons). Training took a long time, as we had to learn all about tanks (M10 tank destroyers) from scratch. It was every boy's dream to drive a tank and I enjoyed the training, but later switched to turret crew. There was more chances of promotion that way as five sergeants were needed for every troop and as everyone was starting from scratch I felt I had as good a chance as anyone else of promotion. The 86th Anti-Tank consisted of four batteries of which two were armed with M10s, twelve in each battery. I was in 340 Battery and by 1942 I was made up to sergeant and was Number One on an M10 – I felt like a dog with two tails! . . . We embarked for Normandy on 29/30 June. The trip was uneventful (a bit rough) and we landed on Juno beach with the tide out, so no problems there. The first nine days were spent moving around for no apparent reason. Then in the very early hours of 10 July we moved forward in convoy with 7 RTR to a forward area. By this time I was beginning to feel a little apprehensive, I suppose it was lack of sleep, not knowing what we were letting ourselves in for. . . . Whilst we were waiting for dawn to break we came under very heavy artillery and mortar fire. I had my steel helmet knocked off and dented by shrapnel, but my head was undamaged!

'In due course we moved forward as directed by our Troop Commander over the radio. We were now on the lower slopes of Hill 112. The amazing part of the next hour or two is that nothing seemed to happen, except of course for the shell and mortar fire. Eventually I spotted two German tanks, possibly three or four hundred yards away, moving very slowly across our front and pointing slightly towards us. I was surprised that their guns weren't pointing directly at us. I think they must have been just as bemused as we were. After I had given the necessary fire orders, the gunner laid on ready to fire. I gave the order "FIRE!" and the first shot went way over the top of the enemy tanks. The gunner had laid on another target further up the slope but in direct line. This mistake was quickly rectified and two shots later both tanks were knocked out and set on fire. Numbers of the crews were seen climbing out. I reported over the radio what had happened and then things were quiet again. I had a great feeling that at last all the blood, sweat and tears of three years training had paid off. To this day I can't understand why the German tanks hadn't seen us.

'Over the radio, my Troop Commander told me that there were more German tanks ahead in an orchard and ordered me to go forward to look for them. I felt very exposed as we went forward. However, we didn't reach the brow of the hill, because it was a false brow, the hill rising again as we came to the first crest, so I kept going. Suddenly there was a loud BANG! A solid shot passed so close that the airwave bounced into the turret, making a noise like thunder. I immediately ordered my driver to reverse down the hill to get us out of trouble. But the driver missed his gears and they became jammed. The next shot hit the M10 and we brewed up at once. The TD burst into flames and we jumped out. I felt really exposed as I left the TD and ran fifty yards to cover, dropping into a slit trench and apologising to the infantry I landed on! Looking back at the M10 I saw two members of my crew get out of the burning TD, which meant that there were still two trapped. I ran back and climbed up to look inside. I could see the driver struggling to move back inside the turret, but said that one of his legs was trapped. I managed to pull him up to the top of the turret. He was still conscious but in great pain. He had to be got off the tank as quickly as possible as it was likely to blow up at any moment, so it could not be done slowly. After agonising for a moment I decided to roll him off the side of the AFV, knowing that it might cause him further injuries but it was the fastest way to get him to safety. Just then I fainted. I had been swaying on the side of the open turret and real-ised that if I fainted forwards I would be burnt to death, but fortu-nately I fell backwards onto the ground.

'When I came round I was lying beside the driver who was clearly in terrible pain, so I climbed back inside the M10 again to fetch the First Aid Box, which I knew contained morphine. Having got it and returned to the wounded driver, I broke a capsule onto a handker-chief and the driver grabbed at it so fiercely that he almost broke my wrist. Unfortunately it wasn't enough to ease the pain, so I injected a syringe of morphine and he became quieter. We were still too close to the burning M10, so I got an infantryman to help me to make a rough stretcher with two rifles, using their slings to lift him. As we did so I realised that the driver had lost one leg, severed halfway between hip and knee. Splintered bones were sticking out – like the shank bone of a shoulder of lamb. We carried him a short distance when some stretcher-bearers came up and took over. Sadly, the driver died two days later, despite being a big, strong chap. However, I will always remember his look of relief when he saw me coming back to help him and he realised that he would not be left to die alone in the burning tank.'

Sergeant Henle's hands were badly burnt and he was eventually evacuated back to England – despite the fact that, having reached the Casualty Clearing Station, he found that there were so many casualties to be seen that he, as he could walk, was told that he should make his own way back to the beach, and did so, managing to cadge a lift and being put on a landing craft which brought him home. He knew that his wife would be worried when she heard from the War Office that he had been wounded, so, whilst on a train for Scotland, he decided to write to her to say he was OK. He and a travelling companion did so in the railway carriage, using airmail letter forms. They then threw the letters out of the carriage window and miraculously his was found and posted to his wife. John then spent a few weeks in hospital whilst his hands recovered, then, after three weeks' leave he returned to his unit.

'The next major engagement I took part in was Operation ALAN, the relief of s'Hertogenbosch, which took six days and the loss of one M10 – not mine this time. On the last day of the action my troop was sent with 1st East Lancs to clear some barracks on the south-west of the town. Before I go on I should explain that all our M10s had a small petrol engine fixed on the front (known as a "Chore Horse") which was used for charging batteries. When we arrived at the barracks everything was very peaceful, so I was told to move to the square. There were wooden huts all round it and as soon as we got there all hell broke loose! I would imagine that the Germans had pulled back, but had the barracks well covered by artillery, mortars, machine guns, etc. It was beginning to get dark and the barrack square was just a mass of sparks, where bullets, shrapnel, etc., was hitting it. I was beginning to wonder what the hell we had let ourselves in for, when a repeat of Hill 112 happened! A loud bang and the M10 was enveloped in flames. I could hear my Troop Commander in my headset yelling: "Bail Out!" All the crew got out without a scratch. Three ran off the square, but myself and the RO went into a big bunker which was just alongside the M10. We kept an eye on it and noticed that the flames had almost disappeared. A shell had hit the chore horse, spraying about a gallon of petrol over it. We then decided to get back into it and to contact HQ, but found that the rubber-mounted aerial was US [unserviceable]. After some difficulty we got the M10 into a safe spot in the town, replaced the aerial base and made contact again.'

ACTION AT PFAFFENHECK

The next battle action demonstrates the importance of the all-arms team, with infantry, armour and artillery, etc., all working together in a difficult situation. 'Having crossed the Moselle River, we spent most or all of the day clearing the high ground on the east bank.' That is how Sergeant Byrl E. Rudd of Elmer, Oklahoma, who was a platoon sergeant in 'C' Company of the US 712th Tank Battalion, began a letter to one of his wartime buddies, who had written to him to ask what had happened at a German village called Pfaffenheck. He continued: 'There were two companies of infantry with the second platoon of 712th, Company "C" (me) as tank support for either infantry company that might happen upon a machine-gun nest. The Germans were backing up, supposedly, for a last stand at the Rhine River. We were giving them plenty of time because our left flank was lagging behind. From the sound of rifle fire, they were meeting more resistance than we were. We moved slowly eastward all day. About sundown, we hit a spot of open terrain. This area was three to four miles square. On our right flank, the trees extended to a small village approximately two miles ahead, so there was no problem to get there with cover all the way. This village was Edenhausen. A little farther east and one to one-and-a-half miles north was another village, Pfaffenheck.

'After a pow-wow, Snuffy Fuller informed the infantry companies that the tanks would not be split. One infantry company would occupy each town for the night with all the tanks in the higher town of Edenhausen. A blacktop road ran north and south on the east of these two towns, and there was not one building on the east side of the road. There were tall pine trees twenty-five yards or less east of the road and our left-flank buddies were still progressing too slow for me. So here we are, mission accomplished. Two towns exposed to a blacktop road and miles of tall pines. I checked to see if all the tanks had a good field of fire and where the infantry outposts were. Nothing to worry about. The Germans have crossed the Rhine. WRONG!

'Guards are out. The infantry is bedding down. Lieutenant Fuller looks out. I am looking out. He looks at me and I at him. Nothing is said. I feel like ducks in a pond and so does he. Good houses to sleep in, but I am up making a noise. Guys are griping. Then about 2 a.m. I hear people running near the rear of the town. I jump on my tank and listen. An infantry guard stops them. All are excited. They wake the officers and convince them of a horrible massacre in Pfaffenheck. Those boys, five or six of them, are the only survivors of the company. The infantry officers are furious and want to attack right away. Lieutenant Fuller and I have a pow-wow. We present a plan to avoid the road and attack with five tanks abreast with the infantry on the backs of the tanks across the open ground at full speed to the apple orchard. The time would be at sun-up. We are hoping that the big guns would be looking at the blacktop road. Plan accepted and carried out.

'The apple orchard was full of SS troops. All had American guns. The second section soon cleared the orchard and three houses on the left side of the street for the infantry. I then had to go forward to get a field of fire down the street. It curved or made a couple of angles. The infantry was taking a beating, which I thought was coming from the right side of the street. There was no big stuff up to now. At the first intersection, I saw Lieutenant Fuller moving and firing at the second intersection. I saw him stop. We were both firing across the blacktop road into the tall pines that were thick with Germans. We had them running, I thought.

'Lieutenant Fuller's tank was hit by an anti-tank gun. He got out and made it to the buildings. About the time he got there and looked back, Lloyd Hayward came out of the top hatch. One of his legs was limp. Lieutenant Fuller started after him. Machine-gun fire stopped him. The fifth tank was not able to fire in that direction. I jumped out to get Lieutenant Fuller while my gunner kept them pinned down across the road. I got Lieutenant Fuller to go back down the street to find a medic. I found Russell Harris, the tank commander, was slowly dying from a bullet that had just grazed the top of his head when he was in the orchard. The medic told me his life might have been saved if we could get him to a hospital within four hours. The boys had got him out of the tank. He seemed to be in no pain. They tried to get him with a jeep, but the SS drove them back. They tried again later with a halftrack and the SS drove them back again. While I was there, I learned that the driver of the Number Two tank had been killed about fifty yards after leaving the orchard. This man was Jack Mantell. Those SS troops were tough.

'Being under strength going into this action, the infantry company was very slim on men able for combat. I had seen their officer killed. Upon getting back to my tank, I found the roof of the house protecting me to be on fire. Lots of SS were moving about in the pines. I decided to try the anti-tank gun again. He was still there and he knew where I was. Time to try something else. The field artillery had been firing all day, but their shells were going too far to help me. I went to find an infantry NCO who knew where the phones were. He would not call the field artillery, so I called someone and got to talk to the field artillery fairly soon. He agreed to bracket one gun. The first shell hit between me and the Number Five tank. I told him to raise it two hundred feet. Since the two tanks were the only men near the road, he agreed, with a promise to pull it down if the SS tried to come back into town. The field artillery went on until an hour or more after dark. The SS had quit shooting at us. They were still milling around in the trees across the road.

'After doing my job on the ground I got back on my tank. The roof had fallen in on the house protecting me from at least one anti-tank gun. While trying to get my nerve up to try him one more time, I noticed that the one rifleman to my right was not an infantryman but was a tanker. This was Aaron C. Brown who had gotten out of Number Five tank and had picked up a rifle and came up where my tank was. Standing in the corner of the house, he picked off a number of SS when they moved from one tree to another. After more than an hour of field artillery, I got nervy and decided to try to get one more shot at the anti-tank gun. He knew what I would do and was waiting. If I had pulled out one more inch, he would have gotten my gun shield. Then I tried backing up again, but the space between the two houses was too wide. He would have gotten two shots at me. There were probably two of them anyway.

'After dark, I got my tank backed up to the disabled crews. I organised three tank crews ready to go at full strength. Together with the few infantry boys left alive, we set up our defence for the night. I called the field artillery again. I told them our position and said that I would tell them if the SS tried to re-enter the town, to shell the east half of the town. We had accomplished our mission. However, at dark there were a lot more men on the other side of the road than there were on our side, so every man pulled guard all night long. We got no information from anyone all day or that night. The medics finished what they could do by about 2 a.m. (too late for Harris).

'The next morning, the first thing we saw move was twelve or fifteen American tanks coming down the blacktop road from Edenhausen towards us like they were on a pleasure cruise going to Koblenz. When they stopped we found that everything movable in the woods had gone. There had been two anti-tank guns where Lieutenant Fuller was firing when he was hit. One was knocked out, I'm sure by Lieutenant Fuller. The other had been towed away. That morning we were informed that 3,200 SS troops were in the woods when we attacked. It scares me to think what might have been had we attacked down the blacktop that morning.'

Sergeant Otha Martin, from Leguire, Oklahoma, who was a tank commander in Byrl Rudd's platoon, also remembers the Pfaffenheck operation. 'It wasn't far to Pfaffenheck from this little village, maybe three kilometres. We moved across country abreast, not in column, and Number Three tank was the first one hit. I don't know if Number One or Number Two were hit next, but Number Three was hit first. It was in an orchard. We went through the little town, but the Germans had dug in on the road and had their guns camouflaged and they knocked out Number Three. And they cut Hayward's leg off below the knee, I remember him holding it and dragging it with him. He got out on the ground and they cut him down, they machine-gunned him on the ground. Bill Wolfe, the shell hit him somewhere in the midsection and he burned in the tank. He was dead. Hayward is on the ground dead. Wes Harrell, who was from Stonewall, Oklahoma and lives in Hobbs, New Mexico now, he was the driver. He got out. And the bow gunner was a little Chinese boy named Moy. Koon L. Moy. We called him Chop Chop. He got out. And the gunner was John Clingerman. He got out without a scratch. But then he got on Snuffy's tank. The reason I know that was the first tank hit is because Snuffy's tank wasn't hit yet. Clingerman got on it, and when it was hit he lost an eye. And it killed Jack Mantell. He was the loader in Snuffy's tank.

'In that crew, Carl Grey was the driver, a Mexican boy named

Guadalupe Valdivia from Topeka, Kansas was the bow gunner and he wasn't hurt. The gunner was Russell Loop. He lives at Indiana, Illinois, he's a farmer. Jack Mantell was the loader and he was killed. The shell came through the gun shield. Snuffy was the tank commander and lieutenant, the platoon leader. So that's One and Three. Now Number Two tank – which was my tank, but I was the gunner on Number Five tank that day – they put in a man fresh from Fort Knox named Russell Harris and he was one of those gung-ho type fellows. He told me the first time I saw him, "I'm not afraid of the damn Germans. They'll not make me pull my head in." I told him, "Harris. You're a fool. These people here, they're not necessarily afraid of the Germans, but they respect them. They're good soldiers. They'll kill you. If they shoot your head off you're done. But as long as you can stick your head back out and fight again, you're worth something." Well, that's just what he did. He never pulled his head in and they shot him in the head with a 40mm gun. There had been only four men to begin with in that tank. John Zimmer was supposed to be the loader, but he had gone to the medics back across the river and he wasn't there. The driver was Leroy Campbell from Meridien, Mississippi. The bow gunner was Lloyd Seal, but he had got up to be the loader in the turret in John's place. And the gunner was Clarence Rosen, he was from Ogilvie, Minnesota and one of the top-notch gunners too.

'Now that's three tanks gone. That just left Four and Five. I was in Five. Byrl Rudd was platoon sergeant and he was in Number Four tank. Well, the Germans had him hemmed in behind a house with a big dug-in gun up there, camouflaged. So he's hemmed in up there. That just left Number Five tank. And we were the only one that could move. The Germans tried all day to come back across the highway, but they never did get back. But I burned the barrel out of a .30-calibre air-cooled machine gun, we changed barrels. I never counted them but we stacked up a whole bunch of SS troops.

'Although we just had two tanks left, the next morning we moved out with three and I never knew where the third tank came from until the reunion at Niagara Falls [in 1987] and Snuffy Fuller was there. I said, "I've thought about this for a lot of years, I want to know where we got the third tank from." Snuffy said Sheppard got it from "A"

Company. And that answered that. But he came to me that day and said: "Say, do you want to be my gunner today?" I said: "I ain't put in no application for it but I will." So we put Loop over in Number Five and Rudd's tank was still intact. And we moved out with three tanks and moved down through the woods. The Germans had pulled out in the night, took their guns with them. And we pulled through the woods, out on point of a ridge and could look across the Rhine. That's the 16th day of March that the fight was in Pfaffenheck. Billy Wolfe was killed. Russell Harris was killed. Lloyd Hayward was killed and Jack Mantell was killed. And we lost three tanks.'

A RADIO BATTLE IN THE MARSHALLS GROUP

Whilst I was researching for a previous book about US tanks in the Second World War, I corresponded with Brigadier-General Robert L. Denig of Los Altos, California, late USMC, who commanded the 6th Tank Battalion during the Pacific War, and he sent me a lot of information about the battles in that theatre. Included was an account of earlier operations of two USMC tank companies on Roi and Namur Islands in the Marshalls Group in February 1944. What makes this account unique is the fact that he sent it to me still in the original radio conversations as broadcast by the tank commanders and logged by operators on board the USS *Biloxi*, standing offshore. The short extract concerns 'B' Company on Roi Island and the '*Dramatis Personae*' are as follows:

NAME & NICKNAME	APPOINTMENT	CALLSIGN	REMARKS
Captain James L. Dening (BOB)	CO 'B' Company	BLACKIE 1	KIA* on Roi
Lieutenant Roger Seasholtz	Executive Officer 'B' Company	BLACKIE 5	KIA Iwo
Lieutenant Jerome A. Krimbring (JERRY or CRANBERRY)	Platoon Leader, 1 Platoon	Not known; called JERRY	
Lieutenant Thomas M. Horn (HORN)	Platoon Leader, 3 Platoon	BUZZARD 1	

NAME & NICKNAME	APPOINTMENT	CALLSIGN	REMARKS
CWO Charles E. Essko (GUNNER)	Platoon Leader, 2 Platoon	BINGO 1	
Sergeant Ace Oliver (ACE)	Assistant Platoon Leader	BINGO 5	
Corporal R. Rottger (RUTGER)	Tank Commander		
Private first class Eugene McCurry (MCKERR)	Tank Commander		
Corporal Cecil McArthur (MACK)	Tank Commander		

* KIA: Killed In Action

The extract also shows how difficult it was to keep station and direction in thick jungle, and how hard to deal with an enemy who show no fear of tanks, despite having no armoured support of their own to assist them in this particular engagement.

Transmissions

Seasholtz to various platoon commanders
JERRY, this is BLACKIE 5 – move your platoon up to the right.
BUZZARD 1, this is BLACKIE 5 – move your platoon to the left.
BINGO 1, this is BLACKIE 5 – move up abreast of me GUNNER.

Dening to Seasholtz
BLACKIE 5, this is BLACKIE 1 – those infantrymen say there are Japs in a concrete blockhouse. Push to the right. That's it. That's what they told me. We can't do anything about it. Shells bounce off. Use flame-throwers through those cracks.

Seasholtz to 2nd Platoon
BINGO 1 – let's bear right now GUNNER.
GUNNER replies: we'll bear as much to the right as we can.

Seasholtz to 1, 2 & 3 Platoons
When we meet at the beach and start north, we'll line up again.

Sergeant Oliver to Corporal Rottger
RUTGER this is ACE – stand by me wherever I go. Christ, the flame-thrower won't work. Fine and dandy. goddamnit I rammed a tree! My gun either went through it or bent back double. Open up to our men. Open up your hatch.

Seasholz to Krimbring
JERRY – head to the beach. We'll have to start swinging left to get parallel to the GUNNER.

Essko to Krimbring
JERRY – I'm hemmed in, got ditches on all sides of me.
Krimbring replies: Back out and bear out to the left GUNNER. I'll back out with you.
Essko replies: OK. Hey, did you see that goddamned tracer go by me? That was too close for comfort. There he is in that hole. Give him a shot of 75mm. That'll get him out – pull your tank up and put the muzzle down the hole.
Krimbring replies: GUNNER, keep the vehicle ahead of you covered. Someone had a loaded cannister and some Japs jumped him.

. . .

Dening to all tanks
All vehicles concerned, there is a blockhouse to the right. Our troops are in it. I repeat, United States Marines, so be careful.

. . .

Horn to McKerr
MCKERR this is BUZZARD 1 – are you doing any good back there?
(No reply listed)
McArthur to Krimbring
JERRY this is MACK – somebody stopped while going and told me to get this goddamn tank back. We're in a hell of a place.

Oliver to ?
? this is ACE – cut to your left. I'm right over here by these here
stumps.
? – Roger
What's the trouble? Want me to come that way or stay here? Stay
there till I give you the word. I don't know where the infantry is.
Good work!

Horn to Essko
GUNNER – I want to stay over as far to the left of this road as I can
and you can stay as far to the right as you want.

Essko to Oliver
Are those our troops in front of your vehicle ACE?

3rd Plt tank comd to Horn
BUZZARD, this is BUZZARD 2 – are those our troops immediately
to the front about a hundred yards?
BUZZARD 1 – those are our troops ahead of us.
Yes, I know it.
Watch that bush to the left, they're in there pretty thick Roger!
Hey, see that dead Jap down there in front of my tank? Or is he? He's
got bushy hair.

Dening to Krimbring
JERRY – what's the holdup here? What's the holdup?
JERRY – this is BLACKIE 1. I've got eight Japs on my tank. I'll back
up to the beach and drown the bastards.
BLACKIE 1 – this is JERRY. Turn to my side of the road. There are
four black wooden boxes. Inside them are bombs. Don't fire at the
. . . Hold fast where you are. I'll pick those Japs off one at a time.
(Machine-gun fire.)

8

Casualty

Experience in the First World War had shown that some 5 per cent to 20 per cent of all those troops involved in action would be killed or wounded, with the ratio between the two being one in four killed. In addition it was estimated that probable number of sick daily would be some 0.3 per cent of the total number of troops involved, although this figure was known to vary considerably from theatre to theatre. All these casualties had to be dealt with by the 'chain of evacuation', which for most armies was divided into three zones: first was the collecting zone, containing the regimental aid posts (RAP), tented field ambulances and motor ambulances; next came the evacuating zone, containing casualty clearing stations, ambulance trains and barges; finally there was the distributing zone, containing general hospitals, convalescent depots and camps and hospital ships. In the Second World War, although the military casualties were not as high, the general evacuation chain was still approximately the same, except that as the warfare was on the whole more mobile, casualty clearing posts (CCP) or their equivalents, equipped with a light ambulance and a couple of trucks, would be established between RAPs and the advanced dressing stations (ADS) which were normally tented. Almost everywhere the speed and efficiency of medical units improved. In the Soviet system, for example, by 1942 all field medical units were accompanied by mobile surgical and ophthalmic teams, whilst the German medical companies had special motorised units. The US Army system was probably the best of all, there being more medical personnel in most divisions than any other support service. It was normal policy to treat patients in theatre wherever possible before evacuation to the USA, the laid down time limits being ninety days for the South-West Pacific, South Pacific and North Africa (due to the lack of hospital facilities); 180 days for Europe and all other theatres, which was later reduced to 120 days.

In an article headed 'Wounded at Tobruk', published in the German military propaganda magazine *Signal* in November 1941, the writer commented:

> The care of the wounded in positional warfare such as this is, naturally functions without friction. The hospital tents lie not far beyond the range of the British guns. They are equipped with all the installations for first aid and are fitted with double and triple walls to keep out the sandstorms. The planes which convey the wounded to the hospitals in the towns start and land quite close to them. The names of the doctors are famous in Germany. University professors are among them. They are helped by nurses who have been carrying out their strenuous duties for months on end in the unaccustomed climate. They are worshipped by the soldiers.

Without doubt the achievements of the Allied medical services in the Far East, in the evacuation and treatment of the sick and wounded and in the prevention of such crippling diseases as malaria, were a major factor in the successful outcome of the campaign. Casualty evacuation by air proved a tremendous boon. Before facilities were improved, a casualty could be involved in a journey lasting five or six days with many changes of transport *en route*. The HMSO booklet on the campaign gave an example of a casualty who was: '. . . treated at the RAP he was sent off on a stretcher to the Advanced Dressing Station 17½ hours march away. The Naga stretcher-bearers cut steps in the hillside, squeezed through the jungle and slung him over a river with rope and pulley. At the ADS they operated on him and gave him a blood transfusion. The next two days he spent being borne on a litter to a place where medical jeeps could come. From there he travelled down a bumpy track to the Medical Dressing Station and Field

Hospital, he made the last stage of his journey by air to India and con-valescence.'

FLESH WOUNDS

'The only time I got hit with a bullet was right across the back of the hand,' said Lieutenant Snuffy Fuller of the US 712th Tank Battalion. 'I had my hand on top of the ring and we were coming over this hill and a bunch of Germans were dug in in front of us. One of them fired a *panzerfaust* and hit my tank right in the front end on the differential casing. It didn't do no damage, it punched a hole in it and we lost the oil, but it didn't disable the tank. So we stayed where we were and we were firing at these birds, they were dug in in small trenches. But the only *panzerfaust* they had was the one I got. The rest of it was machine-gun fire. So this one German bastard, he'd pull up out of his trench and fire a burst and duck down. And I'd get a shot at him. Well, finally I won. I got him. In the meantime I got stitched across the hand. And there wouldn't have been nothing to it, except I'd been wearing a pair of leather gloves with rabbit fur lining. And when that bullet hit, it drove the fur into the hand. Well, I didn't think nothing of it until about three days later my hand got about that big, I had to go to the vets – the vets, I had to go to the medics, and they cut it open and cleaned it out. That's the only bad injury I got all during the war. Shrapnel was nothing. I got it once in my shoulder and once in my arm.'

PERSONAL FIRST AID

'Cocke and I decided to return and see what had happened to the rest of our force. We again drew fire while we were proceeding across the flat and his tank was hit and burned but everyone escaped without injury. There were no tanks in the olive grove when we reached it but they had all pulled back to the vicinity of Tebourba, many of them having taken shelter in and around the buildings. Some shells were coming in and most everyone had taken cover.' That is how Colonel

Henry E. Gardiner of Bozeman, Montana, who served with 1st US Armored Division in North Africa, began a graphic account of being wounded near Tebourba, when he was the executive officer of the 2nd Battalion, 13th Armored Regiment. They were lucky initially, but not for long, as he explains: 'After some difficulty I got them out of the various positions they had taken and deployed them into line and we started out over the broad hill between Tebourba and the enemy. We drew some fire. As tanks began to appear in the distance I ordered ours to fire on them. Our tanks showed a hesitancy to advance and a movement forward was largely accomplished by my moving ahead fifty or one hundred yards and then their coming up parallel to me. On one such move I suddenly discovered a German tank below me at a distance of about three hundred yards. Since I had used up all my 75, I ordered my 37 gunner to fire an AP and he scored a direct with the first shot. Had him put in another and then the crew started to crawl out and run away from it, whereupon I ordered him to cut loose with his machine gun. This caused them to turn around and run back so as to secure the protection of their tank.

'Just then we were hit. There was a blinding flash in the tank, a scream, and I realised I had been hurt. I jumped out of the tank and ran back a short distance and crouched. There had been seven of us in the tank and I saw four get out. Other shells aimed at my tank started coming in, so I moved to one side so as to be out of the line of fire and walked on down the draw where I took stock of my injury. There was a cut in my left elbow that didn't amount to much and a slight one on my right wrist. The one on my elbow was bleeding quite freely so I got out my First Aid kit, put some powder on it and tried to bandage it. Felt very weak and that I was going to faint. Must have been the combination of fatigue and loss of blood. A tank was going by at that time and I hailed it and the tank commander got out and helped me fix the bandage on my elbow. Then I swallowed some sulphanilamide pills we carried. That was quite a job as I didn't have a canteen. Feeling all right and the enemy fire having slackened off, I went back up on the crest of the hill to take stock of the situation. When my tank had been hit, the others had halted and backed up a short distance but they appeared well deployed and in a position to handle anything that might approach from the front. . . .

'A report came back that someone could hear voices calling from my tank. I went up to investigate. Looked in and could see two dead men. They were the radio operator and the 75mm gunner. Was just about to climb in to recover my helmet and pistol when apparently the enemy saw me and started to shell the place so I beat it. The hit that had knocked us out was on the right front and from the hole it looked like an 88mm. During the shelling, one other tank that was in the group strung along the hill was hit and burned.'

'IN THE SYSTEM'

Peter 'Cosy' Comfort, whose early days in the 13th/18th Hussars we covered in Chapter 2, was wounded during Operation Goodwood, as he remembered: 'This was no picnic area. Operation Goodwood started well before dawn. Here they come. Hundreds of planes, two-engined bombers, large stars of identification, carpet-bombing before us. Twenty Boche infantry, hands on heads, advance towards our tank; I wave my revolver. "To the rear, you bastards." Too late, their own mortars have revenge right amongst them. A Bren-gun carrier is also alongside the tank; I don't believe it; Maurice Orchard sits behind the machine gun; he too comes from Deal, a school friend now in the Middlesex; we wave, grin and part. The radio crackles; tank at 11 o'clock, "A" Squadron I think, in trouble; battery. We run alongside and who's getting out? Guess! They have our range, the terrain's flat and open; mortars, Spandaus, this is the highlife of a kettledrum. The engine of the Sherman roars, co-driver disappears, dive headfirst into the turret but my right leg is still stuck out. A burning sensation; feel sick, sticky in clothes; no, not what you think; it's my leg; that last mortar was a hit.

'Nine hours later, darkness; a peep under the field dressing; it throbs; shrapnel in calf and the knee; someone says, "Got your small release, Cosy?" First Aid post at 6 o'clock five hundred yards, another dressing, this time near the ankle; orderly gives me the metal bit for keeps and ties a label to my tank suit; I was "in the system". Fifteen-hundredweight truck to field ambulance, the marquee, dim lights, wounded everywhere on stretchers. My neighbour is very, very silent, doped; bleary-eyed medics; another two dressings; ambulance; few words spoken. "Always label first", that sticks in the mind and I obeyed them. The beach, tank landing craft, tank deck is now a hospital full of wounded, some Boche, all on stretchers; no food. "Sorry, mate, forbidden."

'Southampton, Basingstoke General Hospital, a bed, first for months, clean sheets; kind nurses; grey, tired doctors in pairs. Red Cross train to the north, hospital near Widnes; Sid Beasley would know. Three months; report to Catterick on draft for Burma with other tankies; 4/7 Dragoons, RTR, other 3 and 8ths. "Where the hell are you lot going?" a passing Lilywhite captain spotted us. "You're not, y'know!" The longest road and saved by the bell. The Regiment has spoken and claims its sons.'

A HONEY VERSUS THE HIGH COMMAND

'It was during the battles of the Gothic Line in Italy,' reminisced John Walker, late of 48 RTR and now Chairman of the 48th RTR Association. 'Our Brigade, the 21st Independent Tank Brigade, were taking a hammering, working with the Canadians. Recce Troop were buzzing around all over the place during various jobs. During one particular action, two turretless Honeys were waiting at the Regimental Command Post which also served as the RAP, bringing back wounded men, our own men, Canadians and some Germans also. The position was getting quite packed with casualties, many to be taken back to the Advanced Hospital, our MASH unit of the day. Unfortunately, no ambulances could get through owing to the accuracy of the German artillery. So our MO, Captain Paddy O'Flynn, ordered me to lay two stretcher cases over the back of my Honey, put two "walking wounded" inside and get them back out of range of the guns. Off I went, with no Red Cross cover, just a Honey on a mission.

'The way to the rear meant crossing open country through to the main road, threading our way through the New Zealand Brigade, waiting to "Go in". Now, as we all know, going forward into the line meant conforming to a strict rule of the road. Every movement was controlled by the clock, nobody advanced faster than the specified time laid down and each column of tanks, guns, vehicles of every type, never broke this rule. In any case you couldn't pull off the road, all the edges were heavily mined, these being left behind by the retreating Germans. The side of the road leading away from the front, this had to be left open for vehicles, particularly ambulances carrying wounded men away from the battlefield.

'So off we went, passing the Kiwis, idly watching us go by. Suddenly in the distance I saw a cloud of dust approaching, breaking all the rules. This vehicle was obviously on an important mission and as it got nearer, I saw it was a Humber staff car. It must have "Top Brass" on board, who else would do such a thing. I kept going and as the Humber drew closer, my driver Johnnie Brerton looked enquiringly over his shoulder at me. "Keep going," I yelled at him, and eventually we both came to a halt, nose to nose. One of the red-braided officers in the back jumped up and glowered at this impertinent Honey blocking his progress. I swear to this day that it was none other than the Commander-in-Chief of the Eighth Army, Lieutenant-General Sir Richard McCreery, although I had never seen the man before, only in pictures in the Eighth Army magazine.

'Preparing for the worst, I sprang to attention, as well as one could in a crowded Honey, unshaven, covered in a few days' grime, saluted and called across, "I've got wounded men on board, sir." With no more ado, he tapped his driver smartly on the shoulder and said, "Back Up." And back up he did, for at least the lengths of half-a-dozen vehicles, before he found room to squeeze in out of my way. Now all this time, the Kiwis were sitting on their vehicles variously watching this little drama unfold. The Kiwis were excellent soldiers and good blokes to be with, but DISCIPLINE, I doubt if they knew how to spell the word. When they saw my Honey pushing a staff car backwards down the road this was too good to miss and I was cheered all the way, with such calls as, "Good boy, Corp, you show them" and shouts of encouragement. Stony faced, but to his credit, the General never said a word, just helping to guide his car out of the way. With a sigh of relief I edged past, saluted the General again and continued on my way.

Johnnie Brerton and I had many a chuckle over this incident. I wonder if the General ever did?'

ON FIRE, BUT A LUCKY ESCAPE

'I was in the platoon,' recalled Grayson La Mar, during the Orlando reunion of the 712th US Tank Battalion in 1993. 'Holmes was the platoon leader. We were on top of this field, we were taking orders from a 90th Infantry Division lieutenant and we didn't run into anything. So we were supposed to take up positions the next morning, and since we didn't run into anything he wanted to go down to the bottom of the hill, in the valley and stay down there. So by daybreak, just all of a sudden all hell broke loose. We had four tanks and a tank destroyer. They threw a shell into the tank destroyer, killed all of them. And one boy we could see, they broke his leg or something, he just tried to climb out, then they threw another round in there and finished him off. Then they got the second tank, I believe it was. So when they got that, that left three tanks. Sergeant Gibson, he didn't know what the rest were gonna do, but he's gonna get the hell out of there and he's the only one that got out. When he left, Holmes followed him; I automatically backed up and followed Holmes. When I got to the top of the hill, his tank was sitting in the middle of the road burning. I couldn't get around, so I had to go off into the field and when I did my back end blew up. The shell came in there and that set me on fire.

'It took three tries to get the hatch open. See, the hatch would hit the gun barrel. The gunner was killed and nobody could operate the gun to get the barrel out of the way. Finally on the third try, I slipped by. If the gun was over a quarter-inch more I'd never have got out. The concussion of the shell blew my helmet off. When I got out, there were blazes all around and I had to keep my eyes shut, so naturally I was in the dark. The tank commander, he was hanging over the side, he said, "Help me." He got his heel blown off.

'I dragged him off into the snow and I just fell in too, about ten inches of snow. I drove my head into the snow. And Holmes, he was just laying out in the field. A jeep came up there and got him and got

197

me and the other guy. Carried us back to some kind of a cave or something, a tent or some kind of a cave. They put some powder on us. Then Holmes got into an ambulance and went back to a field hospital or something and they put stuff on us, it smelled like axle grease, they put that all over our heads where we were burnt. They put him into one ambulance and me into another. I remember them giving me a carton of cigarettes. He says, "Take these. It might be a long time before you get one."

'So they got me in hospital, they put me in a chair, kinda like a barber's chair, I remember that and put some more of that stuff and done me up like a mummy, just wrapped gauze all over my head and I wore them for eighteen days, they just cut holes for my nose and mouth and eyes. Got a shot every four hours, man, I never saw so many needles in my life. Stayed in bed and stayed there for eighteen days. When they took it off, it was just as though you had stuck your head in some ice water. A lot of skin came off. I didn't have no beard or eyelashes or nothing. In fact, I can wash my face now with a rough washrag and roll the skin up on my face, it's just been that way ever since. When I wash I don't bear down, I just rub lightly. It makes my face raw to rub it hard.

'But I had orders there to go by some bivouac area and pick up another tank, and they showed me where to go to find my platoon, I didn't even go back to the company, I went on back out on line. Right from the hospital.'

A SPECIAL CAKE

David Ling, whose graphic account of being knocked out was included under 'First Actions', needed medical attention afterwards as he explains: 'After my accident, the gun got three more tanks in quick succession. Stump turned the squadron into line ahead and moved away to the right and as more trouble was encountered the attack was called off. This was reported to me whilst I paused to collect my wits and my strength and thank God I did not have to climb into that tank, for today, anyway, it was all over. Instead, sitting on the engine louvres with my back resting against the turret, I was taken away on Bleadon's tank to Doc Macaulay, our strangely eccentric but lovable and brave MO. His RAP was snugly below the high, bullet-swept Belhamed feature and there, dimly aware of others around me and my eyes quite unseeing, I waited and shivered. I remember Peter Pike of the New Zealanders, shocked at seeing my condition, came over and chatted happily. He was a big bespectacled fellow whom I got to know well during our long training together.

'In spite of the high desert sun and the thickness that swaddled me, I felt cold – icy penetrating cold. I was most uncomfortable and said as much more than once and at each repetition by me further blankets were thrown around till, with seven of them, I had become almost buried and was yet still cold. The blood of Trooper Bucket soaked over me and caked my face, my neck and hands. Passing my hands over my face I found my moustache, eyebrows and eyelashes had gone – seared off. The hair that showed below my stained black beret was burnt into an acrid, crumbling crust that broke away, denuding me as I touched it. They say my face was a pleasant olive green and so enthused was Doc Macaulay at seeing what he later told me was a perfect, orthodox illustration of severe shock that I suspect he lost no time in pointing this out and lecturing his orderlies and all and sundry he could find, before the effects were neutralised by the returning red.

'I lay in the darkened centre of our tank leaguer now mostly composed of crocks – holed in action but capable of limping home under their own steam. I felt cool and comfortable. My eyes smarted but the pain had been considerbly eased by Doc who had inserted little cocaine pills in my eyelids. I don't think I had any special reactions or emotions except a feeling of anger at being a crock and unable to take part in further action for a time. The ambulance door opened and a cheery voice, unmistakably New Zealand, said: "Here you are, Sir. I brought you a cake. They told me you had caught one, so I took the cake from the NAAFI truck as I thought you would like it." Indeed I would and I thanked profusely the voice which I recognised as the NAAFI truck's attendant. I met him two days before, gaily dishing out twopenny Cadburys and Mars bars to the NZ forces and not half a mile from the fighting, unaware of the drama about him and his incongruity. I had asked for some and, although it's against the rules, he said, he handed me down the chocolate. The cake with roasted almonds atop had a rich moist feel, and its segments the limpet touch of sliced raisins.'

ANOTHER LUCKY ESCAPE

Trooper T. A. Bright, a tank driver in 51 RTR, had a lucky escape during the El Alamein battle of October 1942, after having been 'fairly lifted off the seat by a thousand guns which opened up together and started the battle'. He continued: 'We had brewed up a cup of tea and while we were drinking it an order came through that I had to get ready to move up for a recce of the ground in front of us, as we were going to move forward in an attack that night and wanted to see what opposition we had in front of us. I had a tin mug of tea which I covered with a 75mm shell cap to keep the dust out and put it on the side of the switch panel with my watch as I had broken the strap earlier, and that was the last I saw of them. I was told to move up to the ridge in front and stop there for a few minutes for the officer in charge to get his bearings; then I was told to advance over the ridge and move down the other side into no man's land. We had gone about three hundred yards forward when there was a hell of a bang and the periscope I was looking through vanished and it all went blank.

'After a few seconds which seemed like hours we acted and came to the conclusion that we had been hit by an 88mm shell. The engine had stopped and there was a smell of burning and I found that we were brewing up. I tried to start the engine but it was dead. The intercom system had gone dead so we bailed out. My front gunner in the meantime was getting out so I opened the front cover and got out damn quick. I hit the sand pretty quickly and looked around to get my bearings. I saw a slit trench just to the right of the tank and jumped in – right on top of the front gunner who was already there. It seemed that he had been hit with a lot of shrapnel in his back, but he could move all right. The turret gunner was slightly wounded and the officer was also hit. We found out later that he lost an eye and had shell wounds but not too badly.

'After a few minutes things quietened down and we saw that we were about three hundred yards in front of our positions. A Red Cross armoured car advanced towards us and picked up the officer and sped back to our lines. We managed to walk back. I helped the front gunner and we got over the ridge and sat behind another tank and began to wonder what had hit us. The rest of the crew were transported back by Red Cross ambulances to hospital, while I waited for a truck to take me back to base camp. There were quite a few men from different units who were being sorted out.'

Bright went back into action and was later posted to 46 RTR in Italy. While he was serving there, driving a truck, he had the misfortune to run over an infantry soldier at night in the pitch dark, as he explains: 'It was in this wood that I ran over one of our infantrymen one night. It was pitch black and we were trying to manoeuvre back into a holding position (after being held up by a few 88mm guns) when I ran over the soldier. It was very wet and muddy and the truck squashed his legs into the mud and badly bruised them. They said there was nothing broken and that he would recover all right with time.'

SHELLSHOCK AND BATTLE FATIGUE

'We had one little fellow,' recalled Lieutenant Snuffy Fuller, 'I don't know his name any more, we were in the woods and we were getting artillery pasting the shit right out of us, and he went nuts, screaming and hollering, just went crazy. We threatened to shoot him and every-thing else, it didn't bother him. We sent him back. He got out of the tank and was running around, there was more chance of him getting killed that way than staying in the tank. This was an enlisted man and he was in one of my tanks.'

'We were on the Saar River and the Germans were across the river, in the high ground,' said Jim Gifford of the 712th Tank Battalion; 'they were in a wood over there. We were in an orchard on this side. We had our tanks dispersed. We were getting shelled real bad and the ground all around us was blowing up all over the place. It was dusty, just like going across the desert. When they start shelling, the shells explode on the ground and all that dirt turns to dust. If they do enough of it you get a hell of a dust cloud going. The periscope was up and I'm looking around, because we're all buttoned up. When you're moving you open the turrets because a mine will kill you if you're inside. So we'd close the hatches when we were in a standing position and let 'em shoot, we don't give a damn, those shells used to hit the side of the tank and rock the tank but never bothered us inside, because it was high explosive and not armour-piercing.

'So I'm looking out of the periscope and, Geez, I see this turret hatch suddenly come up in the middle of all this dust and this lieutenant comes flying up out of it, lands on the back, jumps down into the dust, and he runs off, out of sight towards the road. I didn't know, I figured he had some good reason, maybe somebody's hurt in the tank, I mean, I never questioned it. But it turned out that he – I don't like to use that word – he just blew his cool and they found him about three miles up the road in a farmhouse in the cellar. We went down in the cellar and he was there in a corner, crouched in a corner. The guy was a brave man. Prior to all that we had no problems with him at all. But I guess there's a breaking point.'

MAN'S BEST FRIEND

'One evening a soldier was shot in the shoulder, so he started to walk back to the rear to the aid station, but he became lost in the darkness. Finally he crawled into an abandoned foxhole to wait for morning. A short time later he heard a noise and was ready to shoot, when he saw that the noise was made by a little dog. The friendly mongrel jumped into the foxhole and curled up beside the boy, where he stayed all night long. The next morning, after daylight, the soldier started off again in what he thought was the right direction, but the little dog tugged at his legs and made quite a scene, apparently trying to get the boy to go in the opposite direction. This the boy finally did. As it turned out, the dog led him back to the American lines. Had he kept on in the direction he had selected, he would have walked into the German lines, to death or some wretched prison camp. After we had dressed the soldier's wounds and laid him on a stretcher, the little dog jumped up on the boy's abdomen, lay down and would not leave. Since the soldier had formed a strong attachment for his benefactor and did not want to leave him, we loaded the stretcher – soldier, dog and all – into the ambulance and sent them on their way to the hospital.'[1]

DEATH

When asked if he could remember Billy Wolfe who was one of the young soldiers killed in action, Lieutenant Fuller replied, 'Hardly nothing because he was so quiet, just a little farmboy, had nothing to say. He wasn't there long enough to really get acquainted with anybody. How long did he last – about a month? He was in Sergeant Hayward's tank. I went in the next morning to try to find any dogtags or something and there was absolutely nothing in that tank. I guess I was hard-hearted by then – I didn't have any feelings at all. I was just looking to see if I could find the dogtags to prove that he had died and all there were were just little bits of bones maybe an inch-and-a-half, two inches. Because once the gasoline went off and them shells, there's nothing much you can do. There was no smell inside the tank – like some of them after they had been dead for a while there, a sweet smell they called it, no, there was no odour whatsoever. The fire must have consumed everything completely – it was just gutted, all the wiring was completely burnt and there was nothing left.'

SELF-INFLICTED WOUND?

'I was on guard on this particular night with another chap, after we had got back from France with the remnants of the BEF,' recalled J. Ellison of 43 RTR, 'up and down the lines of vehicles, when we were approached by another chap from our regiment. We asked him what he was doing in the vehicle lines as no one was allowed there except the guard. Well, he started to tell us about his wife expecting a baby and that he could not get any leave unless he was sick; so he asked me and my mate if we would break his arm for him so that he could get some sick leave and be able to get home to see his wife. We told him to b.....-off and not be so stupid and go back to his billet and we carried on with our guard duty.

'The next morning I had to go to the hospital in the town for a medical as I was on a draft to go abroad. To my surprise, who did I see in the queue with his arm in plaster? Yes! None other than the chap who had asked us to break his arm. I asked him who he had got to break his arm. He replied: "No one you cheeky b.....' He explained that when he left us that night to go back to his billet, he turned round to look at somebody at the top of the vehicle lines and fell into a slit trench and that is how he broke his arm. I was told that he was sent on leave but I never saw him again as I was sent to the Middle East.'

WORST EXPERIENCE

Captain Ted Player's worst experience was on 31 May 1942, having just reinforced the 150 Brigade 'Box' in the Western Desert. 'Ginger Richings, one of my fellow troop commanders, found a newly dug weapon pit four feet deep, over which his Matilda fitted perfectly. He invited me into this improvised bunker for a break and a smoke. His tank was a recent replacement painted a uniform light sand colour and conspicuously different from the shabby camouflage of the rest. It attracted the attention of the German gunners, who dropped several (75mm?) shells nearby. We felt secure and paid little attention. Suddenly the side of the pit blew in with a huge explosion and a blinding cloud of dust. I felt a blow on the head and was sure I was dead. It is difficult to differentiate between this event in the 150 Brigade Box, being bombed by the US Eighth Air Force whilst a prisoner of war in Oflag 79, Brunswick on 24 August 1944 and dealing with a hat-trick of three successive misfires – cap struck – in the course of a shoot with a 95mm HE at Lulworth post-war in 1947.

'I scrambled out and managed to reach one of the nearby tanks where they patched me up with a first field dressing and loaded me onto a truck *en route* to the ADS. Ginger was loaded after me. Even then I knew he was dead. And the next day, 1 June 1942, the 150 Brigade Box was finally overrun and I became a prisoner of war.

CIVILIAN CASUALTIES

Sergeant Ron Huggins' regiment, the 10th Royal Hussars, fought in France in 1940 as part of the BEF and witnessed, on more than one occasion, the *Luftwaffe* deliberately attacking civilian refugees, presumably to hinder the Allied forces. 'The Regiment continued its forced march to the Somme front and passed through Aumale *en route*. The town was burning as the *Luftwaffe* had attacked that too, possibly thinking that the Regiment might be sheltering there. Outside the town, a tightly packed column of French civilian refugees had been bombed and machine-gunned. It was a shocking sight, with dead men, women and children and their horses lying in the road. We had to mount grass verges to get past.'

And the animals

'Am writing this beneath the tank, in a hole, with mortars falling uncomfortably close,' so wrote Sergeant Richard Greenwood in his diary; 'we are quite exposed in large field of long grass. Many cows around . . . dead . . . vile smell. These cattle are terribly mutilated. A few wounded cows round about . . . gaping holes in their bodies etc. Terribly depressing sight. We ought to shoot them. Heavy smell of foul flesh in 1st night's harbour doesn't improve matters. But nothing really matters there: except a deep hole for cover. Meals today have been hasty snacks prepared in between mortaring; a hell of a business. Have filled two flasks with tea for supper. Will be very welcome in our hole later on.'

TUTTI FRATELLI – ALL MEN ARE BROTHERS

The badge of the Red Cross reached across frontiers and showed no distinction between enemies on the battlefield – Medical Officers treating the sick and wounded of the enemy should the situation require it. Lance-Corporal Sidney Beasley of the 13th/18th Hussars recalled what he said was an 'amazing occurrence' in some thick pine woods in Germany towards the end of the war: 'both Sergeant Charlie Rattle and Corporal Reggie Binns were wounded; by this time I was a Lance-Corporal and following behind them as crew-commander of a 17-pounder tank in pretty thick pine woods. We were moving in single file, I think because of the thickness of the woods. I heard the crack of gunfire and saw chaps baling out in front of me and at that very moment my tank just sank into a trench system and ended up well and truly stuck at an angle of forty-five degrees, so my crew and I went forward to help the wounded. I remember Shuttleworth, Charlie's driver, had a facial wound but could walk. Charlie was minus a boot and had an injury to his heel but could hop along a bit. Reggie Binns had collected some shrapnel in his chest but his was not serious. As we slowly made our way back we passed the Squadron Leader's tank at some point, I believe, but I cannot clearly remember that. What I do remember was an amazing occurrence: a German Medical Officer and a soldier carrying a black box with a large red cross came across a field and joined us. I drew my revolver but the officer spoke perfect English and told me that he only wanted to find a building or shelter in which to set up a medical post to treat all soldiers no matter where they came from. Charlie and I accepted this and our now enlarged group went slowly on until we came to a farmhouse. On arrival there the MO stripped off his jacket and whilst he was washing his hands, shouted "*Essen!*", I think it was and the lady of the house held a piece of black-looking bread for him to eat. From then on he was the organiser and in control in that house which quickly filled up with the wounded, mostly Welshmen. After I'd seen him attend to Charlie – the doctor told him it was only a flesh wound, but I think myself it turned out to be a bit more serious than that – I left. . . . On reflection I remember the Medical Officer saying, as we walked along together, "I am sure the war is lost for us now. We have not eaten for two days." He must have decided to give up. Whatever it was he made a great impression on me, he was obviously a leader and a fine figure of a man. I wish him well.'

BACK TO THE 'ZI'

'I spent just over forty-eight hours in the 38th Evacuation Hospital. When I awakened the first morning I found that the daylight hurt my eye. A cataract had formed in my right eye and, except for an awareness of a light held a few feet in front of my eye, the vision was gone.' That is how Private William G. Haemmel began this chapter in the diary of his wartime years as a tank gunner with the US 1st Armored Division. 'The 38th "Evac",' he continued, 'was one of a number of hospitals which made up "Hell's Half Acre", so named by the GIs early in the Anzio fighting because of the pounding the hospitals received and the casualties suffered. The hospitals were under canvas and marked with large red crosses in white circles. While the Germans generally respected the Red Cross-marked medical aid-men on the front lines, the hospital area was under shell fire and bomb attack from February through May. In February several nurses were killed and later VI Corps' chief surgeon was killed. Along with other non-combatant units usually located in safe areas and only occasionally under bomb attack, the hospitals were jammed into an area devoted to supply dumps and artillery positions and German shells often landed among the patients and hospital personnel. The hospitals dug several feet into the ground and raised sandbag walls around the tents to limit the effect of shell fragments, but the canvas was the only overhead cover and many a combat soldier preferred his covered dug-out on the front line to the exposed tent city of Hell's Half Acre. Very few shells fell on the hospital area during my time with the 38th. The Germans' preoccupation with the Allied advance eliminated the danger of being shelled almost entirely.'

Bill Haemmel had all his meals brought to him in the tent, preferring the dim light inside to the bright sunshine outside which hurt his eyes. After being inspected by a doctor, he was told that he had been earmarked to go to Naples and that he should get ready to leave. As he explains, this was an easy thing to do: 'I had walked away from the front with only the clothes on my back and my side arms, and these had been removed on my arrival. I had retained my diary and had been given a piece of soap and a toothbrush. Accordingly I was "packed" as soon as I had picked up these three items and I was ready to move out in one second flat. A number of "walking wounded" were loaded into several ambulances. After an hour-and-a-half of waiting at the ambulance we loaded and drove to the airport in the south-west corner of what had been the beach-head and we were airborne in short order. . . . We completed the flight in thirty-five minutes and after an ambulance drive through Naples arrived at the 21st General Hospital. The admission procedures moved rapidly and I was checked by a doctor, examined by X-Ray and sent to EENT Ward 8 in Hut 3. We had a light meal in the Ward and retired at 9.30 p.m.'

Bill reached the 21st General Hospital on 27 May and three days later was visited by a clerk from the base section at Naples. He told Haemmel that he had not been reported as a casualty because he hadn't been through the 3rd Battalion Aid Station and, as he had literally 'disappeared', had been reported as missing in action. Fortunately this information was not sent immediately to his next of kin (his mother), so that it was not until 13 June that his mother received the following telegram: 'Regret to inform you your son Private William G. Haemmel was on twenty-four May slightly wounded in action in Italy. You will be advised as reports of condition are received.'

After some weeks in the 21st General, Bill Haemmel received the unexpected news that he was to be sent home to the USA – 'I was going to the "ZI" – Zone of the Interior!' Just before receiving this stupendous news he had been decorated with the Purple Heart, the medal presented to all GIs who are wounded in action: 'At noon on 3 June several of us stood at attention while a lieutenant-colonel pinned the Purple Heart to our bathrobes. I mailed my medal home.

'At noon we went aboard the US Army Hospital Ship *Acadia*. A happier, more excited and boisterous group of passengers never had existed! The laughter, joking and general good feeling were widespread. Each man, regardless of his personal condition, regarded himself as doubly blessed; his condition could have been worse or someone else could have been sent home. Certainly a "white boat" is a dreadful thing to contemplate: a ship full of young men returning from war crippled and maimed, wounded and hurt, broken and torn. But if the physical man was less than complete, the spiritual man was more than whole aboard *Acadia* that mid-point in 1944. We settled in E Forward very quickly and replaced the ODs issued at the hospital with the patient's garb. The doctor who helped us get settled assured us we were bound for the States and a member of the ship's crew told us we would land at Charleston, South Carolina. The *Acadia* cast off at 4 p.m. and we remained on deck to watch the beautiful harbour of Naples disappear, going below only for chow at 5 p.m. At 8 p.m. we were ordered below.

'Several hundred men occupied the double-bunked spaciousness of E Forward. We ate at 8 a.m., noon and 5 p.m. and we had fresh milk, the first since leaving the States. The nurses were young, pretty and almost always cheerful and smiling. Miss Clarke was on duty at night and Miss Marsha by day. Some of the patients had to line up to received medications or dressings and many a soldier joined the line just to share the attention of the girl if only for a brief minute before the quick eye of the nurse detected the fraud who stood before her. Both girls were repeatedly told how lovely and winning they were, how the soldier pined for them and would welcome a smile, or a wink, a hug or a kiss. While such attention from a couple of hundred men must have been wearing, both girls uniformly retained their good humour and poise.

'The weather was perfect and we had sunshine almost every day. The ship travelled with all its lights on and large red crosses were visible on both sides. We crossed the Gulf Stream, moving through floating seaweeds of various colours for three days. The surface of the ocean was like a mirror. . . . The *Acadia* made a fast, twelve-day trip of five thousand miles. We saw the dim outline of Spain the third night out but missed the lights of neutral Spain near Gibraltar. The passage was a period of extreme happiness for the passengers. . . . The rush to the ship's railing was brought on by a soldier spotting a coastal boat shortly after noontime on 4 July. We lined the bow and kept watch after that, for the ship's best run had been twelve days and this was the twelfth day. The day was cloudy and overcast, but the spirits of those on board were bright and happy. I was the first one in our immediate group to spot land in the form of a spire. A low black haze thickened and solidified into home – the USA! . . .

'We went to bed with mixed emotions: thanksgiving at being home, relief at the realisation of our dreams of being State-side again, anxiety for tomorrow and damnation for the Army port authorities at Charleston (because they had prevented disembarkation until the following day). Several soldiers expressed bitterness at the prospect that perhaps the Army port people were simply taking the national holiday off, while the men on the front lines in France and Italy were not observing the holiday.'

Bill Haemmel would go ashore the following day. He would spend a further six months in hospital before he completely recovered his sight and would not leave the 'ZI' again during the remainder of his Army service.

9

Prisoners of War

'I was wounded and captured on Easter Sunday,' recalled Wayne Hissong of the 712th US Tank Battalion; 'we were taking the trucks to get some gas, and we came up a little knoll in the road and there was a pocket of Germans. We never dreamed they would be there. And they hit us. Arnold Marshall and I were in the lead truck and a bazooka came right through the truck. Fragments from it hit me in my arms and I was knocked out of the truck. Mutt – Mel Paul – was right behind and when I fell out of the truck, his truck stopped on my ankle. I hollered, "Mutt! Move the truck!" And luckily he moved it enough that I could get out from underneath it. Marshall and I, we laid in a ditch there. I was hit, and Marshall luckily he didn't get hit. The Germans put me up on this horse-drawn artillery. I had to help myself up. I could hardly get up. I crawled up behind the horses to get up on this seat, and they took Marshall down the road. They had searched all my pockets and everything, took everything and I had a P38 shoulder holster. Luckily I threw the P38 away, but I still had the holster. And I had a German pocket knife that they didn't find. When we were going up the road, I showed it to the driver and he said, "Ach, keep it."

'When we got to this little burg, they dropped me off and took Marshall on. They put me out in a barn and there were two other fellows from another outfit. I don't know what outfit they were out of. The guy that owned the building, he could talk a little English and the only thing he asked was that we didn't smoke, as we could set the barn on fire. The next morning, they carried us into the house. In the meantime, one fellow had died during the night. So they carried this other fellow, he had been shot through the knee, and they made stretchers and carried us into the house and laid us down on the floor, and there was a German soldier in the corner to guard us. About 9.30 in the morning this woman German doctor came in. She was dressed in full Nazi uniform, I mean Nazi everything. She talked to this other guy and she could speak fluent English, better than you and I can. She asked all kinds of questions and we didn't tell her anything. So she gave me a morphine pill to stick up my butt and she said, "I'll be back." She left and pretty soon she came back and when she came back this time, she had taken off her Nazi uniform. She was dressed – skirt, blouse, nylon hose, high heels, I mean she was a beautiful woman. Then she went out and got some hot water and she came in and dressed my arm.

'When she came in with the pan of hot water and set it down, imagine now, you're laying flat on your back, you can move a bit, but here she is with long blonde hair and she comes in with this damn skirt on and she kneels down and she pulls the skirt up when she kneels down. I'm flat on my back and because of my injuries I can't move. And she says "Would you like to have a cigarette?" And I said, "Yeah, I'd like to have a cigarette." She gives me a Lucky Strike cigarette out of a green package. She lights it with a Zippo lighter which I had tried for four goddamn years to get one. Then she starts asking all these questions about what outfit are you out of and blah, blah, blah, blah, blah, blah. All I would tell her was my name, rank and serial number, and she said, "If you just tell me what your folks' home address is, I'll write them and tell them where you are and how you are," and the whole works and I just give her name, rank and serial number, that's all I would give her.

'She went over and talked to this other guy, but she didn't spend too much time with him. She said, "I know that you Americans like fried potatoes." And she went out in the kitchen and fixed us a breakfast of fried potatoes and eggs and bacon. Then, after we ate that, she came back in and she went through this whole rigmarole again with questions, how she would get in contact with the Red Cross and get the word to our parents that we were all right and all this and I wouldn't tell her anything else. So finally she says, "I'm gonna leave, but I will be back." She never got back. And I have often wondered whatever happened to her. Man, I'm telling you, she was a beautiful woman.

'The next night, I could hear these tanks coming. I didn't know whether it was our tanks or their tanks or who it was. And all of a sudden, this tank stopped out front and the next thing I remember is this great big black lieutenant busted through the door and as he busted through the door, right over in this corner sat a German soldier with a rifle guarding us. I said to the lieutenant, "Don't shoot him. He hasn't hurt us."'

Hastenrath continued

In Chapter 7, I covered part of a day's operations at Hastenrath by Lieutenant Henry J. Earl and his company, which ended with him being knocked out and having to bail out of his tank. He then had to get his crew away from the tank and find cover in a nearby cabbage patch. This is how he continued his description – still told in the third person as though he were merely reporting on what went on. 'As they flung themselves down amongst the cabbages, his gunner yelled: "I've been hit!" The wounded man lay only about ten feet away; the tank commander inched his way towards him. An automatic weapon opened up, cutting cabbage leaves off around his head. The leaves trickled down his cheek. When he stopped the gun stopped, when he started the gun started. This procedure continued until he reached the man's feet. Ten minutes to go ten feet! He had been hit in the arch of the foot and it was pretty badly torn up, but the shoe was still on, holding everything in place. He knew that the wound was very painful, but it wasn't bleeding very much. He told this to the gunner, not the part about it being painful, he already knew that – only that it wasn't bleeding badly and that he would be OK. It would soon be dark and they could make a move. My gosh – it was cold! The damp-ness of the ground had already seeped through his clothing and it looked as though it was about to snow. Then he remembered: the artillery barrage. Surely they called that off – they must have, for where they were lying they wouldn't stand much chance under a sixty-gun barrage, oh they must have called it off. That was something to think about. Suddenly he realised how quiet it was. The artillery had ceased firing and it seemed as though no activity was going on around them.

'It was dark enough now. He signalled his crew to crawl over and join him. They lay with their heads in a circle. He explained if they were to crawl over to the rear of the tank, they could follow the tracks back to their own lines. The ground had been soft, the tank had been sinking in four or five inches. He was going to crawl over and join his remaining three tanks. At this point they heard a voice say: "Hands Up!" They looked over to the bank by the road and saw a German helmet barely protruding above the bank and a pair of eyes staring at them. They yelled: "Come on over!" He ducked. Again his head protruded above the bank, again he said: "Hands Up!" This time he was invited over with a string of swearwords. What in the world were they going to do with a prisoner? They had enough problems of their own. Again his head ducked. The next time his head protruded above the bank, two others had joined him, each with a light machine gun, complete with stock, ammunition and bipod. He knew two other words: "You come!" But that wasn't necessary. The crew had already got the point. As they crawled towards the Germans, the tank commander heard six artillery guns fire. He knew that these were 3rd Armored Division guns, as only armored artillery had six guns to a battery. As they tumbled into the ditch, alongside the Germans, the bank completely erupted in from the explosion of six 105mm shells. As they shook themselves free from the dirt, they tried to talk the Germans into coming back to their lines, stating that they had plenty of food and cigarettes. A German pistol was stuck in the ribs of the tank commander and they said "*Raus!*"

'On entering Hastenrath, he saw a prime mover still burning. He recognised that as the vehicle he had hit from Scherpenseel. Here he had knocked out an anti-tank gun he hadn't even known was there. The commander and his crew were led into the basement of the first house they came to. Once inside, he recognised that these houses were not ordinary houses. They were built as part of the German defences. The outside of the building appeared to be made of quarry stone. The basement was reinforced concrete. The entrance was zigzagged so no one could fire directly into the basement nor drop hand grenades inside. The German officer, recognising the tank commander's rank, ushered him to a desk and his crew to a nearby table. It was indicated that they wanted them to empty their pockets. This done, the German officer politely gestured for the tank commander's map case. A look of surprise crossed his face when he went through the contents. This was replaced with a broad smile as he spread the photographs out on his desk. And why shouldn't he smile? He was looking at a pretty girl and he knew it. He looked up and pointed at the photographs and said: "*Frau?*" The tank commander nodded. The German broke into an even broader smile. The photographs were replaced in the map case, the map case closed and returned to the tank commander. All the personal property was returned. Not a thing was taken, not even their cigarettes. The Germans were very polite and handled the affair in a business-like manner. There was an air of mutual admiration in the basement that night.'

Interrogated

Lieutenant Earl and his crew were next put onto a truck and taken to a farmhouse some short distance away from the village where he was interrogated. However, before this happened, he was able to locate a German who spoke English and request that his wounded crewman be given medical attention. He was assured that a vehicle was on its way to take the casualty to hospital. They were then led down the hall to a furnished room, where they were told to wait. 'A door opened, and a German captain, addressing the tank commander in perfect American said: "Lieutenant, would you step in here please." They were joined by a German major who also spoke perfect American. The tank commander was offered a glass of beer; he accepted, but only one. He would have liked more, the day's action had left him exhausted and extremely thirsty. Then the questioning began. He replied with his name, rank and serial number. Further questioning – the same reply. After the third name, rank and serial number, the Major said: "Lieutenant, we have time to kill until they come to pick you up. What would you like to talk about?" The answer was a question: "How did you guys learn to speak American so well and without an accent?" The answer was that the two of them had been sent to the United States, their mission to not only learn the language, but the customs, along with a good solid knowledge of American sports.'

The interrogation was then interrupted by heavy shelling and when he was led from the room, he discovered that his crew had gone. Earl was taken to Durne, then on to Düsseldorf and from there to Stalag 11B outside Hannover. From there he went to Berlin, where he experienced a British night-bombing raid on the railway station. From Berlin he was taken to Poznan in Poland, then to Oflag 64 in the Polish Corridor from where he escaped, spending two weeks behind the German lines. He met and joined a Russian patrol, but his stay with them was brief as they were separated during a firefight with some Germans. He spent another ten days behind German lines, then with the help of a Polish major, he made his way to Bydoszcz in Poland. From Bydoszcz to Poznan, then to Warsaw and on to Kiev, Odessa and then by ship to Port Said. His final journey at this time was to the 5th US Army Rest Camp near Naples.

A PRISONER IN THE DESERT

Captain Edward Player was captured in the Western Desert on 1 June 1942, when 150 Infantry Brigade 'Box' was overrun and he had been wounded: 'After being patched up at 150 Brigade ADS [Advanced Dressing Station], I was parked nearby on a stretcher in a shallow slit trench. "Shallow" means that when I was lying flat, the tip of my nose was just about at ground level. The first few hours passed well enough, although the cold of the night was unpleasant. Came the dawn and hostilities resumed. There was no shade and, after a few hours, thirst became a real problem. A Bren section (probably from the Green Howards) somewhere near me was obviously holding out as long as possible. Every time they fired a burst a couple of mortar bombs came back in reply. I admired their tenacity but have to admit that I wished they would give me a little more space. The next mortar bomb seemed sure to drop in my hole. The next thing I remember is a German lieutenant relieving me of my .38 Smith & Wesson. I suppose at the time I felt resigned relief. The next phase was a bumpy, dusty ride in a three-ton truck with other lightly wounded to Derna, where a brisk female German medic assured me that my wounds were "nozzing". We spent five days there in an Italian field hospital, which seemed to be home for half the flies in creation. My initial feelings of depression and frustration began to lift a little, perhaps partly because we were fairly well fed and because most of our Italian custodians seemed humane and friendly. We were then embarked in the Italian hospital ship *Aquilea* and landed at Naples.' Ted was then in a series of 'Campo PGs' between June 1942 and September 1943, when he escaped and was 'at liberty' in Northern Italy, only to be recaptured in December 1943, moved to Germany and finally liberated from Oflag 79, Brunswick, on 12 April 1945. He commented: 'After the initial depression of capture and the opportunity to mingle with one's own, I don't think I ever doubted the outcome of the war. Whether I would be there to see it was another matter. There were some dodgy moments when we were "on the loose" in Italy and even more so when we were the recipients of friendly bombs at Brunswick.'

UNDER THE REVEREND MOTHER'S BED

Lieutenant-Colonel 'Jumbo' Hoare, MC of Weymouth had a number of lucky escapes early in the war, the first being in France in 1940: 'I was in the 4th Royal Tank Regiment when we withdrew to Arras and then counter-attacked. We held our position long enough to enable others to reach the beaches at Dunkirk. Many were killed and taken prisoner, but I managed to get out of my knocked-out tank and rescue my troop sergeant. Together we walked from Arras some ninety miles to the coast and got back to England safely. "B" Squadron 4 RTR then went out to Eritrea and after successfully winning that campaign against the Italians, we were moved to Egypt to reinforce the Western Desert Force during the "Battleaxe" and "Crusader" operations. I was wounded in the leg and head by an anti-tank mine near Tobruk, where I joined the ever-increasing numbers of wounded waiting for evacuation by sea to Alexandria. We eventually embarked on the *Chacklina* in Tobruk Harbour – it was a very old, but elegant PSNC steamer with all its peacetime trimmings but no Red Cross markings. She had been sent up hurriedly from India to help replace heavy losses in ships and was employed to clear the wounded from Tobruk. Unfortunately, we were sighted and attacked by an enemy submarine, which torpedoed us at about midnight on a very stormy night in December 1941, some twenty miles off Sollum. HMS *Farndale*, under Commander Carlil, RN, came to our rescue and did all they could to help; however, the ship sank in a few minutes, many of the wounded being trapped in the holds. I fortunately heard the order to "abandon ship" and wasted no time in jumping over the side, getting astride a piece of floating wreckage and staying afloat until I was safely picked up after an agonising wait.

'In early 1942 I was discharged from hospital and rejoined my unit, only to be captured in the desert on 20 June. I wondered then what the future would hold, having already performed two jumping acts – the first from a brewed-up tank, the second from a sinking ship – little did I know that my third would be from a moving train! I had been taken over to Italy and when the Allies began advancing, the Germans decided to move all the British POWs to Germany. Some POWs from our camp tried to escape at the station but were re-captured and shot. I, with a friend, decided to wait until dark before trying a train jump. We managed to wrench open a ventilator in the roof of the cattle truck in which we were travelling and when the train slowed down in the mountains we climbed out and jumped off. We could not believe the feeling of freedom, but had no idea where we were. Fortunately we met a friendly shepherd who took us to a cave and gave us food. Unfortunately, the Allied advance slowed and, to make matters worse, I contracted malaria, so the shepherd took us to a nearby convent, where the Reverend Mother was a nurse. She gave me the correct treatment and I eventually recovered, but not before the undertaker had measured me for a coffin!

'We stayed in the convent, well hidden from both the Germans and the local priests, until my health was restored. We then, discreetly, began to join in feast-day processions and even sang in the choir – well disguised! From the convent window we witnessed many acts of brutality by the SS: men being taken from the village, shot and buried in hastily dug unmarked graves. Near the convent was a German barracks. One day the Germans arrived to search the convent. I and my friend were hidden under the Reverend Mother's bed. She refused to let the Germans enter her bedroom with the words: "No man has ever entered my bedchamber!" After the Germans had gone she said to me, "Giacono [Jumbo], I shall have to do a lot of penances for telling all those lies!" The local mayor, who also knew of our presence, became very worried and urged the Reverend Mother to get rid of us; however, the brave and courageous nuns never gave us away. Eventually we were able to join up with the Allied advance, being guided through the minefields by the shepherds. On reaching UK I had a further spell in hospital for plastic surgery to restore the full mobility to my leg. After the war I returned several times to the villages to meet all the wonderful people who had helped us. On one occasion I met the shepherd in exactly the same place on the railway line where we had met him in 1944. I also met the only surviving nun at the convent, the rest having moved on or died. They were very emotional reunions.'

'COME OUTSIDE THE WAR HAS ENDED – OR HAS IT?!'

'At the end of March 1945, what was left of 9th Panzer Division was near Siegen. I was in a Panther company of Panzer Regiment 33 and was sent with my platoon to defend a small town, because it had been reported that the Americans would try to break through there. We had been in our tanks for many weeks and were very tired.' That is how *Leutnant* Ludwig Bauer of Keunzelsau, holder of both the Iron Cross 1st and 2nd Class, began a description of his last few weeks of the war. 'After receiving orders to patrol a certain line, my company commander then changed his mind, told me that we had done enough for that day and ordered me to go to a house in the middle of the village and report to an infantry company commander. He told me where I should position my tank and told me to be alert for the slightest alarm. I then situated myself with my crew in a ground-floor room. The Panther was left in front of the house, so there was just the house wall in between it and us. All went well, then suddenly, in the early hours of the morning I dimly heard shooting and American voices – I thought I was dreaming! My driver, Gustl Medak, who now lives in Canada, woke me up shouting: "The Americans are here!" At the same moment the enemy shot through the window and shouted: "Hullo, comrades, come outside the war has ended!" Quickly I picked up my hat and pistol belt and ran. As I could not get out of the door I ran upstairs. In the commotion I cannot remember if any of my crew had followed me or not. After standing quietly on the first-floor landing for a while I crept up more stairs. Minutes later the Americans followed. As I stood there I realised I had no shoes on! The Americans began to search the house and I ended up in the hayloft. When they came to the door I crawled under the hay. They shouted to me again and I debated whether I should shoot at them through the hay, but decided it was more important to let them go back downstairs so I could discover if any of my men had also managed to hide or whether they had all been taken prisoner – I found out later that this was the case.

'Crawling out of the hay I looked carefully out of the hayloft window. I could see some American soldiers standing talking further down the street. I could also see the door which was the only way back to my tank. There had been a few shots but I didn't think that my tank had been damaged. So there I was, standing without any shoes on, in the top floor of this house, gazing down on my Panther. All the infantry were either captured or lying low. What should I do? First of all I had to find out if any more of my crew were hiding in the house, so I went downstars, calling softly "Pst, pst" in every room, but found no one. Three long hours went past and I watched continuously out of the window to see what the GIs were doing. They began looking in my tank, but they only wanted food and drink. They found and drank a bottle of brandy and ate some cooked sausage. Then they got our packs out. They were not interested in the clothes, letters or photos, etc. I supposed that they would blow up the tank, but they didn't do so. I decided that I must get out of the house. I went downstairs to the kitchen and discovered all our cigarettes and some bread.

'Two GIs were watching the tank from the house, but were using only the kitchen and hall, so it was easy for me to avoid them. I realised that they had both taken their boots off, so I stole a pair, as well as some cigarettes and bread. Then I went upstairs again. I heard a lot of shouting and it was obvious they had discovered the boots were missing! I decided then I should leave the house and try to hide in the barn next door, where I hoped I might find some other Germans hiding. There was no one there. It was being used as a paper store and as the company was suffering a terrible paper shortage I took several boxes and crept to my tank. I went around to the rear and managed somehow to get up onto the back decks without being seen – how I did it is still a mystery to me today! Throwing the paper into the turret I then managed to open the driver's hatch and got in – head-first! I was curled up down at the bottom of the driving compartment when three GIs appeared and looked astonished at the Panther, then they got up and went into the turret, spending ages looking around it, one even put his head into the driver's compartment but somehow didn't see me. I was only a few centimetres away, I could almost hear his heart beating!

'Eventually they got out. It was now or never. Although I didn't have any training as driver, I pressed the starter and the engine started! I engaged first gear, put my foot on the throttle and moved forwards – the GIs in front of the Panther leaping out of the way. I made for the end of the village, having the greatest difficulty in changing up, but eventually I got it into third gear and roared off. I had difficulty driving and knocked into many things at one stage damaging the gun muzzle and causing part of the camouflage net to slide down over the driver's hatch, which made my view a bit restricted! . . . After a while I stopped to orientate myself, then started off again and turned sharply into a meadow, where I stopped to remove the camouflage net so that I could see better. Whilst I was doing this, the tank received a direct hit.[1] I tried to get the net aside and clamber out, but could not raise the energy, falling back in my seat as I tried. However, I then saw the flames through the camouflage mesh and it awakened my feelings of self-preservation and finally I managed to get out. I then saw three German soldiers about 100 metres away and ran over to them, I was safe!'

TAKING PRISONERS

A hillside full of Italians

'The first day ashore at Licata,' recalled Major Norris Perkins, 'two miles inland and we were attacking a strong point. The same place where Lieutenant McCully fell asleep on the ground. Attacking the strong point, my tank was hit because it had three antennas. I jumped out, ran up alongside another tank to get back up on the back deck and an Italian in a foxhole shot at me with a German Schmeisser machine pistol; bullets ran up the side of the tank in front of me; my legs turned to water; I jumped behind the tank. We turned the turret on him. They all put up their hands so, on foot, I ran them out with my pistol. It was a really stupid thing for me to do because the whole hillside was full of Italians. But nobody shot at me. What happened? Several score of Italians came running down the hill waving white flags. So what do you do? Well, we followed orders. We did not take prisoners. They just took themselves. We just pointed to the beach and told them to get going and waved them on down to the beach. So that is what happened there.'

CAPTURE AND ESCAPE

Sergeant Charles Matthews of 42 RTR was taken prisoner in the Western Desert, after having to leave his tank at Knightsbridge: 'Our turret was jammed and we were out of fuel, so we couldn't do much harm to the enemy. I dismantled the breech blocks and fired some shots into the engine. We baled out and ran under machine-gun fire into a dug-out. I found a flask of ice-cold water in a recess and it was like champagne to us.' Unfortunately, however, there would be no escape for Charles and his crew. 'After an hour or so we started walking, looking for some usable transport, without success. Later, as we approached a minefield, there was a burst of fire and we saw a Jerry waving a machine gun at us. There was no escape so we walked through this pathway through the minefield where our guns were snatched from us. An armoured car drove up and this German officer came up and spoke to us (I believe that it was none other than Erwin Rommel himself). After that we were handed over to the Italians, who marched us for miles; we were taken to El Adem air base, then to Derna and on to Tripoli. From Tripoli to Naples in a coal boat, complete with coal dust, to a camp in Capua, when I was taken to Caserta "Ospidale" with a kidney infection and dumped in the diphtheria ward, where I thought I was dying and was left alone. There were no doctors or nurses, only army orderlies who stuck dirty needles into us with great glee.

'From Capua we were sent to Maserata in the north-east near Ancona. When Italy capitulated, the Germans took over our camp and the same day we were shipped out in the usual cattle trucks, through the Brenner Pass into Germany and on to a large camp at Magdeburg, where we were deloused and headshaved. From here to a camp near a large chemical works and then to Halle where we were put to work in a sugar-beet factory, working from 6 a.m. to 6 p.m. Monday to Friday, and Saturday from 6 a.m. to midnight. No work on Sunday. We also had a spell in a salt works and then in a brick factory, putting bricks on a conveyor belt four at a time, until my pal Harry and I decided to go on strike and sat down on the floor and dozed off. We were awoken by a kick in the ribs and told, *"Kommen Zie mit."* As punishment we were given the task of unloading a two-hundred-ton Russian coal truck. After about two hours we had hardly scratched the surface when the foreman sent four Russians to help; they soon made short work of it.

'I often wonder how we managed to work at all on our diet of one *"Kartoffel"* and a lump of the same, made into bread. As for Red Cross parcels, I can only remember receiving about eight in three years. This was blamed on the bombings. In the last year of the war I don't think we had one parcel. We also had the job of building a bridge over the river by the factory; the piles were driven by hand and a winch, some forty feet into the bed, then laying the rail tracks over the concrete span. We decided we had had enough and would try to escape again. Our escape was not very dramatic. One night when we were being marched out of camp and a few miles later, having just passed over a road bridge and not knowing where we were going and hearing stories about POWs being shot in the fields, we decided to jump down this embankment. This we did and clung there while the others had passed over. It was all quiet for a while until we heard above us the sound of boots on the tarmac. This was a sentry on patrol. We took our boots off, climbed up the bank and crept over the bridge. After walking for a few miles, we found a small hut in a field and, as it was getting light, decided to stay there. I opened the door slightly when it was light enough to see and there, about 100 yards away, was a Jerry HQ in a house with staff cars and DRs [despatch riders] racing about. They were also digging slit trenches all round us. Then some Hitler Youth came around, searching the fields.

'Fortunately in the floor of the hut was a trap door; we lifted this and found a well underneath with about eight foot of water and some beams over the top. We closed the trap and perched on a beam until they had gone. Why they did not lift the trap I did not know. We stayed in this hut for the rest of the day. We had some tobacco, no food and no matches but there was on the wall an oil-filled electrical isolator switch, presumably for a water pump. Harry decided to short across the terminals with a piece of wire and a piece of paper to obtain a light for our cigarettes. This he did several times without electrocuting himself. We also managed to make some tea in a can, with a small fire, without making too much smoke. The next night we left the hut and started walking again. At dawn we found a small building with a wire fence around and sand dunes. Whilst investigating the possibilities of staying here we were challenged and a German came charging at us, bayonet fixed. I called out, "Don't shoot, we are English POWs." The German was startled and was shaking. He said he had been watching us for some time and thought we were parachutists and nearly shot us. This place we had tried to break into turned out to be a guard-room!

'They kept us here for about two hours and then one of them took us a few miles to a farmhouse, mumbled something about: "Stay here, I will be back" and rode off on his bicycle. We did not wait and ran off up the road into town. It was dark now and we were walking along this street when we heard boot marching towards us. We dived into a doorway with a courtyard beyond; a torch shone upon us and a voice said: "Who is that?" I replied in my best German, "*Zwei Deutsche Soldaten.*" He replied, "*Das ist gut,*" turned off his torch and went away.

He must have been blind because we were still in khaki and with red patches on our backs. It was now getting light and we walked through the main street of Halle with German lorries, troops etc. passing us without taking any notice. I decided to enter this Bier Keller and ask for a drink. It was full of Germans in uniform and when I asked for *"Zwei bier, bitte"*, we were given strange looks. The barmaid said there was no beer, so I asked for two lemonades and was told, again *"Kein"*. We then left expecting to be arrested any minute, but nothing happened.

'After a few days walking and hiding, we came across a disused POW camp and hid in one of the huts. I cannot remember what we lived on, because we had no food, but we did get some bread from somewhere and the rest we found in the fields, sugar beet and turnip tops etc. After this mortar bombs were dropped all around us and we decided to get out. We walked about an hour from the camp and there came across four young Americans in a jeep, they were the advance patrol. What a relief! Cigarettes, biscuits and "K" rations were devoured. We pointed them in the right direction and warned them of the hazards which we knew of and asked where their HQ was about five miles back. Not wishing to walk any more, we stole a car from a nearby house, against the strong objections from the owner and his family and drove to this house being used by the Yanks as advance HQ. They welcomed us and told us to find a billet in any house for the night. The German family in this house did not seem to mind, I suppose they had no option. The next day we were taken to Nordhausen airfield and, after two days living in a bombed, ruined telephone exchange in the basement of this building, we were flown out by DC3, after the wounded had left, to Belgium, a place named Namur. Here we were fed and kitted out with American uniforms, taken to Ostend and then by boat to Tilbury. This was February 1945. We were then fitted out with British uniforms and sent home for seven weeks' leave. After this I was sent to a rehabilitation centre at Bedlington near Newcastle.'

RESCUED

'In April 1945,' recalled Bob Rossi of the 712th US Tank Battalion, 'we were in a column and we had reached our objective for the night. It was near a bridge, and these two German civilians came up on bicycles and told us there were American prisoners in the next town. So we called up and said we wanted to proceed to the next town. They said American wounded, American sick. We proceeded to the next town and naturally, where do you think you'd go to see wounded, we went to the hospital. There were only German wounded in there, no American prisoners in the hospital. They were across the street. They had these guys lying on the floor of the schoolhouse. There was straw on the floor. These were the guys from the 106th Division, they were captured during the Bulge. Every one was a stretcher case. Every man. A guy told us that all they had for three months was potatoes that they would put a wire through and hold it over a flame, and weak tea, that's what they had for three months. They used to torture one another, like make up a menu, every time they made up a menu for one another, it always had sugar, something sweet. One guy pulled his pants down and showed me his long johns, they thought they were o.d., they were brown from the dysentery. This one guy came from Connecticut, his family owned a roller-skating rink, and one of the MPs came from that area; this guy kept saying, "God bless you, men! God bless you, men!" When I walked in my heart was in my throat, because you can't believe what you're gonna see, these guys were like skeletons.

'One guy was buried the night before we got there and they told us it was the first time any one of them got buried. These guys were being marched away from us and if a guy died, they just picked him up and put him on the side of the road. The night before we got there was the first time any one of them ever got buried. So I went to my tank and I got a box of those Tropical Hershey bars we had. They're called Tropical Hersheys because they wouldn't melt. I was giving the Hershey bars out to these guys and Dr Reiff comes in, he starts chewing me out, he says, "What the hell are you trying to do, kill them? They'll get sick." And they promised him they wouldn't eat fast, they would eat them slow. The GIs that were with us, they shot two SS guards that were left behind to guard them, but the prisoners told us, "Don't let them shoot the medic," the German medic, "he's a good guy. He was decent to us." The next day – we're travelling now, we're still moving, moving, moving – I'm up in the turret of the tank, when I see these two guys come out of a barn. They were part of a group of 150 that were still being marched away from us. Well, these guys figured this is it, and they hid in the barn, they escaped.

'I'll never forget their faces. One guy was a short guy with red hair and he's looking at me up in the turret, I could see the tears were just coming down his face. Like he was in a state of shock, like: "I'm liberated". And the other guy was tall, black hair, had a moustache and wore glasses. I reached down, I said, "You guys want a butt?" Because I was smoking at the time and they couldn't reach me, I jumped out of the turret and gave them each a cigarette, and as I went to light the cigarette, this little redheaded guy, as he cupped the light, I noticed he had a big, festering cut in his hand. I said, "What happened to your hand?" "The Krauts cut me with a bayonet and they refused to dress the wound." I called "Medic! Medic!" Again, Dr Reiff comes . . . he said "What's the matter?" and I told him. With that, Captain Reiff asks the redheaded kid, he says, "What happened to your hand?" He told him and Reiff says, "The sonofbitches" and he starts putting sulphanilamide on his hand and bandaging it and Dr Reiff says, "OK, son, we're taking you back now." And with that he can't move, like he's stunned. So Streeter, Dale Streeter, who was Gibson's driver, he was a pretty big guy, he threw a blanket around him and picked him up and put him in the jeep.'

CAPTURE AND ESCAPE

'A Tommy looked into my vehicle with his sub-machine gun threatening. "Hands up!" he cried. I was so shocked that I just looked up at him and couldn't move.' That is how Karl Susenberger of 21st Panzer Division began his recollections of being captured in North Africa. 'Suddenly,' he continued, 'the Tommy fired a burst into the wireless. That broke the tension and I obeyed his order and got out of the radio command car. As I dismounted I saw our other vehicles about 100 metres away driving off – they had left me! At once a couple of Tommies took me to pieces and searched me. I had to take everything off, even my underclothes. In the radio car they had found all the signals documents – we had received weighty instructions that these

227

should not fall into enemy hands – so what, I couldn't do anything. I was then taken to their position where I had to wait in front of a tent. The sentry gave me a cigarette but I couldn't taste it, I couldn't latch onto the fact that I had been taken prisoner. After about ten minutes I was led into the tent and found myself in front of an officer. He spoke some German and asked me how old I was, I answered that I was nineteen. He had my paybook in his hand, "You belong to the 21st Panzer Division, Third Battalion, Regiment 104." I acknowledged the fact. He produced the signals documents and asked me if I was a radio operator, again I replied in the affirmative, then he said we would talk about this later. I was taken outside once more and led over to a heavy lorry. By the last rays of the sun I could see that the Tommies were loading up their lorries, they obviously wanted to leave their strong point. They took up their marching positions and two sentries were guarding me, but they talked non-stop on the journey and took hardly any notice of me. After a few minutes the column began to move. We drove for about a quarter of an hour when a hurricane of fire broke on us. I never experienced one of similar intensity again in Africa. Immediately we jumped out of the vehicles and hit the deck. I lay between the back wheels and saw the big explosions of the 88s shells, the tracers of the 20mms and the machine-gun fire.

'It couldn't be worse in Hell! The leading lorries were set on fire and the screams of the wounded pierced me to the quick. Total confusion reigned and I saw the Tommies running about in all direction. When I looked around there was nothing more to see of my two guards and that gave me a chance to escape. I crept slowly from the lorry. Then everything was illuminated by the glare of a burning flare. I simply ran for it and after a hundred metres fell into a hole almost on top of an Englishman. His scream of pain was loud as I almost fell on his back. I said "shut up!" and immediately got hold of his weapon. It was no usual trench that we were in – it was much bigger. When the excitement died down a bit I offered the Tommy a cigarette, which he took. He spoke a few sentences to me but I didn't understand. We sat down like that until dawn, then when some of our men came into the area and I made myself known. A lieutenant of a light Flak unit took us into custody, I explained to him what had happened. "Good Lord, you had a hell of a time, which unit do you belong to?" I told him and he said that he would try to get me and my prisoner back to my battalion. I now saw many Englishmen who had been taken by my comrades and realised how lucky I had been in the whole affair.

'After a few hours I was driven back to the battalion where I reported to *Hauptmann* Reissman with the words: "Lance-Corporal Susenberger with prisoner back from the English prison camp." I also reported the loss of my paybook and signals documents. Captain Reissman greeted me with a handshake and said, "that is of course a bit of a bloody nuisance, but it's good that you are back." I had to write a report about the loss of my paybook, etc., and later I had to recount all the details of my escape with the Tommy.'

Another German panzer soldier to be captured in North Africa was Erich Fischer of Karlsruhe, who served in Panzer Regiment 8. He was captured after heavy fighting in Bardia in late 1941. He recalled: 'I was captured by a South African unit and there were a lot of our chaps with me. For a start we had to march, but after a while there was a lorry and it took us to a place where many more prisoners were. In the interrogation I was only asked for my name, rank, regiment and what job I did. We were then taken to Mersa Matruh, picking up more chaps on the way until there were between 200–250 of us. Then we were taken by train to Cairo, followed by a short march then another lorry to a field full of tents that was to be our home for the next few months. Later we were sent to Suez and from there by ship to Durban, followed by a train ride to a POW camp somewhere inland. After a few months we returned to Durban and were put on board another ship and sailed off. During the voyage something went wrong with the ship and we spent a while lying off Rio, which was a neutral port. We were hoping that they would put us off on land so that we could stay in a neutral country, but instead we were soon on our way again and landed in Norfolk, Virginia, from where we were taken by train to a Prisoner of War camp in Lethbridge – one of the biggest camps in Canada. It was so monotonous in the camp, we could only try to make the time go by more quickly with sport, reading and taking part in different lessons. I went to a lumberjack camp in Ontario. In the spring of 1946, we were taken by train to Halifax and thence by ship to Hull, England, where I worked on a farm until the middle of October when we went by ship to Cuxhaven in the British Zone of Germany. We stayed for ten days in Munsterlager and were then finally sent to an American prison camp in München-Dachau, from where we were sent home on 5 February 1947 – six years after being captured.'

10
Victory

'Dear Mother, we do live in stirring times. The events of the last two days from our angle will interest you.' That is how Captain Richard Moore of the 11th Hussars, one of the armoured car regiments of the 7th Armoured Division, which had been leading the advance towards Hamburg, began a letter home, written in the closing days of the war in Europe. He continued: 'After some days of the Hamburg negotiations and standing by for more all the time: finally after delays and hitches, "on a much higher level" as they say on the wireless, in we went. Then yesterday after a night spent in a bank, of all places (no money but primuses on the counter brewing up!) and the "Moffer" [German soldiers] coming by in their hundreds, a message to expect a big cheese and later on other messages to me on the rear link to alert people to meet the big cheese. By and by up came our people and we all (SHQ and the representatives from 21st Army Group) went up to the leading troop on the road to Kiel.

'By now the Moffer were coming past in their thousands, lorries, carts, bicycles, buses and everything, but mainly walking not marching and looking unbelievably lost, every vestige of discipline and smartness gone. There we with the colonels waited – the classic scene being an MP looting some eggs, he in immaculate red cap, the whitest of belts and the shiniest of boots and us in fur coats, corduroys and God knows what, all eating fried eggs and drinking char.

'Finally along came Admiral von Freideberg to negotiate the surrender, as you know, in a car by himself and soon after a *Wehrmacht*

231

staff officer in another; the cameras clicked and they talked for a few minutes. I thought Toby was going to loot the admiral's car, he was chatting away to him and looking into it! Then off they went and we settled down to the business of raking in and organising several thousand POWs, the local police, and so on, including several hundred Russian, Polish, French and God knows what else, in ancient vehicles of all sorts mostly run on wood and coal and *all* on tow, off to a camp one of the other squadrons is running, and so on again until after midnight and early next morning (today) again still as thick as ever. More big cheeses from the other side, including two who came in and more or less offered us the *Luftwaffe* and later on Admiral Hoffmann from Doenitz who wanted to get rid of the Fleet. They all came along and asked for Field Marshal Montgomery most correctly – get shown in to Toby and me who usually give them tea and/or cognac and pass them on. The reaction from asking for the Field Marshal and getting two buckshees in pretty rough kit, is worth seeing. Next the BBC, Vaughan Williams or someone, arrived to see the Moffer coming in; so they had tea and cognac, then went up to Reggie and did a recording. The real highlight of the day was Tom Suggitt, the signal sergeant, with a newsflash from the BBC – "Huddersfield has won the Rugby Cup" and as an afterthought later on: "Two Moffer armies have surrendered somewhere!"'

AN ANTI-CLIMAX

'Victory in Europe Day came as an anti-climax to us,' reflected Lieutenant-Colonel George Rubel, who was commanding the US 740th Tank Battalion. 'There was no hilarious celebration as at home. For one thing, we were too busy gathering up prisoners. Tens of thousands of German soldiers had converged on us in Schwerin a few days earlier and we soon had more prisoners than we knew what to do with. We sent out an SOS to the division to send all available MPs and all unoccupied soldiers up to handle this POW situation. So the war had really been over several days as far as we were concerned and the radio announcement was not news in any sense of the word. We knew there would be an announcement, but we wondered when it would take place. Rather than celebrants we felt more the way a builder would feel after having completed a house – this job is finished, now let's get to the next one. We did have some cognac and wine which had been "donated" to us through the courtesy of the "German Post Exchange Service", but we had drunk most of that on 2 and 3 May and had very little left for the official 8 May date. For most part, VE-Day on the banks of the "Schwerin Sea" passed about the same as the others. We tuned in on the BBC to hear Prime Minister Winston Churchill tell England and the Dominions that: "the war in Germany has ended with their unconditional surrender." Across the lake the Russians put on a good fireworks display by shooting up all their flares, but this had been going on for several days, and, as we found out later, continued for a good many more. Just to the north of us the Seaforth Highlanders got rid of their remaining flares and not to be outdone, some members of this battalion threw a few hand grenades, for we had no flares to begin with.

'There was an unexplainable detached feeling in the battalion about the German surrender. The folks at home and the people in England had heard and read of the victory but we have seen the complete disintegration of the enemy before our very eyes. It hadn't come overnight. It had been a gradual process, more and more discernible as time went on. We had not only witnessed this breakdown but had considered ourselves instrumental in the accomplishment of it. Had an impartial observer looked at both ourselves and the Germans on 2 May he might have had quite a bit of trouble in telling who looked the worst. About the only difference was that we still had the guns in our hands when the shooting stopped. As a matter of fact we probably appeared to be more on the verge of collapse from sheer fatigue than did the Germans for we had been driving forward day and night and they, for the most part, had been sitting at home eating, drinking and sleeping.

'The round-up of prisoners continued to be a great task. The handling of displaced persons took up when the prisoner of war work ended, so that we still worked practically day and night for the better part in the month of May. We did manage to squeeze in trips to the Baltic to see the ocean and to Schwerin to see stage shows and moving pictures. . . . When we arrived in this area we were tired and dirty. The water in the lake was almost ice-cold which precluded bathing and no American shower units had been set up, so I arranged with the British VIII Corps, who were in Wismar, to use their shower facilities which they had brought with them and had in operation. They offered us clean uniforms, but I was afraid United States public opinion would frown on the 740th Tank Battalion if they blossomed out in kilts and British battle kit!'

'BUSINESS AS USUAL' FOR THE FITTERS

'After the fighting finished,' recollected Slim Wileman, a forward fitter in 'B' Squadron of the 13th/18th Hussars, 'we were to move up and take as prisoners the men from a panzer unit. It was known that the main road we would have to go along had been mined with five-hundred-pound aircraft bombs and it was not known if they had been cleared, so we had to go along small roads and cart tracks. One road was built up and ran across very soft and ploughed farm land. The lead tank of one troop using this road slipped off into the soft ground, breaking the road up as it did so and the rest of the troop had to back out causing the road to break down as well. This meant that we could not tow the tank out backwards, nor could we tow it forwards. The tank had gone off the road to the right and was in the soft ground parallel to the road. The only firm ground was about 100 yards to the left of the road, slightly higher than the field, the only trees small and deep rooted. So we had to fix a long wire to the front of the tank, find the strongest rooted tree that we could, fix a pulley to it, pass the wire through the pulley, attach it then to the ARV and then place the ARV vehicle at a ninety-degree angle to the main length of wire. (If we had had a double pulley and more wire it would have been easier). Then one of us would have to get into the tank, a job I lost the toss on! I would start the engine, put the tank into reverse gear and hold the clutch down, and pull the right stick back hard so that the drive would go to the left track when needed. At a given moment the ARV would move off then, as soon as all the slack in the wire was taken up and pull was beginning to be felt by me, I let the clutch out so that the tank reversed back swinging to the left and the front was being forced up the banking. I then knocked it out of gear and released the sticks and got my head down inside the tank and hoped our plan would work. It did and I got covered in dirt as the tank ploughed through the mud throwing it all into the driver's access! From now on it would be bulling up the tanks for flag marches and changing our role, with armoured cars instead of tanks.'

THE WAR IS OVER

Peace for the Lilywhites

Peter Comfort, also of the 13th/18th Hussars, had these brief memories of the last few days of the war in Europe: 'On into Germany, onwards, onwards, onwards, into Westphalia towards Bremen. Overhead the last thousand-bomber raid, with little opposition. Prisoners, prisoners, thousands upon thousands, unshaven, vacant faces; horses, odd-looking carts, a fallen helpless army. Then: "Withdraw to a holding line." Cease fire. Calm. We wait. The first night sleeping not in or under the tank, but beside it, looking up at the stars and hearing a lone plane and not being scared. Peace.

'The last low? "You, you and you, report to Squadron HQ." What now? Eight silent men and an officer, Lee-Enfields, one pistol. "Choose your ammunition, one's a blank so you'll never know", but you did. The dark figure stood in semi-darkness, blindfold and white patch on chest. "Take aim. Fire!" The fifth-columnist was no more. Some said he was the mayor. Tots of rum all round, but it tasted somewhat bitter – or was it just in the mind?'

PERSONAL REFLECTIONS

Dennis Young felt that all he wanted was to be in a quiet spot, alone with his thoughts and to dream of being home again with his family and friends. 'It was hard to comprehend the dark cloud that had hung over us for so long was now lifted, the silence, the quietness and sadness everywhere,' he told me. 'The reflection back to those who had suffered even more, some making the supreme sacrifice, pals who we would never see again, how the family and those back home had worked so hard and not knowing what was happening to loved ones. It was like a nightmare coming to an end and yet not trusting your thoughts that it actually had; could we have acted differently when those amongst us were suffering the results of mankind's behaviour in warfare. Then there was the thought and possibility of having to endure it all over again by being sent out to the Far East. Could we take and survive any more? Could we ever relax and settle down again in comfort and security? How could or would we ever make up those valuable lost years?

MOPPING UP IN ITALY

Major Gordon Bradley of 51 RTR recaptured his memories of Italy at the end of the war in Europe, in May 1945, when they were stationed in the plain enclosed by the rough square – Verona, Ostiglia, Ferrara and Padua, RHQ being at Padua. 'There were said to be numbers of Germans hiding in the surrounding area, being chased by Italian partisans. The powers that be decided to put some order into this. My CO, Lieutenant-Colonel R. B. Holden, DSO, decided that I, his HQ squadron leader, had had it far too easy for almost four years and that he should assist the partisans in rounding up these delinquents. Accordingly I liaised with the *partigiani* with a view to putting a bit of organisation into their meanderings. There were some villians there, but they really enjoyed hunting down the Germans and couldn't wait to sort them out. When the Germans saw the partisans were apparently officered by a major of a Tank Regiment they gave up in droves, thinking perhaps that by surrendering to a British officer they could expect a fair deal, for they knew the partisans had a score to settle. For my help over a few weeks they wished to mark my work with a gift. They offered me a 9mm automatic pistol – a Beretta – a beautiful thing and I graciously accepted it with my tongue in my cheek.

'On getting my release I stowed it away in my kit, wondering what I was going to do with it for I had a suspicion that there was no way I would be able to take such wartime trophies into our home. However, the solution came sooner than I expected, because for my journey home I was made OC Train from Milan to Calais, so I was a "marked man" from then on. On arriving in sight of the White Cliffs of Dover, a voice came over the ship's tannoy warning everyone that they must not land with any illegal weapons. It went on to say that those caught would be returned from whence they came and face courts martial. You should have seen it! Stuff showering into the sea from all sides. Somewhere not many miles from Dover, at the bottom of the sea must be a real arms cache just waiting to be recovered!'

VICTORY OVER JAPAN

At Singapore, on the 12 September 1945, this is how Admiral Lord Louis Mountbatten, Supreme Commander SEAC, announced the unconditional surrender of the Japanese, from the steps of the Municipal Building: 'I have just received the Surrender of the Supreme Commander of the Japanese forces who have been fighting the Allies and I have accepted the Surrender on your behalf. I wish you all to know the deep pride I feel in every man and woman in the Command today. The defeat of the Japanese is the first in history.' One of those who was vastly relieved to learn of the Japanese surrender was Corporal Jack Wood, who at the time was serving in 4 RTR who were training for the anticipated assault on mainland Japan. He had served with 9 RTR in North-West Europe in Churchills and remembered his last few months of the war thus: 'In early April we crossed the Rhine by a pontoon bridge (a hairy experience) and road-marched to Gronau, spending VE-Day on guard at the Dutch/German frontier at Enschede, relieving the returning forced labourers and displaced persons of their transport. Most had big wood-burning lorries loaded with looted furniture and household goods which they were allowed to keep provided they were unloaded at the frontier and the transport left on the German side. It was an experience watching them getting the stuff away from there. I relieved some Signals bods of a Mercedes staff car, despite the pleadings of one of them with whom I had worked prior to joining the Services. He was not pleased; to this day he is not pleased, but we had a Mercedes to run around in for a while until the powers-that-be caught sight of it, when we, in our turn, had to hand it in. Before these guard duties, we had paraded before the squadron commander who had a fit. There weren't more than a couple of properly dressed bods among us. Regulation uniform had been adjusted to suit personal requirements during the campaign, with looted civilian gear mixed with uniform.

'We moved from Gronau to Mettingen near Osnabrück where we received our Age+Service release numbers, and where the younger members of the battalion had "FAR EAST" marked in their Paybooks. The battalion being a wartime unit and no longer required was marked down for disbandment, the older members staying with it until the end of their release dates, whichever came first. Most of the rest of us were transferred to 4 RTR, some to other RAC units. A good "Au Revoir" concert was held squadron by squadron and a fond farewell then off to the Fourth.

'Life in the Fourth Tanks consisted at first of training for the coming operations in Japan. Thirty-fourth Armoured Brigade, of which we were a component part, was to take part in an operation codenamed "Coronet", which consisted of an assault landing on the second largest of the islands which composed Japan itself. The prospect was full of foreboding to say the least, but we had to go via USA and the prospect of home leave, Yankee rations and pay, was, as it is said: "sufficient unto the day". By now I was tank driving and my vehicle needed to go back to workshops for a new clutch. When the transporter arrived I decided to load it on myself and duly crashed it into first gear and mounted the transporter impeccably. However, when it came to stopping, it wouldn't come out of gear and by the time I had switched off it was half-way over the front of the trailer. No amount of persuasion, even with the help of a crowbar could move it out of gear, so it had to travel back like that. I was glad I didn't have to travel with it.

'During that period of time I was sent on a malaria course to, of all places, Great Yarmouth – some twenty miles from home. There I learnt about the nasty habits of the female anopholine mosquito and her attendant malarial parasites, how to deal with the larvae by spraying stagnant water with Paris Green and the delights of Mepacrin. At the end of the course I got twenty-four hours' leave, nice little scrounge, and I learned something, which fortunately I did not have to put into effect. I was on the Tank Training Area at Paderborn, living under canvas, when VJ-Day came. For me, as for many others, the dropping of the A-bombs which ended the war against Japan was a Godsend. I am certain that it saved my life as well as the lives of countless others. Our reward was to be paraded and sternly lectured by the Squadron Leader on the fact that it was not over for us and that we should put aside all thoughts of celebration and continue training.'

GOING HOME

'The most exciting day of my life, I thought, as the train pulled into the station at Villach, Austria.' That is how Brian Brazier began his reminiscences about his demobilisation. After his release from hospital he had been posted to the Queens Bays at Palmanova in North-East Italy, because his old Regiment, 50 RTR, had been disbanded. 'We had walked the short distance from the transit camp, fully loaded with large and small packs and kitbags. We soon clambered on board, almost before the train came to a standstill, and we settled down for the most fantastic journey of my whole Army career, in fact I think of my whole life. Going home. The scenery through Austria, winding up the steep valleys, crossing continually fast-flowing rivers and zigzagging right up into the mountains covered in snow, was absolutely fantastic. What a shame I had not got my camera. We eventually reached Munich where the snow lay quite thickly on the ground. There our journey was broken for a short while in order to have a stretch and a bite to eat before we passed on across southern Germany via Frankfurt and Cologne, where it was possible to pick out the twin towers of the cathedral and so across the border into Belgium, finally arriving at Calais, after a journey of thirty-six hours. The waiting in Calais was minimal before boarding the ferry for Dover and back to Blighty, this time for good. Going through Customs was a fairly simple procedure, only about one in twenty being asked to empty their kit. I was lucky, although I did have a bottle of Irish whiskey in an old ammunition box at the bottom of my kitbag, others were not quite so fortunate. I had been able to buy the whiskey in the Sergeants' Mess before I left the Queens Bays and thought my father would enjoy it when I got home, but he only turned his nose up, saying he did not like Irish.

'Once we had been sorted out into our various destinations, one more train journey brought me to the RAC HQ at Catterick Camp in Yorkshire, evidently I still had about three months' service to do in the Army before my actual demobilisation, but the "couldn't care less" attitude had to be abandoned because they still found us something to occupy our time. But first of all it was home for a month's leave. This was what they called *Python* and mine lasted from 25 July to 21 August 1946. It was great to be home again as I had been away for nearly four years. It went by far too quickly, then it was back to Catterick once again. No sooner had I got back I found out it was possible to apply for more leave if my father was employed in agriculture so that I could help on the land. I immediately wrote home asking him to contact my CO to see if this was possible. I was granted another four weeks' agricultural leave, so within ten days I was on my way home again. This time it seemed to last much longer, but finally I was back in Catterick once again and unable to have any more leave and just had to make the most of my last eleven weeks of army life.

'This did seem to drag now, just waiting for the final day, 6 December 1946. It was a matter of grin and bear it right up to the end. That wonderful day did come around at last and the first stop after leaving Catterick was the station at Darlington with a final railway warrant made out for Evesham. Next stop was York and the demob centre, where a complete new rigout of civilian clothes was issued, suit, overcoat, hat, socks and shoes, and the final documentation was carried out. Now the very final train journey to King's Cross, onto the underground for Paddington and Evesham. And so ended 1,736 days of being a soldier. Not before time either, but I suppose it could have been a lot worse.'

A GI release

On the other side of the Atlantic the demobilisation procedure was very similar. Bill Haemmel, from Waynesville, North Carolina, had served throughout the war as a tank gunner in 1st Armored Division, in North Africa and Italy. He was medically evacuated back to the USA in May 1944 (see previous chapter) from Anzio and spent his last months 'Stateside' in the Army Postal Service. He was at Fort Hamilton, Brooklyn, New York in late 1945 and recalled: 'My release from the Army was probably advanced a week or more because I was undergoing company punishment and on hand when an order to clear twenty high-sixty-point men[1] came through the company and I was able to get on the order. Lieutenant-General Brehan Somerville, commanding general of the Service of Supply, was honored by a parade on Saturday morning, 22 September. While Saturday was my regular day off, we were all ordered to fall out and take part. I did not bother to attend and was AWOL [Absent Without Leave] on the 23rd and 24th and this time I was tagged. My punishment was to report to the company on one of my days off and sweep and mop half of the floor. I reported on Friday, 27 October at 9 a.m. and had finished the job within an hour and was reading a newspaper before leaving for home when the new first-sergeant, First-Sergeant Heine, asked if there were four sixty-point men present who wanted out of the Army. He had only sixteen of twenty and wanted to complete the list. While he was reluctant to include me in the draft as I lived off post, he finally agreed and I rushed home to pack my gear and return to stand by for departure. Once we were on orders, we were relieved of any further duty. . . .

'We just sat around for four days before we moved out. On 30 October we finally departed New York City by the Baltimore and Ohio Railroad's "Blue Royal" to Wilmington, Delaware. Fort DuPont is about seventeen miles south of Wilmington and is located on Delaware Bay. It was a quaint place and almost looked as if the war had passed it by. We were assigned to the oldest, most dilapidated brick barracks I ever came upon. The paint was peeling, the floors were scuffed and heavily marked and each of the two-storey old wrecks contained a large number of two-man rooms. The barracks were unlike any barracks I have ever encountered. Upon arrival we were advised that we would be civilians in three or four days. The timing was perfect, for if we were on duty on the first day of the month, a full month's allotment cheque would go to our dependants

241

and Shurin and I decided we would go AWOL from the separation centre in order to ensure the payment of his wife and my mother. After all, one more day was not going to matter greatly after more than three years in uniform. Actually, we did not have to go AWOL. Shurin and I went into Wilmington the first and second nights without passes. The MPs at the gate merely glanced at the two of us as we walked through. Wilmington was a pleasant town and we went for a swim at the YMCA the first night and to a movie the following night.

'In less than two working days we were through the discharge processing; it was efficient and thorough and marked by much levity and wise-cracking. We moved from the nineteenth-century barracks into a modern barracks and had a very quick briefing in the Post Theatre late the second day. The following day we were up at 6.30 a.m., showered and underwent a complete physical examination. Later we were counselled concerning a civilian conversion of our Army skills. The interviewer to whom I was assigned was an ex-combat infantryman and we laughed at the civilian prospects for a tank gunner. The final decision was to convert the tank experience into bus driver and the Army Postal experience into general clerk. The interviewer also planned to resume his education and we were far more interested in the educational benefits of the GI Bill of Rights. One man in the counselling group sought to encourage enlistments in the Army Reserve programme. The usual response was catcalls and raucous yells. But even as we were moving out of the Army we observed a group of inductees receiving their physicals. It was a changing of the guard.

'At 1500 hours, or 3 p.m. to the group nearing civilian life, we had a signing session. I had to sign seven times in order to complete the necessary paper work connected with being discharged. I went to the movies the last night in the Army and my mind went back to the very first night in the Army when I also sat and looked at a movie screen. The final clothing check was quick and careless and the extra raincoat and trousers I had picked up along the way remained in my barracks bag. It was ironic that two German POWs should sew the ruptured ducks onto my shirt and jacket. Our final pay came at 1.30 p.m. We received pay through the day of discharge, $100 mustering out pay (with $200 more to follow over the next two months) and travel expenses to whatever point we expected to travel to. I had planned to take a trip to Buffalo, New York, and was paid the railroad fare to that point. The final Army formation took place in the Post Chapel, beginning at 2.45 p.m. The chaplain lectured us for twenty minutes on the good work we had done and would be expected to continue in civilian life. We lined up and at 3.17 p.m. I was handed my discharge, along with a mimeographed letter from General George C. Marshall, the Chief of Staff.

'Once the chaplain had completed his task, we crowded onto two-and-a-half-ton trucks and at 3.45 p.m. we passed out of the gates. I did not go into Wilmington, but jumped off the truck in order to hitch-hike to Atlantic City, where I planned to spend a few days with the Garwoods. As the truck disappeared down the road and Harry Shurin and several others waved to me for the last time, I stopped and watched. It was a clear, bright, beautiful fall day and I had finally arrived at the moment I had been looking forward to for a year. Perhaps I should have jumped for joy. But I did not. Rather I looked at the truck until I could see it no longer and then I turned, flung my barrack bags over my shoulder and my overcoat over my arm and walked down the highway.'

THE LAST 'PRISONER OF WAR'

Lawrence Brooksby, ex-3RTR tank driver, from Loughborough in Leicestershire, now lives in Stuttgart and describes himself as being: 'the last British POW left in Germany" – but he is not complaining, as he told me: 'In December 1944 I was with 3 RTR in the Ardennes and after a short stay in Poperinge, we changed our Sherman tanks for a very much better tank – the Comet. A few months later we came to Flensburg where I met and married my German wife. Our two children were both born in England. After living in Flensburg for twenty years we moved to Stuttgart where I came in contact with the NATO Sergeants Club and have been a member for the past seventeen years. I am also a member of the Afrika Korps, Stuttgart Old Comrades Association and of the RTR OCA in the UK. On my seventieth birthday I received the Rommel Medal in silver and in May 1997, the Bar to the Medal. I think I can say that I am the only Englishman to have received these awards. Last year, with two German comrades, I was sent by the Afrika Korps Stuttgart to lay wreaths on both German and British graves at Poperinge and at Cannock Chase, not far from Birmingham. We also laid a wreath on the Blackpool War Memorial during the RTR OCA Reunion in May 1997. As you can imagine I am very proud to have been awarded the medals, so I am a very happy "prisoner"!'

Notes

Chapter 1

1. Although there were a significant number of volunteers it was nothing like the vast numbers of young men who had spontaneously volunteered in 1914. The spectre of the horrendous casualties of the Great War was still too fresh in people's minds.
2. On 4 April 1939, the eight regular battalions of the Royal Tank Corps and their Territorial battalions joined together with the newly mechanised Cavalry regiments to form the Royal Armoured Corps (RAC).
3. 'Hobo' would be responsible for the initial training of another famous armoured division, the 11th, but was considered too old to command it in battle. Then, before D-Day, he formed and trained the amazing specialised armoured division – the 79th Armoured Division, which he then continued to command for the rest of the war.
4. The Tank Destroyer (TD) Force came into existence as one of the United States' understandable reactions to the success of the German blitzkrieg in Poland and France. Peak figures were reached in 1943 when there were a total of 106 active TD battalions – only thirteen less than the total number of tank battalions. Basic equipment was a mixture of towed, halftrack mounted and tracked anti-tank guns. The tracked TDs were the M10 Wolverine, the M18 Hellcat and the M36. The last of these was the most powerful, armed with a 90mm gun. This was the equipment which the 630th TD Battalion would man in combat.

Chapter 2

1. The pre-war Royal Military College (RMC), located at Sandhurst, Surrey, became an RAC Officer Cadet Training Unit (OCTU) for the duration of the war.
2. The Valentine 'DD' was the first British amphibious tank, designed to swim ashore from a landing craft in water too deep for wading (see later for the Sherman 'DD' as used on D-Day).
3. The two amazing prefabricated Mulberry harbours (one located opposite the American beaches at St Laurent and one servicing the British at Arromanches) were the cornerstone of successful supply over the beach-head – designed to deal with 12,000 tons of supplies and 2,500 vehicles daily for at least ninety days. Unfortunately, exceptionally fierce storms between 18–22 June damaged both of them badly and the American one never re-opened, which delayed the Allied stores build-up for some time.
4. 'Grease gun' was the nickname given to the M3 .45-calibre sub-machine gun, the 'cheap and cheerful' replacement to the Thompson sub-machine gun.

Chapter 3

1. The 'coax' was the turret machine gun which was mounted coaxially with the main gun, so that they both could be traversed and elevated simultaneously.
2. 'Hull defilade' means that the tank is protected by the slope of the ground up to but not including the turret, so that the gun can fire over the crest. A tank in 'full defilade' is completely hidden – in British parlance these terms would be: 'Hull down' and 'Turret down'.
3. 'Flowers on Armour' by S. Sosonov.
4. The *panzerfaust* was a hand-held rocket launcher which fired a hollow-charge bomb from a disposable tube. It first appeared in late 1942, had a range of 100m and could penetrate 200mm of armour.

Chapter 4

1. The ubiquitous jerrycan was the name given to one item of German equipment that was eagerly sought by the Allies. The robust twenty-litre (4½ gallons) can was far superior to the flimsy British petrol and water cans, from which thousands of gallons were lost in the desert campaigns.

2. The German tanks were PzKpfw IVs and Sergeant Nick Mashlonik knocked all of them out at a range of 1,200 yards with just one 90mm round apiece.
3. 'Crusader' was launched by General Cunningham's newly established Eighth Army on 18 November 1941, catching Rommel by surprise and reaching the approaches to Tobruk, where the great battle of Sidi Rezegh was fought. Both sides had mixed fortunes.
4. Bill Liardet, who went on to become a Major-General and to be awarded the CB, CBE and DSO, was greatly loved and respected by all members of the RTR.

Chapter 5

1. Every armoured regiment had a Technical Adjutant (RTA), who was responsible for all the vehicles in the regiment, both tracked and wheeled. He also liaised with the EME who commanded the LAD, the R Signals Troop which repaired the radio sets, etc., and a multitude of other important tasks. The RTA was, with the EME the most important and responsible officer in the regimental vehicle repair and recovery 'chain'.
2. CREME = Commander Royal Electrical and Mechanical Engineers, the senior REME officer in the brigade/division, who would co-ordinate the overall repair and recovery plan.

Chapter 6

1. The CDL was a highly secret night-illumination device, in which the main armament was replaced by a thirteen-million candlepower lamp that was 'fired' through a shuttered slit in the front of the modified turret. It was to be used to support night attacks by temporarily blinding the enemy.

Chapter 7

1. The British A9 cruiser tank had single Vickers machine guns mounted in two 'dustbin-shaped' small gun turrets on either side of the driver's compartment.
2. Quoted from *Kransaya Zvezda*, dated 22 February 1997, by Anatoliy Dokuchayev.

3. The German PzKpfw V, probably the best all-round medium-heavy tank of the Second World War.
4. Quoted from *Krasnaya Zvezda*, dated 11 March 1997, by Anatoliy Dokuchayev.

Chapter 8

1. Taken from *Battalion Surgeon* by Dr William M. McConahey, which was privately published in USA in 1966.

Chapter 9

1. Ludwig Bauer goes on to explain that it was a German Hetzer tank destroyer which knocked his Panther out. The Hetzer had been hidden in a wood very close to the meadow and when it saw the Panther leaving the village thought that it must have been captured by the Americans. It was the tenth time that Bauer had been knocked out!

Chapter 10

1. 'Points' depended upon length of service, etc. On 1 October 1945, the required number of points for discharge went down to seventy. Bill Haemmel had sixty-five points.

DATE DUE